# A CHURCH FOR THE 21ST CENTURY

# A CHURCH FOR THE 21ST CENTURY

## LEITH ANDERSON

BETHANY HOUSE PUBLISHERS
MINNEAPOLIS, MINNESOTA 55438

Published by Bethany House Publishers
A Ministry of Bethany Fellowship, Inc.
6820 Auto Club Road, Minneapolis, Minnesota 55438

Printed in the United States of America

Library of Congress Cataloging-in-Publication Data

Anderson, Leith, 1944 –
  A church for the 21st century / Leith Anderson.
    p.   cm.

  1. Church renewal.  2. Christianity—21st century.
  I. Title.  II. Title: Church for the twenty-first century.
BV600.2.A55    1992
250—dc20                                 92–23832
ISBN 1–55661–231–1                       CIP

# To
# Wooddale Church

· · · a place to belong,

· · · a place to become.

LEITH ANDERSON is the senior pastor of Wooddale Church in Eden Prairie, Minnesota. He is a graduate of Moody Bible Institute, Bradley University (B.A.), Denver Seminary (M.Div.), and Fuller Theological Seminary (D.Min.). The author of several books, including *Dying for Change*, he has served as seminary teacher, conference speaker, missions leader and as a member on numerous boards. He and his family make their home in Edina, Minnesota.

# Contents

# Introduction

I HAD JUST finished presenting a seminar in Fairbanks, Alaska, on "Changes and the Church." The topics ranged broadly over social, generational, and demographic changes. A Lutheran pastor with a healthy sense of humor shook my hand and said:

> After listening to all you've had to say, I feel like going home, taking off all my clothes, getting into bed, turning the electric blanket on HI, and assuming a fetal position!

Changes can scare us until we want to at least suck our thumbs, if not return to the security and warmth of the womb.

My experience is that many churches and their leaders *do* want to change. I have been thrilled with the thousands of conversations and correspondence indicating a deep desire to make the church of Jesus Christ relevant and effective. Many of the stereotypes simply are not true. Those who are older, more conservative, rural, or in long-established churches are not always staunch defenders of the status quo. There are large numbers of committed Christians who want their churches to grow and are willing to pay the necessary price for change.

The broad positive response to *Dying for Change* demonstrates the keen interest Christians have in understanding the powerful trends shaping society and their desire for churches to change. At the same time, there remains a strong commitment to essential biblical truth and values. The question is, "What's next?" Lay leaders and pastors are looking forward to the twenty-first century with excitement for a church that is both relevant and rooted in revelation.

The problem is they don't know how. They are looking for leaders who will give permission for meaningful change and then point the way. The purpose of this book is to help established churches renew themselves and become effective vehicles for ministry and outreach.

Although some are looking for simple formulas, the truth is that there aren't any. Every situation is different. There are no patent medicines to cure every malady. In fact, beware of such promises lest you are deceived by some quack. If there is anything close to a universal formula for changing the church, it is this:

$$(D + R)HW + PG = \text{Changed Church}$$

## D refers to diagnosis

Like a patient with a physician, the church must be diagnosed correctly. This includes everything from a case history to diagnostic tests to checking out the environment.

My own physician told me the story of a male patient who was chronically ill. His blood minerals were dangerously depleted, but no apparent cause could be determined. After many tests and nearly as many doctors, one physician took the time to ask the man, "What is your daily schedule like?" The patient detailed a normal day from awakening and brushing his teeth in the morning to brushing his teeth and going to bed in the evening. As an unimportant side comment, he mentioned an hour at the end of every workday sitting in a very hot sauna. That was the problem! Vital minerals were being lost through perspiration faster than they could be replaced with medication.

Churches become ill just like people. The symptoms may be lethargy, spiritual impotence, and losing weight (membership).

These same symptoms, however, may be caused by (1) chronic sin in the lives of the leaders; (2) three successive poor choices of pastors; (3) poor financial stewardship; or (4) a new interstate highway that has isolated the church property from all but the most faithful. Wrong diagnosis and treatment are more likely to kill the patient than cure him. Not all problems are spiritual. Some are sociological. Some are strategic.

Good church leaders, like good physicians, are careful to determine the correct diagnosis.

## ℞ is for prescription

Since there must be a direct and correct correlation between the diagnosis and the drug, a tragic sadness often accompanies a clever analysis of the problem when a cure is mistaken. For example, many churches have correctly determined that they need new leadership in order to be spiritually renewed and become institutionally effective. In some cases the church board fires the pastor and appoints a search committee to find a better leader. But, what if the former pastor was the right leader and the real need was for a new board? Right diagnosis. Wrong prescription.

## HW means hard work

Correct diagnosis and right prescription usually need to be *multiplied* by hard work.

Change within a church is seldom easy. It takes enormous amounts of prayer, time, money, and ministry. There are few shortcuts. Effective churches are most often the product of years of zealous labor rightly deployed.

When I reached my thirtieth birthday, I decided it was time to get into shape. A friend generously paid the initial membership fee at a small storefront health club, which has since gone out of business. On my first visit an instructor asked me what part of my body I wanted to shape up. I said, "The whole thing." Over the next hour, he took me through a series of exercises on an assortment of weight machines that systematically strained every muscle in my body. The next morning I could not get out of bed. I was so sore that I took two days off from work in order to recuperate. The long term results were two: (1) I quit going to the health club; (2) I stayed in poor shape.

There are no one-day wonder bodies. And there are no one-day wonder churches. It takes a long time and a lot of hard work.

## PG stands for the power of God

It is never enough to have just the right diagnosis, correct prescription, and lots of hard work. The church is the body of Jesus Christ. It takes the power of God to make the church strong and successful.

When the religion editor from a daily newspaper interviewed me about the growth of Wooddale Church in Eden Prairie, Minnesota, he started out by asking me to "explain the reason for all the great things that are happening here." I told him that I could give the *real reason* or the reasons he wanted to print. Of course, he asked me for the real reason. I said, "The real reason is God. I can't fully explain it, but God has graciously done something special here. He did it and he deserves all the credit." The reporter then started asking questions about marketing, name change, relocation, and specific programs.

This book is primarily about diagnosis and secondarily about prescription. It seeks to gently and positively encourage churches to ask the right questions instead of answering the wrong questions.

The hard work is up to you.

The power is up to God.

Leith Anderson
June, 1992

## Chapter 1

# What Will the 21st Century Church Look Like?

"WHEN DID the twenty-first century begin?" seems like a strange question to ask in 1992. The common answer to the question is, "The twenty-first century *will* begin at 12:00:01 A.M. on Saturday, January 1, 2000." That is probably when most people will celebrate. The technically correct answer, however, is that the year A.D. 2000 is really the last year of the twentieth century, and the twenty-first century officially begins at 12:00:01 A.M. on January 1, 2001. But when did the twenty-first century *really* begin?

"Class of the 20th Century" is a 12-part TV series hosted by Richard Dreyfus for broadcast on the "Arts and Entertainment" television network. It is an oral review of what happened in this amazing century, featuring interviews with Jonas Salk, Mickey Mantle, C. Everett Koop, Julia Child, and a host of other famous persons. The first segment was aired on Sunday evening, January 5, 1992.

No doubt it has been an amazing century with two World Wars; the dismemberment of colonial empires; the inventions of airplanes, submarines, spacecraft, televisions, and microwave ovens; the eradication of smallpox and the emergence of AIDS; the redrawing of the world's political boundaries; the redistribution of huge populations; and the increase from just over 1.5 billion population to an estimated 6 billion plus.

What I find most fascinating is that the television review of the twentieth century took place in 1992. The twentieth century is history. It's over. The twenty-first century has already begun— the calendar just hasn't caught up with reality.

Meanwhile, it has been a spectacular century for the church of Jesus Christ. The gospel has spread all over the world. Neither unwritten languages nor iron curtains could keep out the message of Jesus Christ. The church has turned Africa south of the Sahara Desert from a heathen continent to a thriving center for new churches, new denominations, and new missions. Korea has become a missionary sending country. The Chinese church is mushrooming by the tens of millions. New Protestant churches are beginning in South America at the rate of more than 50,000 per year.

The American church has also experienced an unprecedented growth during this century. It is 375,000 churches strong and a major force in the life of the country. More than 90% of Americans say they believe in God. One fourth say they are born-again Christians. If next Sunday is typical, 43% of the population will worship in a church or synagogue. It has been an especially successful century for conservative American Christianity. In the 1920s the Fundamentalist-Modernist controversy promised to leave liberals the victors and conservatives the vanquished. As we near the end of the twentieth century, it often appears to be the other way around, as many liberal churches and institutions hemorrhage while their conservative counterparts flourish.

That, however, is all history. It's past twentieth-century history, and the twenty-first century has begun everywhere except on the calendar. What is happening with the twenty-first-century church?

*In Search of Excellence* by Peters and Waterman analyzed forty-three of America's best-run companies like IBM and 3M. But, did you know that two years after the publication of that bestseller, fourteen of those businesses were in financial trouble? *Business Week* magazine explained the reason why: "failure to react and respond to change."[1] One of the realities of the emerging twenty-first century is that yesterday's successes are no guarantee for tomorrow's survival.

I am a Christian who loves the church of Jesus Christ. I grew up in the church and have lived all of my adult life ministering within the church. I am committed. And, I am concerned. I very much want the church of the twenty-first century to not only survive but also to thrive.

## Paradigm Shifts

We are experiencing enormous structural change in our country and in our world—change that promises to be greater than the invention of the printing press, greater than the Industrial Revolution, and greater than the rise and demise of communism. Our world is changing so quickly that we can barely keep track of what is happening, much less figure out how to respond.

Jeff Davis, author of an article entitled "Breathing Space: Living & Working at a Comfortable Pace in a Sped-Up Society," says, "My premise is that time management is no longer valid in society as we know it. There is no keeping up. There is more produced (to read, watch, etc.) in one day than you could comfortably take in the rest of your life."[2]

The only way to cope and be effective during this period of structural change in society is to change some of the ways we view our world and the church. It is what some call a paradigm shift— a new way of looking at something. Such a shift will allow us to view our changing world with new perspective. It is like a map. Old maps from 1950 may have sufficed before the construction of interstate highways and the expansion of major cities, but new maps are needed now. Likewise, we need a paradigm shift for the future.

In the beginning of his book *The Seven Habits of Highly Effective People*, Steven R. Covey tells about a memorable personal experience:

> I remember a mini-paradigm shift I experienced one Sunday morning on a subway in New York. People were sitting quietly—some reading newspapers, some lost in

thought, some resting with their eyes closed. It was a calm, peaceful scene.

Then suddenly, a man and his children entered the subway car. The children were so loud and rambunctious that instantly the whole climate changed.

The man sat down next to me and closed his eyes, apparently oblivious to the situation. The children were yelling back and forth, throwing things, even grabbing people's papers. It was very disturbing. And yet, the man sitting next to me did nothing.

It was difficult not to feel irritated. I could not believe that he could be so insensitive as to let his children run wild like that and do nothing about it, taking no responsibility at all. It was easy to see that everyone else on the subway felt irritated, too. So finally, with what I felt was unusual patience and restraint, I turned to him and said, "Sir, your children are really disturbing a lot of people, I wonder if you couldn't control them a little more?"

The man lifted his gaze as if to come to a consciousness of the situation for the first time and said softly, "Oh, you're right. I guess I should do something about it. We just came from the hospital where their mother died about an hour ago. I don't know what to think, and I guess they don't know how to handle it either."

Can you imagine what I felt at that moment? My paradigm shifted. Suddenly I *saw* things differently, and because I *saw* things differently, I thought differently, I *felt* differently, I *behaved* differently. My irritation vanished. I didn't have to worry about controlling my attitude or my behavior; my heart was filled with the man's pain. Feelings of sympathy and compassion flowed freely. "Your wife just died? Oh, I'm so sorry! Can you tell me about it? What can I do to help?" Everything changed in an instant.[3]

Just as Stephen Covey shifted the way he looked at a slice of life in a New York subway, we who enter the twenty-first century need to make paradigm shifts in the way we look at and understand our culture and the church.

## Seeking the Supernatural

America is spiritually thirsty. After decades of advancing secularism, oppressive communism, and declining spiritual interest, a spiritual awakening is sweeping the world. America is part of this awakening. There is a fascinating mix of disillusionment, post-secularism, generational depression, fear about the future, and return to fundamentalism.

Atheism is out. In October 1991, Madalyn Murray O'Hair announced that American atheists were closing down forty-one of their local associations across America. She said, "Chapter leaders have become mired in the busywork of serving local members, rather than advancing the atheist movement." In 1990 the national organization spent $200,000 on recruitment, resulting in a net increase of thirty-four names to their 50,000 person mailing list. That's a cost of $5,882 per new recruit![4]

Spiritual interest, however, does not mean an interest in Christianity or the church. People want to experience the supernatural. They want to feel God. And they are looking everywhere.

The New Age movement is evidence of this increasing desire for the supernatural. The words "New Age" are well known to most Americans. In fact, the New Age sections of B. Dalton Booksellers and Waldenbooks are among the largest in their stores. Yet there are only 20,000 self-declared New Agers in America. While there are comparatively few who call themselves New Agers, there are millions who believe and pursue various New Age ideas and practices. Channeling, crystals, reincarnation, horoscopes, and paranormal psychology are all quests for the supernatural. Even though New Age ideas and practices run counter to biblical teaching and Christian beliefs, that it is where many spiritually seeking Americans are looking for the supernatural.

This revival in religious interest extends to baby boomers who are returning to the church in large numbers. This spiritual renewal is also revitalizing hundreds of pastors in the Pacific Northwest and the renewal movements in large denominations from the United Methodist Church to the Southern Baptist Convention, while prayer concerts are uniting diverse Christians together for intercession.

Within the American Christian community itself, the popularity of signs and wonders and the phenomenal aspects of the charismatic renewal are further evidences of America's desire for supernatural experience.

All of this is a far cry from the intellectualism of the 1950s and 1960s. We began the twentieth century with the ascendancy of rationalism and liberalism. We are ending the century with a new supernaturalism. Fewer people are looking for careful philosophic apologetic arguments. They are looking for a supernatural experience.

Take a case from the spiritual brushfire burning across Latin America, as reported by the Associated Press:

> Celia Garcia, 49, a schoolteacher and librarian, said she was baptized a Catholic, received first Communion and was married in the church, but "never felt anything in the ceremonies."
>
> When she attended a Pentecostal service with a friend three years ago, "Immediately I felt something very special I had never felt before," she said.
>
> "Someone explained to me that I felt the presence of Christ. It was because I had opened my heart, because I was ready to change my life."[5]

I often hear the same thing in North America. People tell me they are looking for a church where they can meet God, where there is the power of the Holy Spirit, and where their lives can be radically changed. We have a generation that is less interested in cerebral arguments, linear thinking, theological systems, and more interested in encountering the supernatural.

The widespread spiritual thirst means that we have an extraordinary opportunity to reach people for Jesus Christ. The window of opportunity is wide open for effective evangelism and the growth of those churches that really are churches—that is, gatherings of people who have themselves experienced God and who speak for him.

The twenty-first-century church must be less preoccupied with internal issues, petty conflicts, and traditional divisions of Protestant Christianity. Those are all luxuries of affluence and of a religious culture. In an increasingly secular culture, we must be able to lead seekers to an authentic encounter with God, or they will look somewhere else.

The old paradigm taught that if you have the right teaching, you will experience God. The new paradigm says that if you experience God, you will have the right teaching. This may be disturbing for many who assume that propositional truth must always precede and dictate religious experience. That mind-set is the product of systematic theology and has much to contribute (it is my own background and mind-set). However, biblical theology looks to the Bible for a pattern of experience followed by proposition. The experience of the Exodus from Egypt preceded the recording of the Exodus in the Bible. The experience of the crucifixion, the resurrection and Pentecost all predated the propositional declaration of those events in the New Testament. It is not so much that one is right and the other is wrong; it is more a matter of the perspective one takes on God's touch and God's truth.

## Will the Church Be the Church?

One of the most significant questions to be answered is "Will the church be the church?" in this era of spiritual thirst. There is a current philosophy of church ministry that is wonderful and dangerous at the same time.

This philosophy seeks to reach unbelievers starting from where they are rather than where we as believers are. In its implementation some services of the church are minimally religious. There are support groups for adult children of alcoholics, persons with sexual addictions, and couples struggling with infertility. There are athletic teams, dinner clubs, investment clubs, and many more. Language has been purged of much religious jargon—we refer to the "Bible" rather than to "the Scriptures," and we give the page number instead of a chapter and verse. Personally, I not only subscribe to but also practice much of this philosophy. I believe it is incarnational in the pattern of Jesus.

The danger, however, is that the church might abdicate what the church should do the best—communicate God and God's truth.

When I go to a restaurant, I expect to be served food. At a

concert I expect to hear music. In an art museum I expect to see art. In the doctor's office I expect there to be talk about medicine. I am never surprised or offended that these people and places present what they represent. The same goes for the church. Churches are people and places where God is expected to be present and his Book is no surprise. The churches of the twenty-first century that flourish among those seeking the supernatural will be the ones that talk about and offer authentic supernatural experiences.

The definition of these supernatural experiences varies greatly and is hard to define. But most people can tell you when it happens: "I can't describe it, but I know when I feel God!" The practical approach is to encourage people to describe their experiences and check those descriptions with the Bible.

## Looking Future

The 6,000-member Millennium Society has already chartered the *Queen Elizabeth II* to transport 1,800 passengers from New York to Alexandria, Egypt, where they will bring in the millennium on December 31, 1999, at the Great Pyramid of Cheops. Other celebrations are planned for each of the twenty-four time zones of the world—including events at the Great Wall of China, India's Taj Mahal, Mount Fuji in Japan, and Times Square in New York City. They are not the only ones. Major hotels and restaurants around the world are already booked for Millennium Eve parties.

We are all beginning to wonder what the future will look like. Christians are wondering as well. We know that the church has survived and flourished for almost 2,000 years, but we also know that it looks a lot different than it did in A.D. 33.

Eschatology was "hot" among evangelicals in the 1950s and 1960s. Amillennialists argued with premillennialists, and pre-, mid-, and post-tribulationalists wrote their books and fought their battles. Holding one position or another became a litmus test for ordination in some denominations. Churches accepted or rejected candidates based on their eschatology. Prophecy conferences, books, and films were very popular.

That particular focus all changed in the 1970s and 1980s when the baby boomers took over. They were more concerned about the present than about the future, especially about their current marriages and families. Thus, the focus shifted to marriage books, family seminars, and sermons about child rearing.

Well, the future is "in" again. But this time the interest is different. Unlike the last time, it has not been triggered by the 1948 founding of the modern state of Israel and its relationship to Bible prophecies. And it does not primarily focus on the continuing conflicts in the Middle East. It is not limited to the religious community. This time around it has been ignited by the coming turn of the millennium. The whole world is beginning to wonder what the future will be like.

Some fundamentalists date the creation of the universe around 4000 B.C. They tie this date to a theory that the history of the world will be seven "days" of one thousand years each. The seventh or final day will be the millennium when Jesus Christ rules the earth for 1,000 years. Start putting those numbers together, and the arithmetic reveals that the end of the sixth day and the start of the millennium is around A.D. 2000.

Another segment of the Christian community sees the year 2000 as the target date for world evangelization. The goal is to establish a viable and growing Christian church in every "people group" (variously defined as an ethnic social grouping identified by language, culture, race, etc.). Careful analysis plus aggressive plans indicate that such a universal spread of the gospel is indeed possible by the end of the century.

At the other end of the spectrum are the New Agers, who believe that the next millennium brings such cosmic convergence that we will enter earth's golden era. Life will be very different and will be much better.

Historians tell us that there has been a measure of eschatological interest at the turn of every century, but there was especially great interest approaching the year A.D. 1000.

Prophecy books are making a comeback. In 1990 Hal Lindsey's *Late Great Plant Earth* went into its 108th printing. Zondervan Publishing Company re-released John Walvoord's 1974 book *Armageddon and the Middle East Crisis*.

To some, all this renewed interest in the future is an irritation. They remember the divisiveness of eschatological battles in the past.

To those with a broader perspective, this renewed interest is welcome. This time we're not talking about an internal interest among Christians in the church. Instead, we're talking about a worldwide interest that crosses religious, political, cultural, and other lines.

The church at the turn of the century will be surrounded by people with a growing fascination and fear of the future. It is an extraordinary opportunity for the church to address the trend and answer the questions from the authority of the Bible and a Christian world view.

## Changing Demographics

By the year 2000 whites will be a minority in the state of California. Whites are already a minority in the schools of stereotypically Scandinavian Minneapolis, where the combination of African-Americans, Hispanics, Asians, and Native-Americans adds up to 52.5% of the student population. Dade County, Florida, including the city of Miami, is bilingual with signs and public announcements in both Spanish and English.

By comparison, the white population is growing older in average age, while minorities are growing younger; whites have a lower birth rate, while minorities have higher birth rates; whites have comparatively fewer immigrants, while minorities have a proportionately higher number of immigrants.

The United States accepts more legal immigrants than all of the other nations of the world combined. Moreover, illegal immigrants are estimated to exceed half a million each year. It is comparatively easy to enter the United States and become a citizen, either as a student, a political refugee seeking asylum, or by marrying an American citizen.

Although there are cluster centers that gather more Asians in California, Cubans and Haitians in Florida, and Europeans in the Northeast, immigrants are amazingly widespread throughout the country.

Changes are more than racial mix. There are changes in roles and social positions. Many Asian-Americans have achieved higher education, business ownership, and financial stability within the first generation. African-Americans have moved into the middle class in large numbers. Hispanics, on the other hand, have often struggled with illegal immigration status and other handicaps that have precluded socio-economic rise. Whites have wondered about their own identity as they change from majority to minority position in many parts of the nation.

The populations gap is closing, though the financial gap is growing. The Census Bureau reported on January 7, 1991, that white households in America have ten times the median wealth of black or Hispanic households. The median white household (in 1988) had net assets of $43,280, compared to $4,170 for blacks and $5,520 for Hispanics.

As minority groups increase in number and power, increased social tension may be anticipated. Deep prejudice and racism still exist in the corporate American life. Issues like wealth distribution and allocation of public funds will run into dangerous age-race clashes. The voting public is more white and getting older—they still want money spent on seniors programs, Social Security benefits, and Medicare provisions. They neither will want greater public debt to renew the infrastructures nor will they support higher taxes. On the other end, deprived minority groups will clamor for the same style of spending that financed the earlier (and whiter) generation's college education, interstate road system, and other social programs.

The coloring of America has and will have a far-reaching impact on American church life. The African-American churches are growing at the high rate of 13.5% per year. The number of African-American theology students increased an average of 5.5% for the first five years through 1989, bringing the total to 3,814 (6.8% of all theology students in the USA). By contrast, the number of Hispanic theology students has grown more slowly (2.8%), while the Asian student numbers have grown more quickly (12.9%). There are 38% more Asians than Hispanics pursuing theological education, even though there are millions more Hispanics than Asians in the country. Hispanics have significantly swelled the ranks of Roman Catholicism, which already exceeds 55 million, although large numbers of Hispanics are switching to charismatic Protestant churches.

If these trends continue, the church of the twenty-first century will experience huge shortages of educated pastors, far wider gaps between the size and impact of white and minority congregations, and probably more segregation than ever.

Integration still lingers as an unresolved issue in American society. Certainly there is more of a mix in churches than there was before the civil rights movement of the 1960s. But, churches remain highly segregated institutions. One study indicates that upwardly mobile African-Americans often choose black churches rather than primarily white churches. Integration and equality is desired for employment, housing, and civil rights, but the historic character and quality of the black church is desirable and maintained.[6] The same often applies to Asian churches, at least among first-generation immigrants. Minority churches are viewed as vehicles for maintaining identity and continuity of heritage.

The challenge to the twenty-first-century church will be to behave Christlike and justly as persons of color grow in power and number in society. It will be a challenge facing every variety of church and Christian organization. New means must develop to express solidarity and unity in Jesus Christ without requiring dilution of racial identity and ethnic heritage.

## Importance of Money

Money has always been important, but it became more important with the opening of the decade of the 1990s. Economics is increasingly setting the agenda for businesses, nations, charitable organizations, churches, families, and individuals. Persons born before 1940 nod their heads and say, "Of course!" without any note of surprise in their voice. Many born after 1950 are shocked that money is becoming such a serious problem.

Baby boomers were born into prosperity and have lived most of their lives with economic growth. The 1980s were years of freewheeling spending when jobs were plentiful, extravagances were common, and borrowing came easy. The Reagan era set records for successive years of an expanding economy. It also set records for national, corporate, and personal debt.

We are just beginning to understand the extent of profound economic realignments occurring in North America and throughout the world.

One recent radio news program compared the 1990 disparity

between the rich and poor in the United States, claiming that the total annual income of the richest 1% of the American population is equal to the total annual income of the poorest 40% of the American population. The very rich are few, but they have as much money as all of the poor and much of the middle class combined. What was especially startling about the report was the comparison to 1980 when the richest 1% earned as much as the poorest 20%. In other words, the rich are getting richer while the poor are getting poorer. With the middle class disappearing from the center, a few are rising to wealth while increasing numbers drop into poverty. Because this country has thrived from a strong middle class, the future economic implications may be ominous. Likewise, most American churches are middle class and exist on the contributions from middle-class members.

The recession that started the decade of the 1990s forced a major contraction of many parts of the economy. Layoffs and extended unemployment became common. Debt reduction replaced borrowing as a national priority. The lesser availability of cash dictated many business, political, and personal decisions.

The combination of various economic circumstances forced government to decrease services and increase taxes. Connecticut added its first state income tax and was forced to declare its need to borrow from the federal government to replenish its exhausted unemployment compensation fund. New York City closed fire stations that had been in operation for more than a century. The District of Columbia laid off large numbers of municipal workers as part of an effort to trim over one-hundred million dollars from its operating deficit. Since states cannot have budget deficits like the federal government, they must mandate higher taxes and lower services in order to balance their budgets.

The point is not that tough times have come nor that the economy does not go through cycles of highs and lows. The point is that economics increasingly is the basis for our decisions. Hospitals send patients home on the basis of cost, when the decision was once made on the basis of individual need and medical opinion.

Because the church and para-church organizations are part of the world economic system, economics will increasingly set the ecclesiastical agenda as well. As small business bankruptcies increase, so will churches go bankrupt. Congregations with large debts and dwindling attendance will face hasty decisions about survival. Many schools, publishing houses, service agencies, and similar organizations will be forced to close or merge.

Denominations may be especially hard hit. Denominational loyalty has long been in decline. When local church leaders must choose between paying the mortgage and paying the denomination, the mortgage will win every time. Missions utilizing personalized support will fare better than those who have unified budgets—because donors are slower to cut off individual missionaries whom they personally know. But it may become even harder for new appointees to raise initial support. In 1980 missionary sending agencies worried about having enough new recruits to replace veterans approaching retirement. By 1990 many of those same agencies wondered whether enough money could be raised to send out the new recruits they had.

Expect increased calls for lean staffs, increased efficiencies, getting more for less, and general fiscal responsibility. Money matters will dominate the board meeting agendas of religious organizations more and more. Para-church organizations that once hired executives with a Master of Divinity degree will wonder whether they should instead look for someone with a Master of Business Administration degree. Pastors will choose churches and churches will call pastors on the basis of salary packages, housing affordability, and eligibility to qualify for health insurance programs. Financial questions won't replace theological questions, but they will increase in importance as decisions are made.

There will be some clear winners and losers as economics becomes more important. Those who appear to be unstable, irresponsible, and constantly facing financial crisis will be losers. Donors will wonder whether the leadership is competent and whether the organization deserves to survive. During earlier years of greater institutional loyalty, fund-raising letters declaring a "crisis" brought in generous contributions. Increasingly, such fund-raising tactics turn away donors who see no point in giving money to losers.

The winners will evidence stability, integrity, high ministry return for every donated dollar, and meaningful servicing of the donor as a consumer.

Religious organizations have not traditionally viewed donors as consumers. On the contrary, churches and para-church organizations have seen themselves as the consumers. Stewardship sermons, fund-raising letters, and other solicitations are most often institution-centered rather than donor-centered. It is "What you can do for us" more than "What we can do for you." Expect that donors will want their needs at least considered if not met. Consider some positive examples:

The Chapel at University Park in Akron, Ohio, and the Colonial Church of Edina, Minnesota, both have received national recognition for servicing persons who are unemployed, underemployed, or in job transition.

The Baptist General Conference based in Arlington Heights, Illinois, periodically sends personal letters to pastors asking for individual prayer requests and telling them that they will be prayed for by name at the headquarters on a certain date.

A veteran missionary to Africa regularly sends small gifts of appreciation along with personal letters to supporters.

When such efforts are primarily self-serving, they border on manipulation. However, when the organization and its leaders are genuinely seeking to serve through discovering and meeting needs, they will strike a responsive chord.

Combined with meeting donor needs is the importance of being "missional"—driven by a positive purpose. Twenty-first-century donors are far less interested in giving to institutional perpetuation and to operating budgets. They are motivated by missions they believe in and purposes with which they can identify. When challenged to give to feed starving children, to alleviate the problems of urban teenagers, to evangelize their community, or to prepare leaders for tomorrow's church—they want to contribute and be a part of something significant.

The church has always talked a great deal about money. Perhaps too much. Often the number one criticism of churches by the unchurched is, "They always ask for money." But the church has not adequately developed a popular theology of money. Materialism has been condemned in sermons without fitting into a popular system of Christian economics. Attempts to develop a theology of money have ranged from academic treatises to "health and wealth" prosperity preaching. Some good thinking has occurred; some good writings have been published. But none has adequately captured the ordinary Christian's biblical understanding and lifestyle. The 1990s offer the best opportunity since the Great Depression of the 1930s for the church to develop and communicate a biblical theology of money that seeks to serve the needs and answer the questions of the average Christian during unstable times.

The evangelistic potential of economics is enormous. Tough times bring more people to spiritual decision than prosperity. When money is not plentiful, people look for a God who is dependable. Those in crisis know that the building with the cross on top may provide food, clothing, shelter, and hope when all the other social service agencies say no. They should also know the church as the place where practical money management is effectively taught.

## Old Look; New Look

The twenty-first-century church will look a lot like the twentieth-century church, and yet it will look a lot different. Casual observers see the similarities between a propeller driven DC–3 and a jet engine Boeing 747. Both have wings, pilots, seats, and wheels. Yet the differences are many—speed, capacity, cost, complexity, and noise. They are different versions of the same thing. They share the same purpose of transporting passengers from one place to another as quickly, safely, and economically as possible.

The new-century church will be an updated version of the old-century church. It will differ in everything from cost to complexity. But both are the body of Christ and share the purpose of doing God's work in God's way, evangelizing non-Christians, and edifying Christians.

Anticipating some of the differences will help us deal with the changes.

# Chapter 2

# *What's Going to Be Different?*

ONE SUMMER AFTERNOON I was driving alone through downtown Minneapolis looking for "my kind of music" station. I wanted to hear the popular tunes of my younger years. Finally I found a station playing a song I remembered and liked. I even sang along with the music. It was "me." After the song concluded, the station played a commercial—for caskets! I quickly changed stations and erased both its call letters and the song from my memory. The casket company had figured out the best station to reach people *aged* to buy a casket. And they had targeted me!

Have you ever revisited your childhood grade school since you graduated from the sixth grade? I did, and it was another reminder of how much I have aged. And I wasn't sure I liked the changes. All my favorite teachers were gone—no one I asked could even remember their names. Some of the classrooms were so completely remodeled that I couldn't tell the way they used to be.

I was saddened by some of the differences and delighted by others ("I wish they'd done that when I was here!"). As I reminisced, I realized that I too was different. No longer did I fit in those chairs. Besides, would I really want everything to stay the same?

Differences may be good or bad, comfortable or uncomfortable. Either way, we must recognize them and deal with them. Sometimes we adapt. Other times we resist. Every time changes happen and differences appear.

## New Diversity: Segmentation Into New Niches

Segmentation is not new. India has a long history of segmenting its society into a strict hierarchy of castes. Even in America we have long pictured society with lower, middle, and upper classes. The traditional segmentation by gender, age, race, economics, and marital status is only the beginning of a very long list.

Segmentation is also not new to American religion. We have greatly divided over Arminianism and Calvinism, infant baptism and anabaptism, exercise or non-exercise of charismatic gifts, form of church government, instrumental or noninstrumental music, high or low liturgy, reformed or dispensational theology, and a host of other issues and idiosyncracies.

Many of these points of segmentation will not disappear. Some have been around for centuries and will still have their vocal adherents in the future. However, there is a fast-growing church population that considers most of these distinctives to be irrelevant. They really don't care about these differences, and they demonstrate their attitude by easily moving from church to church with differing ideologies. Many perceive that these distinctives are the creation of denominational bureaucrats and highly theoretical theologians. They do not have loyalty to the historic distinctives of their churches and denominations—to the contrary, they see these distinctives as barriers to effective Christianity.

I see this when couples with a Roman Catholic background show up at our Protestant church because they like our children's program. The differences between Catholicism and Protestantism don't matter very much, if at all, compared to the importance of a Sunday school they and their children like. Sometimes they say, "When the kids are grown we'll think about going back to the Catholic Church."

The ChurchGrow program at Wooddale Church seeks to assist

other churches, averaging 300–1500 worship attendance, to develop through a process of self-study, mentoring, and a three-day
seminar. Half a dozen churches participate at one time—often
including charismatic and noncharismatic, mainline and independent, young and old. No attempt is made to change doctrinal
or denominational distinctives. There is a spiritual unity and sharing that transcends the differences.

The day is fast disappearing when people choose churches
because of the name of the denomination, the mode of baptism,
or the system of theology. But that doesn't mean that diversity will
disappear. The new diversity is based on style of worship, socio-
economic status, racial/ethnic/language background, the variety
of services that a local church offers, and the list keeps getting
longer.

America is fragmenting. We are increasingly heterogeneous.
Variety abounds. The twenty-first-century church must recognize
the new diversities and minister to people where they are and not
where we have been. This will mean de-emphasis on many old
distinctives, offering of many new ministries, and recognition that
we cannot reach everyone—we will need to target specific audiences more and more.

Every indicator is that the culture and the church are entering
an extended era of greater diversity, increased segmentation, polarization, division, and even hostility. It is just that the segmentation will follow new directions and create different niches. The
church of the twenty-first century may be less divided over mode
of baptism and more divided over race, money, abortion, homosexuality, and gender roles.

The new diversity also means that more than one approach to
ministry will work. Under our old mode of thinking we were
always seeking the "right way" or the "best way" to do ministry.
Conferences, articles, and seminars offered the latest methods:
tent meetings, altar calls, Sunday school, social action, expository
preaching, camping programs, busing outreach, and so on. We
need to understand that what works well in one situation is not
always transferable. Everything always seems to work well at
churches that are a thousand miles away. When we get closer to
home, it's a different story.

It frightens me to see how many naive pastors and church

leaders attend conferences, read books, or visit churches and conclude that they have the answer to take back home and implement.
Imagine a medical doctor going to a training conference on some
new wonder drug therapy. She then returns to her practice and
prescribes this new drug for every patient without prior diagnosis.
The results prove wonderful for some, nothing for many, and
death for a few. As inane as such an approach seems, we have
suffered from twentieth-century pastors and lay leaders who have
taken this approach to their churches. They go to a conference at
the Crystal Cathedral or Willow Creek Church or at denominational headquarters. They pick up the approach to worship, music, visitation, preaching, evangelism, or some other ministry.
When they return home, they try to apply a very good but inappropriate method to their churches. In some of the saddest cases,
the home church not only rejects the method and fires the pastor,
but also is inoculated against any future change. Tragically, a
church that desperately needed to change now has greater resistance to change because of a bad experience.

Segmentation by music preference is largely a generational
matter. People often prefer the music that was popular in their
teens and twenties. With the diverse styles of musical expression
acceptable in the church today, there are many more niches into
which people can move.

When *Newsweek* magazine wrote a cover story on religion in
America, it took for granted, as an established trend, something
that many churches haven't yet undertaken. Referring to the Unity
Church of Chicago, *Newsweek* wrote, "Like most churches these
days, Unity is full of support groups from, Women Who Love
Too Much to Overeaters Anonymous."[1] Whether or not most
churches have support groups, the small-group movement is a
major social trend that reflects the micro-segmentation of American society. Americans are seeking meaningful relationships out
of deep-felt loneliness. Decades of mobility, divorce, blended families, and individual isolation have multiplied the list of legitimate
felt needs, driving people together into groups to help one another
meet these needs.

The neighborhood pub in England is the stereotype of a place
where people go to meet and make new friends. It is a safe place
where they can laugh and cry and be themselves. That portrait

has been popularized in the American TV show *Cheers*, which is a series of conversations among a small group of friends in the same place for every show. They go to their Boston bar because they feel welcome and because "everybody knows your name."

In earlier generations the family unit provided many of the services now sought from small groups. When families stayed for generations in the same locale, a measure of family cohesiveness was provided by traditions, multiple generations, love, confrontation, and support. The church was the gathering place where family units met and interacted. The church primarily provided opportunity for worship, education, and social fellowship beyond the family unit.

As families have either fractured or taken on different forms, they function less as small groups. Many people are geographically removed from their nuclear families. Due to death, divorce, or other tragic circumstances, many have no families. Isolation and loneliness are common. Consequently, the church is increasingly composed of individuals rather than families.

Add to this situation American preoccupation with individual problems and the widespread optimism that every problem can be solved if you get the right kind of help. It is no wonder that support groups have arisen to try and address so many issues.

Many of these people who have felt this social fragmentation have found that support groups provide lasting relationships, escape from loneliness, and opportunity to address and resolve their personal problems. Alcoholics Anonymous was an early entry and is now a well-established veteran in the support-group movement. There you will be accepted—not only in spite of your problems but also because of your problems. Everyone is on a first-name basis. People care. You are not alone. People have many of the same problems you are facing.

Commercial enterprises have recognized the power and even the profit from small groups targeting special needs and niches. Weight Watchers and NutriSystems use small support groups to bring people together for fellowship and weight control. Counselors have established support groups for rape victims, for families going through grief, and for executives coping with stress.

When a Quest group for couples facing infertility was started at Wooddale Church, there was enough newspaper interest for a

feature story. Couples came from beyond the metropolitan area
and even across the state line to participate.

A national organization trains and accredits facilitators of support groups for grade schoolers who are the children of divorce.
Many hospitals sponsor support groups for cancer patients, those
who have undergone mastectomies, and parents of children with
terminal illnesses.

The interest in groups for Adult Children of Alcoholics has
been so large that in many places the numbers have stretched the
usual definition of a "small" group. These ACOA groups are composed of adults who grew up in alcoholic or otherwise dysfunctional families and are seeking to come to terms with their painful
backgrounds. The group provides a combination of support and
instruction—often focusing on learning the skills and handling
the emotions in ways that were not learned and handled appropriately in childhood.

The small-group movement is more than support groups. It is
a grass-roots movement of people gathering together for friendship
and common interest. In churches, the variety is unlimited:
MOPS (Mothers of Preschoolers), athletic teams, choirs and other
musical groups, evangelism teams, boards and committees, dinner
clubs, prayer fellowships, investment clubs, parents of teenagers,
travel groups, social action committees, and others.

A generation ago pastors and other church leaders feared
small, uncontrolled groups within the church lest they become
centers of dissent or heresy. Now, the mood has switched dramatically. There is a growing recognition that many people resist
central control and will meet in small groups with or without
church permission. Many fast-growing churches promote small
groups and have full-time staff to facilitate them. They have become a means to integrate and connect individuals into otherwise
large and impersonal congregations. The small-group movement
is also consistent with the trend in businesses toward hierarchal
organizational structure and greater democratization of institutions.

Small groups are not for everyone. Even those churches that
heavily promote them often do not exceed 50% of their overall
constituency who regularly participate in small groups. However,
it is an important, if not essential, experience for those who do

participate. And, many of those who do not actually join a small group choose to be affiliated with churches that make small groups available—just in case they ever decide to join one.

There is a whole other side to the segmentation of the culture and churches into new niches. It is the polarization that increasingly characterizes our segmented society.

## Polarization

The following conversation in a Sunday school class couldn't have been imagined ten years ago. Heather suggested that everyone go to lunch at Burger King after the Sunday morning worship service. Karen objected because Christians were boycotting Burger King. Heather said, "Oh no, that's over. ClearTV called off the boycott when Burger King agreed to stop sponsoring shows with violence and profanity and sex." But Karen wasn't convinced. She said, "I'm sure I saw Burger King on some other list I got in the mail."

Polarization over moral and political issues is threatening to paralyze the effectiveness of many Christian groups. The polarization is not always because of different moral convictions but often over different methodologies.

In many of the old-line denominations, including the Episcopal Church, the United Church of Christ, and the Presbyterian Church USA, the recent polarizing issue has been church policy toward homosexuals. Some argue that there must be a shift from a traditional biblical hermeneutic to a new "justice hermeneutic." They say that in the name of justice the church should not discriminate against persons on the basis of their sexual preference. On the conservative side are those who insist that homosexual behavior is condemned as sin in the Bible. With such opposite views, it is no wonder that there is sharp disagreement on the blessing of same-gender marriages and over the ordination of practicing homosexuals. The oncoming battles promise to be so fierce and bitter that many churches will attempt to withdraw from their denominations, and withdrawal may precipitate protracted court battles over church property.

Equally divisive in some traditional denominations is the definition of the role of women. Most old-line denominations and churches accept, if not mandate, that women be fully represented on church governing boards, be considered for all ministerial positions including senior pastorates, and be ordained when qualified. The Roman Catholic Church, the Orthodox churches, and many conservative Protestant churches are the primary ecclesiastical groups withholding full leadership and participation to women. In many cases, churches are forced to take positions in one camp or another—either opening all positions to women or restricting top leadership and ordination to men. It is a sensitive issue in which there is very little middle ground or room for compromise.

The potential for future tension and conflict is already great. Women are coming into top positions in business and politics. They are significantly represented, if not a majority, in many seminaries and medical schools. Yet the present structures often leave little room for the top leadership positions for which these women have prepared. Even those denominations that strongly promote calling women as senior pastors have few, if any, large churches with women preachers.

No issue polarizes more than abortion. In the general population 33% of Americans say they are pro-life, 39% are in the "middle," and 27% are pro-choice. Few political or religious leaders have the option of choosing the "middle." Churches have become primary gathering grounds for pro-lifers. Because abortion is called murder, it is perceived as a moral not a political issue.

However, not every Christian feels as strongly as the activists. Growing numbers resent the regular use of the pulpit for pro-life sermons and feel intimidated by fellow parishioners who insist that they sign petitions, protest, and join in "rescues" at abortion clinics. Both sides make points when they say that (1) Christians must act righteously against shedding innocent blood; or (2) the church is not a one-issue activist organization unless the single issue is evangelism.

As the seemingly unresolvable political debate continues, the line between pro-lifers and pro-choicers is more clearly drawn. Neither is persuaded by the other's rhetoric. Their methods keep raising the stakes and drawing every aspect of community life into the debate.

One of the battlegrounds has been the Dayton Hudson Corporation. In 1990 the Dayton Hudson Foundation canceled its $18,000 per year support of Planned Parenthood at the insistence of pro-life activists. Planned Parenthood is one of the nation's primary providers of abortion services. Even though the $18,000 was a comparatively small amount and designated for nonabortion programs, all money given to Planned Parenthood was considered by pro-lifers to be directly or indirectly supporting abortions. The Dayton Hudson Foundation discontinued the support because it wanted to be "neutral" in the abortion debate. Board members quickly discovered that neutrality may be an impossibility. Within hours of their decision, there was an uproar from pro-choice activists, who picketed the retail department stores of Dayton's and cut up their Dayton's credit cards. Dayton Hudson agreed to reconsider and subsequently reinstated the $18,000. Following suit, the pro-lifers started picketing, boycotting, and cutting up their credit cards for reversing the original decision.

The debate enters the church when members quiz one another on their shopping habits. Many pro-lifers insist that Dayton's, Target, Mervyn's, Marshall Field, and all other Dayton Hudson stores must be boycotted—because shopping at any of them is indirectly supporting Planned Parenthood. Joining such a boycott becomes a practical test of commitment and even of fellowship among church members.

We recognize how strong the emotions are when analyzing how far the issue has been taken. Church members are polarized over boycotting Target stores because: (1) Target is owned by the Dayton Hudson Corporation; (2) Dayton Hudson Corporation funds the Dayton Hudson Foundation; (3) trustees of the foundation authorized $18,000 for a nonabortion program of Planned Parenthood; (4) other programs of Planned Parenthood provide abortions; (5) abortion is murder.

In earlier generations churches polarized and denominations were formed over mode of baptism, meaning of communion, consumption of alcohol, and form of church government. Today, many Christians are willing to leave those differences behind because they have taken up new moral and political issues for polarization.

At the same time, while churches divide over these issues, some unlikely and unexpected new alliances are being created.

Pro-life Protestants and Catholics, who might not otherwise have met, now have a strong bond in their opposition to abortion. Many are finding fellowship and service together outside their churches, which is more meaningful than the relationships they have within their respective churches.

Environmentalism shows up as the number one issue among Americans responding to several surveys. It is also a source of polarization within and between churches. One congregation has a group of adults who are convinced that issues of global warming, rain forest destruction, and ozone depletion are scientifically un-verified and based on politically liberal politics. In that same church the children are crusading for recycling soda cans, planting trees and promoting environmental responsibility as an expression of Christian commitment. One group considers Earth Day to be evil, while the other views it as a celebration of God's creation.

These polarizing issues will not soon disappear. Rather, we may expect the positions to become more entrenched and the vol-ume of rhetoric raised. New issues will arise that will draw others into the battles who now sit on the sidelines.

A national proliferation of special interests and a growing re-luctance to compromise compounds this climate of polarization. The result could be anarchy, in which everyone acts on individual convictions, with little regard for common cause or consensus. The church does not stand alone in this trend. The same tendency is regularly seen in the Congress, where members become uncom-promisingly focused on party loyalty, fiscal policy, constitutional interpretation, environmental stewardship, or hundreds of other matters of public policy. Because of so many different issues and such uncompromising commitment, the Congress often cannot act. It is increasingly difficult to agree on a federal budget or pass legislation. For example, even though there has appeared to be a broad-based agreement on reduction of the federal deficit, there is such political polarization that the government has been para-lyzed and unable to act to solve the problem.

The twenty-first century is opening with a sharp focus to single issues, no compromises, and the blaming of others who disagree. The dangers of such polarization are obvious—making the mis-sion of any organization or government harder to fulfill. The twenty-first-century church is caught up in this polarization because people do not leave their convictions and positions outside. Even more significant is the mentality of extremes and polarizations that will increasingly be imported into the church from the culture. Churches will be shaken by a decrease in Christian consensus and an increase in individual competition.

Leaders will increasingly be forced to take firm positions on matters they would rather not address. As those positions are taken, they and their organizations will pass the litmus test of acceptability for some and alienate and disenfranchise others. It will be increasingly difficult to keep many churches and parachurch organizations mobilized by purpose and loyalty to Jesus Christ.

## The Way We Learn

The old paradigm of education centered on time and place. The time was from age 5 through age 18. The place was the classroom. After the "student" passed kindergarten and twelve grades, he or she became a "graduate" and moved on into life as someone who *was* educated. Those who lacked a high school diploma were considered less educated, and those who went on to college were assumed to be more educated because they spent more time in another place. A select few persevered for more time and more places to be officially pronounced masters and doctors of their field.

The old paradigm served well when most information was old and when knowledge was crowned king. But the twenty-first century is an era of information explosion. Some estimate that human knowledge doubles every five to eight years. That means that half of the knowledge in the world was not even available when today's twenty-three-year-old finished high school.

On my first day of class lecture in a university Biology 101 class, the professor started out by saying, "Ten years from now the things I am going to teach you will no longer be true."

Educators designing courses talk about "scope and sequence," which is logical but not always practical. The scope of courses now must reach into the future, far beyond the limits of information now available. Sequence decreasingly fits with our culture—younger people often do not think sequentially. Nor do students always attend school sequentially because of family moves. Some urban school teachers finish the school year with a completely different roster of names than those they began with in September. The same happens in churches. Few Sunday school teachers or pastors would assume that listeners to this week's lesson or sermon were present the previous Sunday. In fact, a class of children may not even have the same teacher week after week.

Twenty-first-century education must emphasize lifelong learning. Systems must be established to access and process new knowledge as it comes on line—long after the school day or graduation is past.

An easy-to-understand example comes from physical education. When I was a high school student, we played football during our physical education classes. Football is a great sport, but very few play the game after graduation. Instead, we watch it on television or go to a stadium—neither of which helps condition our bodies. Modern schools teach tennis, golf, and aerobics in high school physical education classes. Macho fathers may fear that their sons will turn out wimps and won't understand what is going on at the Super Bowl, but the physical education teachers know that tennis, golf, and aerobics can be lifelong physical activities.

But the challenge facing us is bigger than that. Education must equip people to think, to grow, to be, and to do. Peter M. Senge explains it in his popular book *The Fifth Discipline:*

> Learning has come to be synonymous with "taking in information." "Yes, I learned all about that at the course yesterday." Yet, taking in information is only distantly related to real learning. It would be nonsensical to say, "I just read a great book about bicycle riding—I've now learned that."
>
> Real learning gets to the heart of what it means to be human. Through learning we re-create ourselves. Through learning we become able to do something we never were able to do. Through learning we view the world and our relationship to it in a new way. Through learning we extend our capacity to create, to be part of the generative process of life. There is within each of us a deep hunger for this type of learning.[2]

There is no doubt that this lifelong learning, which prepares for the future, accesses new information and generates understanding that is needed for the twenty-first century. But this type of learning isn't easy to teach.

We have assumed that the best way to educate is through reading. This is particularly true for those of us who read books, which includes you. But reading is in decline. Less than 10% of the population buys all of the books sold in America, although that's no guarantee that purchased books are read. The United States has become increasingly post-literate. Twenty-three percent of the US population is illiterate.[3] Newspapers are facing large financial losses as readership declines, which is largely due to less reading by baby boomers (born 1946–1964) and baby busters (born after 1964). Research by the *St. Louis Post Dispatch* revealed that if a person reaches age 18 and doesn't read a newspaper four times per week, there is only a 33% chance of converting him into a regular reader. It is even less likely for *him* than for *her* because women read more than men. When the paper ran six focus groups to check out the views of 18–44 year-olds, they posted pictures of different people around the room and asked which ones were most likely to read newspapers. The winners were a 70-year-old grandmother because "she didn't have anything else to do" and a gray-haired businessman because "he needed to keep up with the news for his job."

How does a newspaper (or a school or a church) convince people who don't want to read to access new information? Here's what *The Boomer Report* suggests, working off the example set by Dan Cotter, marketing manager for the *St. Louis Post Dispatch:*

> Cotter's paper has dumped the usual bland, sober marketing campaign in favor of TV and radio spots using MTV-type music and upbeat themes.
>
> Many papers are experimenting with content and format changes like shorter stories, more features on parenting and environment (boomer favorites), expanded local coverage (boomers want more depth on hometown issues), and tabloid-style graphics and color.[4]

MTV is an interesting comparison. The Music TV channel combines vivid visual experience with popular music. It is a multi-sensory experience. We are increasingly becoming image-oriented. While TV watching has somewhat declined, video rentals have boomed. Laser shows are stunning displays at rock concerts, major league sports events, and even building dedications. A generation that is accustomed to intake of sights, sounds, ideas, emotions, and information all at once tends to become bored with single-sense communication and learning. That reality is hard for an older generation to understand.

Do you remember when the multi-screen audio-visual presentations were popular in the 1970s? Several large screens were set up in an auditorium and banks of slide, movie, and video projectors aimed multiple pictures on the different screens at the same time. Simultaneously there was a sound track that mixed music, background noises, and talking with narration and captions. The first time I watched one of those shows it nearly made me sick. I tried to take in every picture, listen to every sound, and make a logical connection between them all. That's the old paradigm. The new way is to "just experience it all at once," missing some while getting much—with the multi-sensory experience central to the event. That is the way the post-World-War-II generation tends to experience, listen, see, and learn.

The old approach was more theoretical, time-and-place oriented, deductive, linear, sequential, process-oriented, long-term, and standardized (everyone fit into the same schedule and curriculum).

The new approach is more practical, experiential, inductive, rooted in relationships with models and mentors, short-term (like field trips, seminars, and retreats), interactive, hands-on, product-oriented, issue driven, and customized (offering options that fit individual needs).

What does this changing trend mean for the church? Worship services will be increasingly multi-sensory. And yet, multi-sensory worship is not new. Visit an Eastern Orthodox church where the service includes the sounds of music and message but also the sights of art, candles, architecture, vestments, and movement, as well as the smells of incense. Before the invention of the printing press, the church educated with statues, stained-glass windows, plays, and stories. Many twenty-first-century churches will incorporate drama, art, video, interaction, varied music, monologue, dialogue, and other sensory experiences. In certain cases, many of these forms of communication will be happening at the same time.

Sermons in series won't make sense to listeners who attend every other week. In a nonsequential world every sermon will have to stand alone as a complete communication unit.

Discipleship will be outcome-based. The criteria for success will be changed lives that reflect Christian behavior rather than learning a prescribed curriculum.

Content will be clearly tied to the present practical interests of the listener/learner. Theoretical knowledge will be presented in terms of current issues. Relevance will require a local application—how does it relate to my life right now in my community? This is not to say that absolute truth or historic revelation is lessened or minimized, but it will be presented differently. It is like a marketing decision made years ago by a cannery in LeSueur, Minnesota. Since sales were not what they should have been, a product analysis was ordered. The report said the company's vegetables were as good or better than anything else on the market—they should not be changed. Instead, the little known company changed the shape of its cans, which gained better attention on the supermarket shelves. Sales increased until, in 1991, the Jolly Green Giant products were the number one sellers in the nation. The point is they didn't change what was inside, just the way it was presented on the outside. That is a model for the communication of the historic Christian faith in the twenty-first century.

Relationships with role models and mentors will have growing impact over books, quarterlies, or lectures. It may be better to meet with a mentor off-campus than have a class for an hour on Sunday in the basement of the church building. Retreats, seminars, and ministry trips will also prove highly beneficial and life-transforming when they are well planned and well executed.

I was impressed by the testimonies of teens at a baptismal service I recently attended. Nearly half of the fourteen mentioned a specific time and place when they became Christians or experienced a significant spiritual change. Not one was in a church building on a Sunday. They were summer missions trips, weekend retreats, special seminars, or other out-of-church-on-Sunday events. Many, if not most, new career missionaries already have had a previous short-term missionary service experience. It's hands-on, see-it-for-yourself, be-there, real-life education.

Stories will replace a lot of outlines—especially stories that show how Christianity works and how to live. Today's learners are much more inductive than deductive.

Clergy education has already begun to undergo a revolution. Expectations of the clergy have increased. We have had a clergy surplus for the past twenty-five years as a result of the baby boom, the Vietnam War, and the huge number of graduates from Bible colleges and seminaries. But we have a clergy dearth coming. Fewer are preparing for the ministry, and many are moving toward retirement.

The church of the twenty-first century promises to place a premium on performance rather than on credentials. There is less concern over degrees, accreditation, ordination, and other credentials, but an increased asking of the practical question, "Can he or she do the job?"

Anticipate a growing division between scholarship and practice. It has already affected most professions and will have a growing impact on clergy education.

Twenty years ago when I sat in planes at the airport gates, I often saw pilots get out and do a walking inspection of the aircraft before takeoff. That doesn't happen much anymore—because many pilots don't know a lot about the highly sophisticated technical systems that fly their planes. If a light goes on in the cockpit, they call in a technician. The technician doesn't fly the plane, and the pilot doesn't fix the plane.

Medical doctors are trained to be practitioners (often highly specialized) more than research scientists. They prescribe medicine but leave the pharmacological research to the Ph.D.'s (most of whom are not M.D.'s).

Traditional seminary education is designed to train research theologians, who are to become parish practitioners. Probably they are adequately equipped for neither.

Already we have seen an enormous switch from the traditional Master of Divinity degree to various Master of Arts degrees offered by seminaries. I believe we are on the front end of a long-term trend. We will see more and more students choosing either academic scholarship (the theologians) or parish practice (the pastors).

The institutions will change. They must. Few schools have the resources to train both. We will need comparatively few graduate schools of theology and comparatively more professional schools of ministry. Both must move away from the traditional notion of education being time and place, but this switch must especially apply to the preparation of practitioners. They want to be (and the church wants) men and women who can *do* something, not know everything.

## Networking Instead of Incorporating

Incorporation, institutionalization, and bureaucratization have characterized the twentieth-century American culture. We learned it as children. As soon as five or six guys from the neighborhood got together, someone suggested organizing a club. There was an election for president, vice-president, and treasurer (no secretary because the boys didn't want too many written records and thought only girls were secretaries). Rules were chosen—the number one rule was always "No Girls!" As soon as possible, a clubhouse was borrowed or built in someone's backyard, basement, or tree.

We continued that same mind-set as adults. Laborers organized unions. Vendors formed trade associations. Professors incorporated academic societies. Veterans established their VFW and American Legion Posts. Churches had their denominations.

Even established organizations formed other organizations. Unions affiliated with the AFL-CIO. Denominations founded the National Council of Churches, the World Council of Churches, and the National Association of Evangelicals. Nations tried the League of Nations and then started the United Nations.

Most of these organizations quickly incorporated, established boards, hired staff, elected officers, wrote budgets, built buildings, and multiplied rules (sometimes still including "No girls!").

During this period we established much of our personal identity and credibility with organizational affiliations. We categorized one another by the clubs to which we belonged.

While some organization is obviously necessary, the culture is turning away from this long-established tradition. Many people don't want to formally affiliate. They may go to church but not join the church; they like the job but aren't interested in the labor union; they may vote Republican but not register Republican. Masonic lodges have been hit by this non-affiliation trend to the point of advertising on the radio.

Many are fed up with organizations and institutions that they perceive as cumbersome bureaucracies that are slow, expensive, legalistic, and unresponsive. They are just too much hassle. There is a broad-based perception that too many organizations live for themselves and not for their members or customers—the college is more interested in survival than in education, the government exists to serve itself and not the citizens, the church is for the clergy and its traditions but not for the average person.

At the same time people still want to be connected with one another. Perhaps more than ever we want to belong. In rapidly changing times we like to associate with others like ourselves for mutual support. We intuitively sense that the best way to learn is through information exchange with others facing similar problems and opportunities.

We network. We initiate loose connections with people and groups on the basis of some common denominator. Networks are voluntary associations. As long as the network meets our needs, we continue the association, knowing that we are free to leave at any time. Generally networks don't have formal membership, own property, incorporate, or otherwise establish traditional business-type structures. Networks tend to be loose in organization, simple in structure, highly flexible, and comparatively temporary.

Increasingly, when I am invited to a gathering, there are advance promises that there will be no agenda, no minutes, and no formal organization will be established. Such promises are made because the conveners know it is the only way the invitees will come.

Informal networking is taking precedence over formal organization among churches. There are many common denominators among churches and Christians that are stronger than denominational ties, such as church size, geography, race, language, political issues, or socio-economic status.

I belong to a lunch group of seven pastors from larger metropolitan churches. We come from six different denominations. We have no agendas or minutes. Meetings are scheduled from month to month. While our traditions are different, we find we have a lot in common outside of our traditions. I seldom miss a meeting, although I rarely attend any denominational or other institutional meetings on a regular basis.

Some pastors network within their denominations. They attend all the denominational conventions (although they may gather with friends in the coffee shop instead of showing up for the formal meetings).

People are choosing churches not denominations. They view local churches more as networks than formal organizations. Many come and participate but never join. Those who do become members often insist that they may belong to that local church, but they don't consider themselves part of the denomination.

The church of the twenty-first century will be a networking church. Christians will choose their churches on the basis of personal recommendations rather than denominational affiliations. Financial contributions will be controlled more by networks than by denominational assessments, para-church fund-raising, or traditional loyalties. Denominations, colleges, seminaries, missions, and other para-church organizations will continue to exist (at least the larger and stronger ones will), but they will compete for money, members, and followers. Their diminished authority and influence will further decline.

People will remain in churches and educational institutions as long as they sense a personal benefit. If their needs are being met, they will worship, serve, listen, and learn. They will see churches and Christian education as consumers see stores and service businesses, not as patriotic citizens see their country.

This attitude does not mean that they are less committed Christians. The church will be viewed as a means to an end rather than an end in itself. Frankly, we have had many years of church history in which the leaders of the church have seen the church as the end and the people as the means. Those institutional days will increasingly give way to the days of the network.

## New Iconoclasm

The Iconoclastic Controversy of the eighth century was one of
the causes of the division between the Eastern (Orthodox) Church
and the Western (Roman Catholic) Church. Icons (or images)
were traditional in religious life until many attacked them as shams
and literally destroyed them.

The Christian church has had various periods of iconoclasm
when traditions were smashed. Sometimes it has been good; sometimes it has been tragic. Whether good or bad, we are in an iconoclastic period today. Many are attacking and doing away with
long-time traditions of the church, ranging from Latin in the mass
to pipe organs in the sanctuary. The list of today's icons under
attack include traditional hymns, Sunday evening services, Sunday morning services, congregational singing, robes, liturgy, offerings, altar calls, church buildings, denominations, clergy, seminaries, and mission agencies.

In some cases reformation is long overdue. The church could
no longer expect to communicate to a modern generation where
no one understands Latin, wouldn't listen to Elizabethan English,
and excluded women from ministry. However, new is not always
better and old is not always bad. Traditions are essential to human
nature and social stability. When old traditions are abandoned,
new traditions must be established. Furthermore, there are historical precedents for extreme swings of the pendulum. We know
of some of the excesses of the Protestant Reformation followed by
opposite excesses in the Catholic Counter-Reformation.

Take music as an example. Congregational singing was itself a
product of the Protestant Reformation. There was a strong emphasis on doctrine as evidenced in Martin Luther's "A Mighty
Fortress Is Our God." In the 1800s and 1900s doctrinal hymns
gave way to experiential hymns like "Since I Have Been Re-
deemed" and "What A Friend We Have In Jesus." More recently,
the switch has been against experiential hymns and toward worship choruses and the singing of Scripture—or, in some circles,
the abandonment of congregational singing altogether. Is there not
a place for all types? Few churches are tolerant enough to allow
such variety.

As we seek to fashion the church for evangelistic response to the spiritual awakening at the end of the twentieth century, we must be careful to manage the iconoclasts. There is the repeated danger of becoming entrenched in reactionary traditions on the right or such abandonment of traditions on the left that the church is no longer Christian or even religious.

A subcategory of this new iconoclasm is a new anticlericalism. It is a tough time to be a pastor. The expectations are extraordinary. Pastors are expected to be strong leaders at a time when all leadership is suspect, expected to communicate with the skill of Jay Leno, be as socially informed as George Gallup, and as effective managers as the best Harvard M.B.A.'s. Often the expectations are hopelessly unreasonable. Yet those who do not meet the expectations are at risk for termination.

The good news is that laypeople have high expectations and often respond well when much is expected of them. They are far less willing to settle for ineffective churches. I talk to a lot of people from a broad cross section of North American churches and am convinced that large numbers of Christians really want their churches to change for the better. They want their pastors to perform well, but they want to perform well themselves. They want to be spiritually vibrant, evangelistically effective, and socially responsible. I see more openness for change and for effective leadership than at any time I can remember.

These and other differences are already pressuring old churches to change on the inside in the way they relate to the culture on the inside and the outside. Some will cope, some won't. Some will thrive and some will die.

In the twenty-first century many new churches will come that are born into this generation. A few old churches will be reborn—practically dying and starting over again. Among the new and the reborn will appear new shapes and forms of the church.

## Chapter 3

# *What New Forms and Shapes Will the Church Take?*

THERE IS A MCDONALD'S on the Near North Side of Chicago on Ontario Street, just half a block east of LaSalle. It has a 1950s decor, including a classic 1954 white Corvette convertible inside. There are ads, posters, radios, records, and juke boxes from the 1950s. The lines are long and the sales must be in the millions as customers come to step back in time. It appeals to the traditional, reflecting back to a time when life was supposed to be simpler and more stable.

And yet, that McDonald's has some very modern features and services: drive-through window; home-delivery service (the delivery vehicle is a 1955 Chevy station wagon painted red); you can charge souvenirs on your Visa Card; there is an automatic teller machine for cash withdrawals before you order your food; and there is a larger variety on the menu than other McDonald's restaurants.

That Chicago McDonald's is a model for the traditional church in the twenty-first century—doing yesterday better than it has ever been done before.

The shapes of the twentieth-century church have not been unlike the shapes of the seventeenth-, eighteenth-, and nineteenth-century churches of America. Most are small, democratic, denominational, and identified by their buildings and pastors. Church services have been very predictable within denominational traditions. We have had "franchise churches" that are very similar wherever you go. And yet, changes have begun, indicating some of the new shapes and forms of the twenty-first-century church.

## New Shapes and Forms of the Church

MEGACHURCHES have 2,000 or more people at worship services each weekend. They are like large shopping malls offering a broad array of services to enormous numbers of people. Megachurches have large staffs, require expansive facilities, operate on multimillion dollar budgets, provide an impressive variety of services, tend to be leader led, and often have excellent preaching and music. No one knows everyone; most parishioners know others because of associations with groups within the megachurch. These churches operate with a high degree of autonomy even if they are affiliated with a denomination. At the beginning of the century, there were only a handful of churches in North America with more than a thousand at worship. Today there are thousands of churches with over a thousand, and their number is growing. A few megachurches average 10,000 and more at worship services.

It is important to recognize that megachurches are not large versions of minichurches, just as a train is not a large car. They are different kinds of churches. They relate differently. They minister differently. They see themselves differently. Because they are so different, there is a growing shortage of senior pastor candidates for large churches. It used to be that pastoral ministry began part-time while in seminary, progressed to a small rural church, and eventually the successful pastor was promoted to a larger urban congregation. However, the skills to pastor a church of 50, 500, and 5,000 are not the same. Expect megachurches to seek their new senior pastors more and more from the associate pastoral staff of other megachurches because these associate pastors know how the megachurch operates.

Megachurches are especially attractive to baby boomers who are comfortable with large social organizations. They also appeal to persons who seek anonymity, specialized services, or sophisticated programs and methods.

More megachurches are on the way since they fit well with a large part of the coming twenty-first-century culture and lifestyle.

METACHURCHES are relatively few in North America but are becoming more popular. They are based on a network of small groups that function as centers for assimilation, training, pastoral care, and evangelism. Each group has a leader but also trains another leader in anticipation of generating another small group.

The metachurch gathers for worship services but doesn't expect to accomplish most ministry through the Sunday morning gathering. They are decentralized into homes, offices, and other meeting places. Because so much of the ministry is lay led and small-group based, the professional staff of the metachurch may be very small.

The growth potential for the metachurch is far greater than the megachurch because it is not limited by land, buildings, budget, and staff. It can grow indefinitely.

Most famous of the metachurches is the Full Gospel Central Church in Seoul, Korea, with 600,000 members. But there are other Third World metachurches also numbering in the tens and hundreds of thousands of members. So far there are none in North America of such large size, but there may well be metachurches with tens of thousands in the twenty-first century.

Converting traditional churches to metachurches can be very difficult if not impossible. It is such a radically different structure that it is most likely to succeed if it is instituted when the church is first born.

SEVEN-DAYS-A-WEEK CHURCHES are not mutually exclusive from other forms of the church, but they are new and fit in well with the twenty-first century.

To understand how the seven-days-a-week church works requires some history on how Americans have entered churches throughout the twentieth century. Early in the century, a primary entry point for unbelievers into the church was the Sunday evening service. It was often billed as an evangelistic event. Back then there was a perception that Christians went to church on Sunday mornings, but anyone could attend on Sunday night. Thousands of churches from coast to coast and border to border inaugurated

Sunday evening services. Many of them were outreaching, vibrant, effective, and well attended. But they ran their course, and the primary entry point switched after World War II.

In the 1950s the Sunday school became a primary entry point for unbelievers and the unchurched. In those years Sunday school attendance exceeded worship attendance at most churches. Newcomers first tried a Sunday school class and later bridged over to the worship service and other church programs.

During the 1960s and 1970s another switch occurred. This time the Sunday morning worship service became the primary entry point for unbelievers and the unchurched. Only after extended worship service experience might a newcomer venture deeper into the church by connecting with Sunday school, Sunday evening service, midweek meeting, or small group.

In the last half of the 1980s, another switch began when the midweek activities became a primary entry point. The first experience of the church happened in a support group, weekend retreat, Mom's Club, athletic event, party, counseling session, wedding, funeral, or other weekday activity. If the midweek event was a positive experience, the newcomer would risk venturing into a Sunday event.

This fits in well with our culture—its busyness, fatigue, and multiple choices.

The outreaching church now offers many small doors (a variety of midweek events) instead of just one or two big doors (Sunday school or Sunday services). This multi-program approach requires the church to operate seven days a week in order to house and schedule a broad variety of events and programs. We will increasingly see Saturday, Wednesday, Thursday, and Monday worship services (almost all in the evening). There will be education and fellowship activities during every night of the week. The aging population will move into many of the daytime slots. It is the seven-days-a-week church of the twenty-first century.

HOUSE CHURCHES are hard to number because they tend not to be affiliated with denominations, incorporated with the government, or counted in any church census. They are usually small gatherings of Christians in homes and cater to family relationships or special interests. Sometimes they are clergy led, but the pastor will probably be part time or bi-vocational. It is more likely for the house church to be lay led.

The variety of house churches is almost infinite. Some are seasonal, tied to gatherings of summer-home owners. Some are ethnic, gathering the few in the community who speak a foreign language. Some are doctrinal, centering their church on one or two doctrines not common to the other churches in the community.

House churches can be very durable. Budget shortfall or clergy resignation have little effect on them. Their reason for existence is often independent of their existence as a church. For example, the family-system house church is durable because everyone is related to everyone else. Those relationships don't go away. The problem is that house churches can begin or become to be exclusive—the only way to get in is to marry a member.

CHRISTIAN MOSQUES are an example of a new form of the church of which few are aware. These are churches where the Bible is taught and orthodox Christian doctrine is believed, but God may be called Allah, there is no furniture in the room, and the paint on the walls is green. The Christian Mosque targets Muslims much as Messianic congregations target Jews. Until an Arabic Christian friend explained to me that "Allah" is the Christian word for God as well as the Muslim word for God, I didn't know.

TV CHURCHES do not now exist as they might in the twenty-first century. But imagine a form of the church that might develop. Millions of Americans are aging into retirement. There are already more people over 65 than there are teenagers—for the first time in the country's history. Many will become shut-ins who can't or won't leave home for a church service. At the same time, the rise in crime in some sections of the country has turned homes into fortresses with bars on the windows, gates at the doors, and electronic security systems connected to the police department. Those people don't go out any more than they have to. Some work at home via computers with modems. Many have at least their pizza, if not all their food, delivered. Why not stay home for church as well?

TV churches in the twenty-first century need not be the spectator exercise of the 1990s. Interactive TV through cable (or fiber optic, telephone line, or small satellite dish) hookups will enable direct responses and ongoing communication between the viewer and the broadcaster. Actually, the word *broadcast* is better replaced by *narrowcast* for the members of the TV church of the twenty-first century.

Because of many changing factors that will be characteristic of the twenty-first century, new forms and shapes of the church are appearing and will continue to appear. Some of them we cannot imagine now any more than the microwave oven, VCR, and cellular phone could have been imagined in 1960.

WAL-MART CHURCHES are few now, but they may be the most promising prospect for rural America in the twenty-first century.

Rural America has undergone extraordinary changes in the twentieth century, but more changes are on the way. Towns of under 2,500 population are an endangered species.

Many small towns have already lost their schools. It is estimated that the United States will close the century with less than half of the school districts as in 1900 because of consolidation. What happened with schools is now happening with gas stations. State and federal laws are being enacted by Pollution Control Agencies to regulate Underground Storage Tanks. Many old UST's are leaking gasoline, diesel fuel, and fuel oil into the ground water system. Regulations require regular reports, inspections, and repair or replacement of leaky UST's. Such measures are very expensive. Only high-volume stations can meet the regulations and remain profitable. Unless a small-town station is along a major highway or in a resort area, the likelihood of high volume is almost none. Gas stations will close. On November 1, 1991, Peter Jennings reported on "ABC World News" that the number of USA service stations has dropped from 200,000 to 100,000 in the past two decades. Big oil companies are shutting smaller stations and building bigger stations to service larger areas. One of the effects of the UST regulations will be very few small towns with gas stations. Rural residents will have to drive ten or twenty or more miles to a larger town in order to buy gas.

The same thing is happening and will happen with churches in small towns.

Recently our family drove through a rural Kansas town early on Sunday morning. The sign read "Population 131." On the right side of the road sat a lovely church building with red brick walls and stained-glass windows. It represented fine early twentieth-century church architecture. The sign in front read "City Hall and Community Center."

My guess is that the church went out of business because the town didn't have enough people and money to support it. My second guess is that in another ten years the building will be completely closed because there will be a population of less than 131—too small to support a city government and a community center.

I've seen a lot of rural America lately. While some areas flourish, others languish. Many stores are boarded up. Downtown areas are deteriorating. The economy is tough. Most of the jobs to be found are in the cities.

But I've also seen a lot of Wal-Marts. Where there is no Wal-Mart, there always seems to be a large truck with "Wal-Mart" on the side, driving down the highway to a Wal-Mart. Wal-Marts are huge stores with lots of employees. They are highly successful in rural America, where other businesses are closing.

Wal-Marts are a fascinating rural phenomenon that has now begun to penetrate the cities. Until a year or so ago, I had never shopped in a Wal-Mart store because I live in a metropolitan area where none exist. But, a Wal-Mart is being built near my home, and the established urban retailers had better watch out. In 1991 Wal-Mart surpassed Sears and Roebuck to become the number one retailer in America.

Why? Wal-Mart gives a lot for the money. Wal-Mart has a friendly and helpful greeter (a grandparent type) to welcome customers coming in the front door. Wal-Mart gives lots of choices—more than any of the little stores around. Wal-Mart offers excellence. Wal-Mart is user friendly and consumer sensitive. One Wal-Mart employee told me about the "ten-foot rule"—every employee is to greet and offer assistance to any customer who comes within ten feet of that employee. Since the first Wal-Mart opened, all employees, from the late Sam Walton at the top to the part-time stock boy of the newest store, have gone on a first-name basis. Perhaps most of all, Wal-Mart has given permission for rural residents to move outside of their traditional retail relationships into a superstore with new and different relationships.

We need Wal-Mart churches: churches that will serve regional rural markets; churches that are friendly, carry lots of programs, are customer-driven rather than institution-driven; churches that transcend the deep traditions of small communities and give permission to worship without alienating family histories and relationships.

NEW CHURCHES are beginning in North America at a wonderful rapid rate. Such rapid growth is a very good thing because new churches are the most effective means of evangelism.

New churches are flexible, open to newcomers, entrepreneurial, outreaching, and not burdened with servicing old internal relationships and demands.

Unfortunately, new churches tend to be outreaching for a maximum of twelve years. When they are young, they are excited and need new people to survive. As churches become older, they quickly show signs of aging and decline. After a dozen years, these churches tend to become so burdened with budgets, buildings, and pastor and people problems that they no longer have the energy for outreach. The once outward churches have turned inward.

Over a century ago many denominations established comity agreements that limited the locations of new churches. If a church already existed in a community, another one would not be started. Some denominations wouldn't plant a new church anywhere near an existing church of any denomination. More often, denominations stay away from existing churches of their own denomination. It is a territorial notion of the church. The result has often been terrible. For example, a denominational First Church has been in New Town for seventy-five years. It is old and ineffective. New Town begins to grow with urban sprawl. The population skyrockets by thousands every year. There are enough people for dozens of new churches, but the denomination won't start another church in First Church territory. The consequences are either thousands of unreached people or thousands of people reached by other churches who *will* move in.

In the twenty-first century few people choose a church by location. Most Americans drive by several churches, often at least one of their own denomination, on their way to their chosen place of worship. Churches are selected for personal, demographic, psychographic, and other reasons—but seldom just for geographic reasons.

Churches that recognize this reality aren't afraid to have other new churches emerge nearby. The new church is likely to minister to people whom the old church could never attract. Healthy churches near one another often help each other. Have you noticed that Arby's, Wendy's, Burger King, Subway, and McDonald's are often within less than a mile of one another? That's because different customers have different tastes.

NON-CHURCHES may seem like the strangest new form of all. A research project out of Collegeville, Minnesota, indicates what we probably already know. A large and growing segment of America's population has a spiritual experience outside of established churches. The "church" for many is a 12-Step Program. For others it is individual Christianity tied to a spiritual director. There are many home and family churches to match home schools. These people say their spiritual needs are being well met without anything that resembles a structured church.

Some churchgoers will be quick to quote "Forget not the assembling of yourselves together" or argue for the necessity of church organization, elders and deacons, baptism and communion, church discipline, and spiritual gifts. They are correct. But they are also theoretical and philosophical and may be talking to nonchurch people who are primarily practical.

TRADITIONAL CHURCHES will be one of the major growing segments of the twenty-first century to the surprise of many.

We have heard so much about nontraditional churches with new music, contemporary styles, and iconoclastic attitudes that we have ignored America's growing interest in the traditional. The marketing analysts are keenly aware of what is happening—people are reacting to change, frightened by losing control, and worried about the future. There is lots of interest in the way it used to be. As a result, the divorce rate has dropped back to 1970s levels, the birth rate is the highest since the baby boom, and styles from the 1940s and 1950s are coming back into vogue. Nostalgia is in! Many Americans are trying to recapture yesterday. Faith Popcorn subtitles the first chapter of her bestselling *The Popcorn Report* "The future bears a great resemblance to the past, only more so."

Do not underestimate the power of this phenomenon. There is a significant positive future for traditional churches with flavors and styles from the mid-twentieth century. However, two necessary ingredients must be added to the mix:

1. Successful traditional churches will need to incorporate many contemporary elements, including services to consumers and meeting modern needs.

2. Successful traditional churches will need to do the traditional with a high level of excellence. Many people remember the past better than it actually was; and, younger adults who weren't part of the past idealized it to be far better than reality. Yesterday must be even better than today if it is to have a place for tomorrow.

## Christian Creativity, Not Details

While the New Testament speaks often about churches, it is surprisingly silent about many matters that we associate with church structure and life. There is no mention of architecture, pulpits, lengths of typical sermons, or rules for having a Sunday school. Little is said about style of music, order of worship, or times of church gatherings. There were no Bibles, denominations, camps, pastors conferences, or board meeting minutes.

Those who strive to be New Testament churches must seek to live its principles and absolutes, not reproduce the details. We don't know many of the details, and if we reproduced the ones we do know, we would end up with synagogues, speaking Greek, and the divisive sins of the Corinthians.

Each church in the first century had its own personality and style, fitted to its time and place. The Ephesian church was not a franchise of the Jerusalem church. Change and creativity were welcomed.

No Christian or church has the right to deviate from the Bible, but each has the freedom to respond to the creativity of the Spirit.

## New Leaders for a New Century

The twenty-first century will require some new types of leaders. Personally, I find that threatening.

Peter Drucker says every time an organization doubles in size, half of the leadership becomes obsolete. I am a leader, and I fear obsolescence.

I also know how hard it is to change. Many of the old ways are my ways—I like them and feel comfortable with them. I struggle to distinguish between what is absolute and what is relative—because I do not want to compromise God's absolute truths on the altar of current fads.

Sometimes I wish everything could stay the same until I retire, and then all this new stuff can be someone else's problem. That way I would be free to reflect on yesterday's successes and free to criticize the new ways of doing things.

But I'm not called to be comfortable. I'm not called to a denomination, a Sunday service schedule, or to any particular methodology. I am called to Jesus Christ and have been commissioned by him to reach my generation for him. That means *I* must change.

What qualifications must the new leaders for the twenty-first-century church have?

New leaders must be *attuned to their culture*. It is not enough to know the Bible. We must also know our culture and our people. We must have incarnational ministries in the pattern of Jesus, who was the eternal Son of God before he came to earth. His *incarnation* put God into a human body. He was no less God. The difference was that he became human, bringing Deity to humanity. Incarnational ministry today does the same thing—it brings God to humans—without compromising God and with fully relating to human form and need. In the first chapter of the gospel of John, the apostle John explains how the Son of God did it when the Word became flesh and lived among us. The book of Acts and the rest of the New Testament also explain how the early church lived and ministered incarnationally in its era and culture.

New leaders must be *flexible*. Rigid people with inflexible methods are going to bend and break in the years ahead. In changing times we need leaders who are able to adapt.

New leaders must be *relational*. Relationships are more important than ever. Churches want leaders who are real and approachable. This does not mean they must be extroverts or always working the crowd. Leaders must live where their people live, feel their emotions, and intuitively sense their thoughts. Another way of saying it is that leaders must relate. The people in the church and community must be attracted to a leader enough to identify, listen, and respond.

New leaders must be *good communicators*. In stable times communication isn't quite so important. But when society is threatened and the world is experiencing drastic political, social, and economic upheavals, we need people like Abraham Lincoln and Winston Churchill who can communicate the vision and move the people.

New leaders must be *entrepreneurs*. Entrepreneurship is not just starting something from scratch. It is the ability to make something succeed. They see the opportunities in the changes and strategize to turn those opportunities into good for God's kingdom and Christ's church.

New leaders must be *risk takers*. Those who seek to avoid risk and conserve may end up with nothing. Risk takers are willing to fail in order to succeed.

Along the Main Street sidewalk in Longmont, Colorado, there is a plaque marking the spot where a butcher opened a store and went bankrupt. He moved north to Wyoming after leaving Longmont, where J.C. Penney tried again with a dry goods store that succeeded.

Henry Ford went bankrupt three times. Thomas Edison tried 10,000 times before his light bulb worked. Sister Kenny was rejected by the medical community for her unconventional rehabilitation methods before she moved to Minnesota to establish the world-renowned Sister Kenny Institute. They were leaders who were risk takers.

New leaders must be *godly*. Most of all we need leaders who are men and women of God. Those who have Christian integrity. Who have suffered enough to be tested and proven. Those who have their prayers answered. Those who have died to self and who live for Christ. No fakes. No mere professionals. We need leaders who are genuine disciples of Jesus Christ.

## Driving the 21st Century Highway

I was an eighteen-year-old college student when the measles canceled my summer study program at the University of Minnesota. So I sat behind the wheel of my 1961 Volkswagen beetle and started the long drive to my parents' home in New Jersey.

After driving all night, I was finally on the hilly, twisting, tunneled old Pennsylvania Turnpike. It was morning, but I was so tired that I fell asleep behind the wheel. I was awakened with a jerk, only to see the front of a huge Mack truck directly ahead of me. I thought I would die. But—it was being towed backward.

Obviously I lived to tell the story. I also stayed awake for the rest of the trip.

Drivers need to stay awake.

Leaders of the twenty-first-century church are headed down a road to the future that moves very fast. The map hasn't been drawn yet. There will be surprise curves and sudden stops and starts. It will be exciting!

So, don't fall asleep.

Stay alert, and lead the church of the Savior into its best century yet.

## Chapter 4

# *Would You Recognize Success If You Had It?*

THE SOUTHERN CALIFORNIA pastor started a new program to reach younger families. The genius of the plan was the Wednesday night meeting time. First, there was a dinner so parents could pick up their children on the way home from work. It was subsidized so that the price was not prohibitive. Next, there was an informal church service, which significantly varied from the usual Sunday morning liturgy. Finally, everyone was invited to stay afterward for conversation and fellowship.

Lots of people came. Far more than anyone anticipated. The attendance grew over the first two months of the trial period. Those who came loved the whole concept and spread the word among their friends.

The pastor, however, was disappointed. Since he felt that the program had failed, he closed it down. To his surprise, its appeal had not been to younger families but to senior citizens. They had come by the hundreds. Some say it was a success that the pastor could not recognize.

Management expert Peter Drucker cites a similar situation with Apple computers. The original dream was to produce a line of computers that had broad appeal and application within the business community. Apple's greater appeal was to schools. Most of America's schools scrambled to raise funds to buy computers for at least one laboratory. Millions of American children were first introduced to computer technology on an Apple. But that market wasn't good enough for some company executives. They were determined to make their computers into business machines. In a sense, they succeeded but didn't like the results.

Some succeed and call themselves failures. Some fail and call themselves successes. Few step back soon enough or long enough to define what is failure. Such definitions go a long way toward enabling a church to change.

## Success Is Difficult to Define

Success tends to be highly subjective. What looks good to one looks bad to another. Different perspectives are nowhere more painful than in the words of a divorced husband who says, "I thought our marriage was going well. I thought we were both really happy. Then she served me with divorce papers, said that she's been miserable for years, and probably never loved me in the first place. I was devastated."

Every year a famous bicycle race is held in India, where the goal is to come in last. Cyclists, who are not allowed to touch the ground with hands or feet, go as slowly as possible. A visitor who doesn't know what winning is might pedal fast, reach the finish line first, and declare victory.

The same thing happens when employees are fired or quit. The surprised employee defensively argues, "I thought I was doing a great job and that the boss was pleased with my work." Or the boss who just lost a valuable team member to the competition explains, "I was sure she would stay until she retired here. She was well paid and happy and fulfilled. I still can't believe she just up and left!"

It is no less common in churches. Every year hundreds of pastors are surprised by involuntary termination. They thought they were doing okay. Even more common are Christians who think everything is going great, while their pastors are trying to convince them to change their church before it dies. Meanwhile, there are some churches calling themselves successful that I would consider cultic. Some very famous American churches thought they were doing well until their leaders were exposed by the press and convicted by the courts.

Success scares some Christians. One pastor told me, "Our bishop believes a successful church must be out of God's will." Some assume success means sin. Obviously that is not the case when we say, "Jesus successfully defeated sin and death on the cross and through the resurrection." No Christian would want to call Jesus a failure. So it depends on who means what by the word "success."

Why are there such discrepancies in the definition of success? Sometimes it is merely a matter of preference. A used car salesman once told me, "You can negotiate the price, compromise on the delivery date, and even agree to put on new tires, but if she doesn't like the color, you don't have a sale." Some people like blue. Others hate blue. It is a matter of personal preference. If the preference is strong enough, nothing else matters.

The far greater problem is when no one has made the effort to define success in advance. Without a well-defined target, it is hard to determine if someone is a winner even if he or she hits the bull's-eye every time.

When seeking a new music director in the 1980s, I was part of a search committee that wisely asked the question: "How will this person know whether he or she has succeeded after a year on the job?" A list included "100 in the choir" and another half-dozen specifics. Admittedly, there was much more to success than checking off each accomplished item on the list. It would be possible to have one hundred monotones. What is significant is that an effort was made to name specifics of success in advance.

Some individuals and organizations balk at the notion of defining success in advance—especially churches. Some believe there is a lack of spirituality about such definitions. The reality is that all persons and organizations define success whether they admit to it or not. Comedian Woody Allen says, "Eighty percent of success is showing up." There are many for whom that is not a joke. They really believe if they have shown up for school, work, or church, they are successful.

Early definitions of success are usually perpetuated and reinforced unless there is a special undertaking to change prior definitions. When threatened, we are all likely to revert to our earlier concept of success even if that concept is now inappropriate and will make matters worse.

One example is a church that was founded fifty years ago as an outgrowth of evangelistic meetings in a rural community. Success was defined as bringing in an itinerant evangelist for several weeks of meetings. The church has had such events almost every year since. Most recently the congregation has gone into decline, and there have been six consecutive years without "revival" meetings. As the leaders gather to face the future, the temptation to seek solution in another round of evangelistic meetings is almost irresistible. It is much more difficult to admit: (1) the community has changed from rural to suburban; (2) the appeal of outside evangelists and special meetings has disappeared among the present population with busy schedules and too many events to choose from; (3) the time and money invested in evangelistic meetings have been diverted from the programs that would have far greater effectiveness in today's community; (4) a new definition of success is needed.

Pastors are subject to the same temptation. Many were trained with the belief that the definition of success in a parish is the number of pastoral calls made. In some communities and churches this is still the case. Many churches that once flourished through pastoral visitation now need a fresh preaching style, expanded program options, and a different style of worship service. When Pastor Matherly recognizes that the church is not going well and feels ill-equipped to make the changes others request, what does he do? He redoubles his visitation efforts among the faithful.

Because of the tendency to self-perpetuate definitions of success, it is crucial to carefully define success from the beginning and remain open to new definitions of success along the way.

Even though defining success is difficult to do, it is worth the effort. Even if the definition must later be amended or changed, the process itself can make for increased effectiveness and far better relationships.

## Success and the Pastor

The 1990s have turned out to be a tough time for pastors. The North American church is traveling through a transition period in history. No one knows where we are going. Nevertheless, church members expect pastors to know.

During the 1960s and 1970s, seminaries and other pastor-training institutions skyrocketed in enrollment. There were more graduates than church jobs available. Churches seeking clergy had a buyer's market. It was not unusual for some churches with an average Sunday morning attendance of 100 to have 125 nominations presented to the pastoral search committee. The competition became fierce among baby boomer pastors.

Consumerism soared over the past four decades as customers began to demand more from suppliers. University students petitioned for less competent professors to be fired and demanded that their favorite instructors be tenured. Grocery shoppers insisted that labels reveal all ingredients and that questionable products be recalled. Television viewers pressured networks to meet their demands. And churches adopted a consumer mentality as well.

Many older pastors resigned or retired in deep discouragement. They were unable to understand, much less adapt to, the new ways of doing church. Often they tried harder at what they had always done, only to find they were criticized for doing the wrong things. The conflicting demands of highly vocal parishioners sometimes immobilized ambitious new pastors, who also became discouraged, and many left the ministry.

It is not exclusively a North American phenomenon. A significant study of former pastors in Australia has sought to determine why so many leave the pulpit and where they go. "Some observers believe more pastors and priests are leaving parish ministries than are lost to any other profession," says Rowland Croucher, founder and director of Australia's John Mark ministries.[1] According to Croucher:

> There are possibly 10,000 Australian men and women who were once in pastoral ministry, and now, for a variety of reasons, are pursuing another vocation. For a few, the transition is relatively stress-free, but for most the emotional and spiritual strain associated with exiting what was

intended to be a life-long vocation is considerable. Divorce and suicide rates among this group are high, and up to half are no longer worshiping regularly in any church.[2]

There are many specific reasons why pastors feel like failures, leave the ministry, or otherwise collapse in their vocation. Here are half a dozen of the more common causes:

## 1. *Unrealistic expectations*

Some call it the "walk-on-water syndrome." It is the belief, too often shared by both the pastor and the congregation, that the clergyperson can do anything. Syndromes are not single-symptom maladies but composites of many symptoms. When factors such as clergy glut, consumerism, and pastors who are achievement-motivated exist, the volatile mix is present to believe he or she can and should be nearly perfect.

It is not that any one expectation is impossible. A scintillating sermon most Sundays might happen. Visitation of parishioners is not unreasonable. Competent counseling is not unusual. Church growth is certainly desirable. Fund-raising is part of the job. But no one is able to fully meet all of the expectations. Our increasingly pluralistic and fragmented churches are multiplying the list of unrealistic expectations. There are fewer who have a sense of the whole and more who are bent on their special interest.

Maybe the challenge is largest in the Roman Catholic Church with its growing shortage of priests. "A priest is expected to be spiritually deep, theologically wise, and fiscally clever, while being good at preaching and counseling with young and old. Each person in the congregation expects only a limited something, but the conglomeration can be overwhelming," says Father David Brinkmoeller, director of Priestly Life and Ministry at the National Conference of Catholic Bishops in Washington, D.C.[3]

Peter Drucker suggests that among the most difficult jobs in America today are the presidency of a university, administering a hospital, and pastoring a large church. In each case the demands are many. Usually, a university president comes from the academic ranks with an earned doctorate and credibility in a particular academic field. Nevertheless, she or he must also be an adept manager, articulate spokesperson, and gifted in dealing with diverse groups that range from alumni to students to parents to politicians. Few can do all well.

As hard as running a school or hospital may be, few presidents are well known to the average student, and almost no hospital patients know the name of the administrator. But it is different with a church. The pastor is highly visible to almost every member, and he or she must fulfill the triple roles of scholar, priest, and shepherd. Candidly, very few persons are fully gifted in all areas.

Too many times the spotlight focuses on failures rather than successes, on weaknesses rather than strengths. The parishioner says, "I wish he would preach better sermons," or "the new pastor certainly isn't as good an administrator as the last pastor," or "the sermons may be good, but I don't feel my pastor cares for me as a person." What happens next can be sadly predictable. The pastor also focuses on the weakness and pours energy and time into improving in an area where he or she will probably never be strong. At the same time, what the pastor does best is neglected and is no longer done as well. It becomes a downward spiral of unmet unrealistic expectations.

## 2. Difficult churches

"There are congregations that are widow makers," according to *Leadership Journal* editor Marshall Shelley. "I would say if two pastors in a row don't stay in a church more than three years, it's probably not the problem of the pastors."[4]

These churches are like dysfunctional families that entangle the pastor into the system. It becomes harder and harder to think and act objectively and independently. The church has a history of criticism, undermining, or even pervasive sin. Often those in such a church do not recognize their own sicknesses. They really believe it has always been the pastor's fault.

When there is an oversupply of pastoral candidates, difficult churches have great freedom to perpetuate their damages. As soon as one pastor leaves, another is always waiting with a resume and anxious to pick up the challenge. Seldom do pastors who become the victims and casualties of such churches fully recognize the situation. Unfortunately, there is usually a high level of self-blame. Both the devastated pastor and the difficult church lose out.


## 3. *Dysfunctional families*

The other side of the coin is pastors who come from difficult homes. They bring emotional and psychological baggage with them that may undermine from the beginning their likelihood of effectiveness and success.

Paul Rasmus, an Episcopal priest who left the ministry in the wake of alcoholism and divorce and later returned, says, "I find that a lot of us, growing up, wanted to save our families—but, when that was impossible, we went out to save the world. We're generally workaholics, and we're great at fixing other people, but we don't have the foggiest notion of what to do for ourselves."[5]

While it is inappropriate to classify all clergy into certain personality types, there are some common threads among those who struggle the most. Dr. Wayne Fehr, director of spiritual care at the Saint Barnabas Center in the Milwaukee area, explains that "they share an excessive compulsive absorption in work to the neglect of their personal needs. There's a deeply rooted, overwhelming need to please others, to take care of everybody else, to avoid conflict—but at some point it becomes too hard, and everything breaks down."[6] The consequence, according to Dr. Glen Gabbard of the Menninger Memorial Hospital in Topeka, Kansas, is that "they try to be loving to others in hopes of getting love in return—but often, to their surprise, they're met with a host of problems and become the target of complaints, resentment, and disappointment."[7]

In other words, the pastor's own problems do him or her in, even in an average church that has average people with their own average problems. The pastor can't get beyond personal issues to be an adequate agent for ministry and change in the parish.


## 4. *Inadequate training*

There is a growing realization that classical theological education has not appropriately prepared men and women for leadership in late twentieth-century American churches.

One well-known evangelical seminary has developed a continuing education module, which insiders have dubbed the "recall program." Like cars being recalled by Detroit for correction of poorly designed brakes or fuel lines, this seminary is trying to bring back graduates from the 1960s and 1970s before they experience failures in the church. Like all recall programs, it is based on the recognition that many have already failed and the reason is in an initial design error.

Much theological education is based on the "academy model" of classical European universities. Students are trained to be scholars. They are given the tools for research and analysis, and then are trained to be theoretical theologians. Certainly there is a need for such specialized training. Without careful scholarship the Christian church would probably repeat the heresies of earlier eras within a generation.

The rub comes when graduates face the realities of parish ministry. There is little time for the more leisurely life of scholarship. People aren't asking for academic alternatives, they are expecting practical answers to life's problems. Too often the pastor is like an emergency-room physician trained in genetic research but surrounded by patients with gunshot wounds.

Pastors are among the few generalists in a society where most specialize. The system may need to adjust in ways that will train some to research the theology and others to pastor the churches. The researchers will need to know the basics of practice, and the practitioners will need to know the basics of theology. Few, if any, will know both in depth.

Larger churches even now are working out their own new approaches. Rather than look to the seminaries to provide program staff, these churches are recruiting laypersons from their own memberships—usually those who have already demonstrated practical skills in their churches.

Some of the greatest stress is being experienced by those who were trained a decade or more ago to be scholars, and now find that their scholarship is unappreciated and the skills they need are absent. Current demands on pastors focus on leadership, communication, administration, and interpersonal relationships. These skills often were not learned at seminary. Or, perhaps, it is better to ask: "*Can* these skills be learned in a school?" New formats are now developing in which churches and schools work together in training clergy; schools emphasize theory while churches emphasize practice. Internships and "field education" are being added to the curriculum. The student then implements theory in a practical setting of a church under the guidance and supervision of one with experience.

Fortunately, seminaries and other institutions are offering effective means for pastors to retool their skills. They include continuing education classes, doctor of ministry programs, sabbatical leaves, books, videos, and numerous conferences. Churches should require and fund their pastors in these growth and change opportunities.

## 5. Stress

All of the above relates to stress. Yet there is a sense in which stress must have a category of its own.

Roy Oswald is a senior consultant of The Alban Institute in Washington, D.C. In his work with churches and synagogues he estimates, "Seventeen percent of the parish clergy he has worked with in more than 20 years of consulting are suffering from long-term stress or burnout."[8]

In 1989 the Southern Baptist Convention paid out $64.2 million in medical claims for pastors. The number two cause for claims was "stress-related illness."[9]

This is not a phenomenon limited to any one denomination. It is a characteristic of what is happening in the entire society. Stress is taking its toll as crimes increase, unemployment rates fluctuate, and problems multiply. Thirty years ago newspaper and magazine articles predicted the myriad of ways Americans would use all their extra leisure time in the 1980s and 1990s. The forecasters were wrong: Working hours have increased, not decreased.

For pastors, who are people and have their own stresses and problems beyond their profession, the problem is compounded.

Oswald says, "When stress on the culture rises, people bring that pressure to their church, along with higher expectations of the clergy. But at the same time, it's less and less clear what it means to be a pastor. As a result, clergy are trying to live up to these expectations by covering all the bases, but it's never enough.

They can't quit at the end of the day and feel they've done everything, because there's always someone else in need."[10]

Economic pressures in the ministry are not unlike those that working people face. Salaries are generally lower than other professions with comparable education and responsibilities. (In 1988 Protestant ministers averaged $23,000 in income, or a total of $38,000 with housing and all other benefits, according to the U.S. Department of Labor estimates.) Many enter parish ministry with heavy education loans. When recession or other economic setbacks hit a community, church income and clergy salaries are affected.

But it's much more than money. There are marriage strains, adolescent children, aging parents, infertility, illness, self-esteem, and everything everyone else is up against. What is different is the frequent congregational expectation and self-expectation that pastors should be better equipped to handle these problems than anyone else. And when they are not able to cope as well as others, many pastors become self-declared failures.

## 6. Success

Success is an unlikely item to end a list of failures, but success is a potent cause of failure for some. Take the tragic story of Rick Chollet. Here's the way *Newsweek* reported it:

> Saying that Rick Chollet had it all doesn't quite say it. Chollet, the son of struggling French immigrants, built a small mail-order tool business called Brookstone into a hugely successful national purveyor of adult toys and gadgets. He was handsome, happily married, loved by his employees and colleagues—and, it turned out, deeply despondent. Last March 18, out of the blue it seemed, Chollet took his life. "Please forgive me, but the thought of going through the torture of living is just too much to bear," he wrote before locking the garage door of his New Hampshire house, climbing into his BMW and turning on the engine. His wife, Susan, later revealed that Chollet had been depressed for half of his adult life. People put him on such a pedestal, she said, that he constantly feared letting them down. "He swung from feeling totally powerful to totally helpless."[11]

Analysis of cases like Chollet's provides multiple reasons for the destructiveness of success. One is loss of personal identity in success. Do people like me for who I am or for what I have done? Another is "encore anxiety," worry about trying to repeat a successful performance. Often the expectations get greater and greater. As one pastor put it, "If our church keeps growing at the current rate, by the year 2020 our average Sunday morning attendance will exceed the population of the world!" Those who expand a church or a company 100% in one year must eventually face the mathematical reality that such growth cannot continue indefinitely. Then there are those who sense they have succeeded far beyond their competence and live in dread that people will discover how weak they really are. In other words, they think they "lucked out" in getting to where they are but want others to think that it was because of their talents and expertise.

As a result, successful people sometimes try to find an acceptable way out. Steven Berglas is a psychotherapist and the author of *The Success Syndrome: Hitting Bottom When You Reach the Top*. He explains that executives may adopt "self-handicapping" behavior so that they will have something to blame other than their own incompetence. So they gain weight, become ill, or find some other excuse that gives them a means of "quitting without appearing to quit."

In church terms, those considered to be successful are often the pastors of megachurches and the heads of well-known parachurch ministries. The casualties among their rank have been many and well-publicized. Often it is because of such self-defeating behavior as moral sin.

Some argue that God never intended churches to be so large, pastors to be so famous, or Christians to be so popular. Their demise is therefore reckoned to be the judgment of God. While that may be true in some cases, it is certainly not a valid universal explanation. Most well-known Christian leaders do not fail. Some have stood in the limelight for a lifetime without straying from the highest standards of Christian virtue. As the nineteenth-century London pastor Charles Haddon Spurgeon explained, "It takes a steady hand to hold a full cup." There have been and are many steady hands among Christian leaders. Those who shake and fall include some who simply could not handle success. They were afraid of failure, afraid of being found out, or simply afraid of success.

Nevertheless, there are some hopeful signs that the environment for the clergy will improve over the next ten years.

## 1. *A clergy dearth is coming.*

It is predictable just in terms of those approaching retirement and the greatly reduced number of ministerial candidates. Almost all seminaries and Bible colleges have lower enrollments. Many have merged or closed. There is little sign that the decline will soon stop. Many of those who are currently enrolled in seminaries and Bible colleges will never end up in vocational ministry. A large number are studying for degrees that do not lead to ordination. Many are laypersons who are already in a vocation and are going to school for expansion of their biblical and theological knowledge rather than preparing for full-time ministry. Some long-time observers say the quality of seminary students is less than it was twenty and thirty years ago, and that many now in school will never make it to a pastoral call.

All of these factors point to a coming shortage. There will be a switch from the recent buyer's market to a seller's market. Churches will have a much more difficult time finding pastors, will probably expend more time and energy to find effective pastors, and will work much harder to retain those they have.

## 2. *There will be fewer and newer churches.*

This will result from the current trend of weaker churches closing (or merging) and the great upsurge in starting of new churches. The combination of trends will tend to eliminate some of the struggling parishes and replace them with younger, stronger churches.

## 3. *A new period of stability will begin.*

Perhaps this is only hopeful thinking, but it would seem that the new upheaval and changes of the 1990s will not go on indefinitely. New forms of worship, evangelism, associations, and "doing church" will emerge and stabilize. Like forms before them, they will serve a generation or more before a new period of transition begins.

Since upheaval has often served the church well, the present may be the era of far greater opportunity for evangelism, innovation, and growth. If there is a subsequent period of stability, it may lessen the stress level of pastors, but it may also be a time of spiritual and ecclesiastical stagnation.

Meanwhile, it must be stated that by no means do all pastors currently fail. There are 537,379 clergy persons of all different faiths in the United States, according to The National Council of the Churches of Christ. An estimated 325,000 of these are serving churches or synagogues. It is impossible to count accurately all those outside of the statistical system, especially laypastors. However, there are over 300,000 serving parishes, and most don't quit, are not fired, and probably don't consider themselves to be failures. Those who see themselves as successes usually have a clear definition of what success is and a personal sense that they measure up. They are more than survivors. They are the leaders of the religious community, which makes the U.S. one of the most religious countries in the world.

12/15/92

## Chapter 5

# What Are Successful Churches?

THE CAPTION of the *Leadership Journal* cartoon said it well: "All the great churches are 1,000 miles away."

Distance seems to make successful churches more successful. Those nearby are close enough that their flaws can be examined. Thus, pastors and other church leaders frequently travel a thousand miles or more to attend a conference or study a successful church in order to learn how to replicate the principles and programs back at home. Sometimes this works well; sometimes it is divisive and destructive. In many cases it depends on the definition of success. If the mentor church and the home church share a definition of success, there is a much greater probability that replication will work well.

Different churches have defined success in different ways:

1. *Success is numbers.*

This is one of the most popular definitions for obvious reasons. Americans tend to define financial success by how much money a person has, athletic success by how many points are scored, business success by how many employees, products, and offices a company has, and health success by the right numbers for weight, blood pressure, and cholesterol. Numbers are tangible, measurable, and objective. They are easy to see and easy to understand.

When denominational directories arrive in the mail, the listed numbers establish a clear pecking order by size of attendance, membership, or contributions. At conferences, pastors artfully communicate the size of their churches until everyone knows where everyone else stands.

We all know the problems with this approach. Among countries, for instance, the numbers prizes go to such central African nations as Rwanda and Burundi for density of population or to the People's Republic of China with more than a billion citizens. Switzerland barely makes the list by comparison. Except Switzerland does dramatically better in per capita wealth and life expectancy. Thus, bigger is not necessarily better.

Although we know the flaws of measuring success by size, we still perpetuate the system because it's so easy to do so.


## 2. Success is representation.

This was a more popular measure in 1950 but still claims a large following today. It is the notion that every community should have its own Presbyterian, Lutheran, Baptist, Catholic, or Methodist church. Some go a step further to insure that each community has one of each kind of Baptist church and one from each synod of Lutheranism.

When denominational loyalty is high, planting new churches or maintaining old churches for representation is very important. With declining denominationalism and an increased sensitivity to demographics, this definition of success has taken on new expressions. Today, it may call for a particular style of worship to be represented in that community. A church with the Latin mass must be maintained in a metropolitan area because all the other Catholic churches have switched to the vernacular. A new Vineyard Fellowship church is needed because there are no similar charismatic churches around.

Ethnic churches often define success by representation. Many immigrants come to North America unable to speak English or fit in with the culture. A long-established pattern has concentrated immigrants in certain geographic areas (Cubans in Miami, Chinese in San Francisco, Koreans in Los Angeles, Mexicans in the Southwest, Hmong in St. Paul, Dutch in Michigan, Polish in Chicago). Immigrants tend to be very open to the gospel of Jesus Christ and a fertile soil for starting new churches. Success is seen as having a church for each ethnic group in a city. It not only works well, but it may be the only strategy that will effectively reach first generation immigrants. The downside comes with the immigrants' children and grandchildren, who may want to disassociate from the old culture and language. Within only a generation they may not even know the language and culture of the old country, which forces the ethnic church to negotiate a new definition of success or die with the old generation.

This raises an important secondary question. Is there anything wrong with a church serving a single generation and then closing down? It may be that the practical life of most churches is thirty-five to fifty years. After that they become obsolete and ineffective unless they are renewed. A church that intends to serve a specific audience (ethnic, generational, or other) may be highly successful for one generation and then close its doors. State governments, for example, have what are called "sunset laws" that have the termination date of the law built in from the beginning.

Among conservative Christians the words most often heard are "there is no Bible-teaching church" in that town. There is interest in a denominational label only as long as there is systematic (usually "expository") Bible teaching as a central part of the Sunday morning worship service as well as other important programs of the church.

The effect of this definition of success has often been good. New churches have started and old churches have maintained. The problems arise when a new generation arrives with a different set of loyalties and no mechanism exists for either renewing the old definition of success or negotiating a new definition of success. In an increasingly pluralistic society, multiple diverse churches may serve to broaden the basis of appeal for the many different kinds of people in the community. There is, however, the danger of also clinging so vehemently to ecclesiastical idiosyncrasies that most people are turned off.

3. *Success is faithfulness.*

Typically, these are churches with highly defined systems of doctrine or tradition. They may be creedal with carefully written theological beliefs. Often they say they are noncreedal (that the Bible is the only rule of faith and practice), but a powerful understanding of the church's beliefs and behaviors underlies all that they say and do.

There is no shortage of examples of such definitions of faithfulness—from Roman Catholic dogma and loyalty to the pope to various Protestant positions on the mode of baptism, Calvinism, Arminianism, or a particular lifestyle.

As the culture and constituency changes, there is pressure on churches to alter doctrine and lifestyle. Some churches are more effective than others in either adapting to the culture or affecting the culture. When neither works, there may be a movement to define success as staying faithful to the old beliefs and behaviors no matter how few adherents that church may retain. Efforts are then made to insure that the organization and assets will not fall into the hands of the unfaithful. These efforts sometimes include the requirement that church rules cannot be changed or can be changed only by unanimous votes or that church property will be taken away from any who deviate from the established system. Almost always such "faithfulness" is construed to be faithfulness to God.

Of course, faithfulness is a wonderful Christian virtue. When it is in short supply the orthodox Christian faith has been jeopardized if not sacrificed. The danger is never in genuine faithfulness to God. It is better to be the only one left and still faithful to God than part of a popular majority and unfaithful. Faithfulness is what motivated martyrs in the first century and still motivates the estimated three hundred thousand Christian martyrs who now die every year because of their faith in Jesus Christ. Faithfulness may be the highest possible definition of success. The tragedy occurs when unfaithfulness parades under the guise of faithfulness—when churches perpetuate extrabiblical traditions as faithfulness to God.

4. *Success is survival.*

Church survival is a growing concern, especially for the estimated two hundred thousand churches with fewer than seventy-five at worship on Sunday morning. Many are financially unable to have a full-time pastor. Some are dwindling in numbers and struggling to continue programs and maintain older church buildings. They face the same plight as hundreds of rural school districts. It is a part of the town's identity, cohesiveness, and even its economic survival. But it is too expensive, thus school districts are forced to consolidate. Urban school districts are not as likely to consolidate as they are likely to close neighborhood schools to save money. Each time there are painful neighborhood meetings with threats and tears.

Church survival is threatened for different reasons. Sometimes it is economic—keeping the church going is more expensive than the congregation can afford. For some churches it is an issue of age. As a congregation grows older, it may become more difficult to attract a younger generation. Finally, the church literally dies off. Survival may even be a geographical matter. New highways, changing housing or commercial real estate use, or even rezoning of church property have strangled churches in every area.

In all of these and other cases, churches move into a survival mode, which causes them to set directions and make decisions primarily to perpetuate the institution. Success is defined as making it until tomorrow.

## What Success Isn't

Many understand a concept by describing its opposite. Because health is harder to see than illness, we may say that health is "not being sick." Most of the pastoral and church descriptions above are examples of what success isn't. But there are more.

### 1. Success is not achievement.

The American culture is highly competitive, and achievement is promoted from earliest childhood. It is common to consider only the winner of the race as successful. Being number one is everything. Finishing second is never good enough. In other cultures self-identity may be found in family, tribe, or tradition. Those connections can be shared; there is enough for everyone. But in a culture where identity and success is equivalent to being the best, most are left out.

Christians have written, preached, and taught that identity should be found in Jesus Christ. Since the Reformation, Protestants have strongly insisted on "salvation by grace through faith" rather than a "works salvation." Theologically, what goes for salvation also goes for Christian living and church life. But the culture is strong, and our emotions keep telling us that winning really is most important.

The Special Olympics is that most unusual athletic event that features mentally and physically disabled athletes from around the world. One of the most memorable events has been relived thousands of times in Special Olympics videos. It was a foot race among persons with Down's syndrome. The runners were close together as they came around the track toward the finish line. One of them stumbled and fell. The rest of the contestants stopped, helped the fallen runner to stand, and then resumed the race. Their success was wonderful, and it wasn't in the achievement of being better than others.

## 2. *Success is not agreement.*

Among many Christians, consensus is success. Certainly agreement is desirable and unanimity has powerful benefits. Yet it is possible for everyone to be wrong. A common belief among churches that require unanimous votes among elders (or other church leaders) is that everyone agreeing proves that the mind of the Holy Spirit has been determined. Is it not possible that everyone has agreed to a wrong conclusion?

Much has been made of conflict management, but little is ever said about agreement management. Jerry B. Harvey, professor of management science at George Washington University, helps us face the issue. Harvey tells a story from his own experience:

> My wife's family lives in Coleman, Texas, which is 53 miles from Abilene, and is like the town in the movie "The Last Picture Show." If you saw that movie, you've been to Coleman . . . We were visiting her parents . . . Her dad ran a pool hall and domino parlor right outside of town. The Baptists would get upset if he tried to run it in town. . . .

It was the middle of the summer—106 degrees, with a dust storm howling—and we were sitting there playing dominos. Suddenly my father-in-law stood up and blurted out, "Let's go to Abilene and eat at the cafeteria." I thought, "Man, is that dumb," but I didn't say anything. My wife said, "It sounds great, but I don't want to go unless you go, Jerry." I said, "I was hoping that somebody would invite me, but I won't go unless your mother goes." Mamma said, "Of course, I want to go."

So we all get into this '58 Buick and drive 53 miles to Abilene, where we have the worst meal you can imagine. Then we drive 53 miles back, and nobody says anything. It takes an hour for us to scrape off the dust. . . .

I didn't know what to say. Finally, with all the dishonesty I could muster, I said, "Well it was a great trip." My father-in-law responded with an expletive. I said, "What do you mean by that?" He said, ". . . I didn't want to go to Abilene. I was just making conversation, and you all made me ruin my day." I said, "I never wanted to go." My wife said, "Who would want to drive 106 miles in a dust storm? Not me." Mamma just cried. She didn't want to go either.

Nobody wanted to go, but we all thought the others wanted to. To avert a fight, nobody was willing to say, "No, I don't want to go."[1]

Most of us can readily identify with that story because we have traveled the road to Abilene with our families, churches, and other relationships. We agree in order to be agreeable when everyone was hoping someone would have the courage to disagree. Agreement does not mean success.

## 3. *Success is not numbers.*

Christians have always made that statement. It's an axiom that is almost guaranteed to be spoken whenever the topic of church successes and failures is discussed. Someone is sure to say, "In the Lord's work numbers aren't everything." Everyone agrees, and then the conversation goes on.

Numbers *are* important because they are a measurable means of comparison. A child is not necessarily sick or healthy because she has a temperature above or below 98.6 degrees Fahrenheit. That temperature is merely an average for comparison purposes. Some very healthy people have normal temperatures of 98 or 99 degrees.

The Bible has a book called Numbers. The history of the early church in the Book of Acts gives frequent counts as proof of God's blessings and the success of the first-century church. But all numbers must be evaluated and explained in relationship to their context. A very healthy church in a declining community may have declining numbers. A sick church in a booming population center may have increasing numbers. Numbers are only one helpful means of evaluation.

Social scientists are warning Americans that the 1990s may be a decade of "no growth" for many sectors of the economy and population. Contraction has replaced the economic expansion of earlier decades. Thousands of churches will have level, if not lower, budgets. Many para-church organizations will restructure into smaller ministries with fewer personnel and less expansive goals.

The numerical stability and aging of the Anglo population will shrink the pool of people from which churches can draw membership if they limit themselves to whites. By contrast, churches targeting African-Americans, Asian-Americans, and especially Hispanics will have a growing population to reach.

Numbers are important, but much more is needed to determine success or failure.

## Recognizing Success

Every time I am asked to pick up a stranger at the airport, I request a description in advance. I like to have at least the basics: gender, approximate age, size, special characteristics (color of hair, "wearing a blue suit with a red tie," carrying a green briefcase). Ideally, I prefer to have a recent photograph. Even with a full description, some people are hard to recognize. Without any descriptions they would be missed in the crowd.

The best way to recognize success is to get a description in advance. Then you will know what to look for. Here's the basic definition:

Success is reaching the right goal, using our resources according to specified standards.

### 1. *Success is a right result.*

There is no success if nothing happens. "Faith by itself, if it is not accompanied by action, is dead" (James 2:17).

Process is important. But results are most important. *How* we do something is important. *What* we do is more important. There is a temptation to misplace the emphasis of the church on the way we do things rather than on what we do. Management teachers explain, "Efficiency is doing things right; effectiveness is doing right things." God calls on Christians to do both.

Recognizing success begins with defining the goal. The concept can be expressed with many synonyms: mission, purpose, target, objective. It is carefully answering the questions: "Why do we exist? Where do we want to go? What do we want to happen?"

The pastor, church, or other organization that has a clear definition of where it is headed will not only have an improved chance of getting there but will also know when they have arrived.

New churches often accomplish this the best. For example, the pastor and organizing team have a clear picture of starting a new church of their denomination in their community, which will become self-supporting with at least 200 members within three years. Thirty-six months later everyone knows whether the goal has been reached or not. If success is the result it will be celebrated.

What about the process? As Christians, isn't it more important that we behave Christlike even if we don't end up where we are headed? The problem with this attitude is that it assumes that process and product are not connected. God calls us both to travel his way and to arrive at his destination.

In some cases, the process may indeed be the result. As an example, there were three men in their nineties who ran the 1990 New York Marathon. Having never run a marathon, I would say that entering and starting the race would be a success for anyone over 90 years old. In this case, just running was a victory.

*2. Success is using our resources.*

That is the point Jesus makes in Luke 14:28–32:

> Suppose one of you wants to build a tower. Will he not first sit down and estimate the cost to see if he has enough money to complete it? For if he lays the foundation and is not able to finish it, everyone who sees it will ridicule him, saying, "This fellow began to build and was not able to finish."
>
> Or suppose a king is about to go to war against another king. Will he not first sit down and consider whether he is able with ten thousand men to oppose the one coming against him with twenty thousand? If he concludes that he is far outnumbered, he will send a delegation while the other is still a long way off and ask for terms of peace.

Success requires a prior inventory of resources to determine whether we have what it takes to do what we propose. If not, then the objective needs to be modified to match the available resources.

The danger always exists that some will misuse this principle. Some conclude that their resources are minimal and therefore set low goals. It is not uncommon for church boards to have at least one member who says, "We don't have much, and we need to hang on to what we have. So let's not set any unrealistic goals and get ourselves into trouble." Most of the time the comment refers to money. At the other extreme, many boards have someone who is prone to overlook the absence of adequate resources and insist, "We must have faith and trust God to provide what we don't have."

The biblical balance is to assess all the resources, be responsible in the stewardship of those resources, and trust God to show us what to do and how to do it. An underlying assumption is that God always provides the resources for us to do what he asks.

Resources, however, entail much more than money. For example, a pastor needs to know oneself well enough to assess realistically his or her gifts, skills, strengths, and weaknesses. Some churches require strong relational skills; others demand better communication skills. It is foolish to overestimate one's ability and then embark on a task that cannot be accomplished.

A very general "rule of thumb" is that suburban churches may grow to an average Sunday morning worship attendance of one hundred times the number of acres of land. A church with a five-acre campus probably will not exceed five hundred in attendance. While there are some notable exceptions, most churches should take this ratio into serious consideration when defining and planning success. An unwise approach would be to build a two-thousand-seat auditorium and incur a heavy debt that requires growth to two thousand, while owning only seven acres. A better use of resources would be to buy more land, build smaller, and lengthen the timeline to reach such high attendance. As Jesus taught in the parable of the talents (Matt. 25:14–30), God may later supply greater resources to those who demonstrate responsibility with their initial resources.

### 3. Success includes standards.

Since it is a challenge to establish standards, this aspect of success may be the most difficult to implement.

The restaurant industry has many well-known standards. The kitchen must meet Health Department rules for safety and sanitary conditions. The food must use USDA-approved meat products. The cost must be competitive with other restaurants. The service must be courteous and in reasonable time.

Restaurants have ways of measuring their compliance with these standards. The Health Department inspector comes to evaluate and gives a written report. The USDA stamp appears on all incoming meat products. The back of the check gives opportunity for customers to rate the server in terms of courtesy. Some restaurants invite timing—Denny's puts a timer on your table and starts it running when your order is placed; Domino's promises thirty-minute home delivery, or your pizza is free. In each of these cases there are not only standards but also external means of determining whether the standards have been met.

The thermostat on your wall is another example. It is set to a standard, perhaps 68 degrees. It also reads the current temperature in the room and sends a signal to the furnace or air conditioner for more hot or cold air to raise or lower the room temperature to a desired standard.

The same concepts apply to success in ministry. Effort is made to determine the standards in reaching the goals. Some are easier than others. For example, the church worship service will start at the announced time and finish one hour later. That is easy to measure. When the standard is not met, adjustment is necessary the next time. Standards can also be set for leadership (1 Timothy 3 specifies the standards for elders and deacons), for music (words appropriate to the service theme, musicians adequately prepared, performers demonstrate credible Christian faith, vocalists sing on key, etc.), and for finances (approved budget, expenditures according to budget, and a published public report of receipts and expenditures).

Some standards always remain the same; some standards change. The biblical standards of love, forgiveness, and honesty do not vary. However, the musical standard may be much more demanding for a large urban church with a telecast worship service than for a small family-centered country church. Changing non-biblical standards is not only permissible but also advisable. They need to be regularly updated, but everyone should know when the changes are made and be made aware of the standards in advance.

The church that is serious about pursuing success can involve its leaders by asking, "What will success look like?" Then they can write out the standards by which success will be attained and measured.

Consider a practical example. A significant factor in pastoral success is *fit*, which is tough to define but valuable to have. Some pastors *fit* well with aggressive churches; others *fit* better with more laid-back churches. Some speakers communicate well with blue-collar workers, and others with white-collar workers. The best single indicator is that pastors tend to do best in the part of the country from which they come. In other words, a pastor raised in New York City will probably fit best in New York City; the church in Montana will get the best fit with a pastor from the Rocky Mountain regions. Thus, in the search for a new pastor, the church committee may require a good fit by listing the following standards: (1) the pastor must be from our area or relate well to people in our area; (2) the pastor's lifestyle, communication style, and priorities should be compatible with those of our church and community.

How can this factor be evaluated? One possibility is to have the pastoral candidate stay in the homes of several church families and meet with several groups of unchurched people from the community. Then those people should be asked to evaluate whether the candidate is "our kind of person"—talks our way, relates to our needs, fits in well with our lives.

## Examples of Success

*Howard Head:* In their bestselling book *In Search of Excellence*, Peters and Waterman borrow a story from *Sports Illustrated*. It is the success story of Howard Head, father of modern snow skis and founder of the Head Ski Company.

> In 1946 Head went off to Stowe, Vermont, for his first attempt at skiing. "I was humiliated and disgusted by how badly I skied," he recalls, "and, characteristically, I was inclined to blame it on the equipment, those long, clumsy hickory skis. On my way home I heard myself boasting to an Army officer beside me that I could make a better ski out of aircraft materials than could be made from wood."
>
> Back at Martin, the cryptic doodles that began appearing on Head's drawing board inspired him to scavenge some aluminum from the plant scrap pile. In his off-hours he set up shop on the second floor of a converted stable in an alley near his one-room basement flat. His idea was to make a "metal sandwich" ski consisting of two layers of aluminum with plywood sidewalls and a center filling of honeycombed plastic.
>
> Needing pressure and heat to fuse the materials together, Head concocted a process that would have made Rube Goldberg proud. To achieve the necessary pressure of 15 pounds per square inch, he put the ski mold into a huge rubber bag and then pumped the air out through a tube attached to an old refrigerator compressor that was hooked up backward to produce suction. For heat, he welded together an iron, coffin-like tank, filled it with motor oil drained from automobile crankcases and, using two

Sears Roebuck camp burners, cooked up a smelly 350°
brew. Then he dumped the rubber bag with the ski mold
inside into the tank of boiling oil and sat back like Julia
Child waiting for her potato puffs to brown.

Six weeks later, out of the stench and smoke, Head
produced his first six pairs of skis and raced off to Stowe
to have them tested by the pros. To gauge the ski's camber,
an instructor stuck the end of one into the snow and flexed
it. It broke. So, eventually, did all six pairs. "Each time
one of them broke," says Head, "something inside me
snapped with it." Instead of hanging up his rubber bag,
Head quit Martin the day after New Year's 1948, took
$6,000 in poker winnings he had stashed under his bed,
and went to work in earnest. Each week he would send a
new and improved pair of skis to Neil Robinson, a ski
instructor in Bromley, Vermont, for testing, and each week
Robinson would send them back broken. "If I had known
then that it would take 40 versions before the ski was any
good, I might have given it up," says Head. "But fortunately, you get trapped into thinking the next design will
be it."

Head wrestled with his obsession through three agonizing winters. The refinements were several: steel edges
for necessary bite, a plywood core for added strength, and
a plastic running surface for smoother, ice-free runs. One
crisp day in 1950, Head stood in the bowl of Tuckerman's
Ravine in New Hampshire and watched ski instructor Clif
Taylor come skimming over the lip of the headwall, do a
fishtail on the fall line and sweep into a long, graceful curve,
shooshing to a stop in front of the beaming inventor.

"That's great, Mr. Head, just great," Taylor exclaimed.
At that moment, Head says, "I knew inside that I had it."[2]

Success! Head knew the result he wanted: "Make a better ski."
He used the resources available to him: drawing board, off-hours,
supplies from the scrap pile, rubber bag, tank, refrigerator com-
pressor, old oil, second floor of a converted stable, $6,000, and
his own ingenuity and commitment. And, Head had a standard
to measure both the process and the product: the approval of a
professional ski instructor.

*Parable of the talents.* In this famous story from Jesus, a very rich man left enormous resources in the care of his servants. Different employees were entrusted with different amounts of money, apparently on the basis of the employer's evaluation of their abilities. The first servant received five talents, the second two talents, and the third one talent. In today's money we might say the distributions were $10,000, $4,000, and $2,000, but by ancient standards of living, each received a fortune.

The employer's expected results were well known to the three. He expected his investment to grow while under their care. The standard by which they were evaluated was clear and external— the current bank interest rate on savings accounts (Matt. 25:27). The first two used the resources well, doubling their employer's money. The third employee buried the money in the ground and returned the exact same amount when his boss returned home.

The conclusion of the story is pointed. The last man had the $2,000 taken away from him and given to his co-worker who had the most. Plus, he was fired for failure.

The formula for success is the same. The first two employees attained the results with their resources according to the established standards. They succeeded. The third employee didn't attain the required results; instead, he improperly used the resources and didn't measure up to the standard. He failed.

*Falls Church.* The Reverend John Yates first rejected a 1979 inquiry to become rector of the Falls Church, an Episcopal congregation in Falls Church, Virginia. The church was not doing well. It had been without a rector for two years. In an interview in *Faith & Renewal*, he explained, "When I visited them, I was bowled over by the tremendous need. There were few people, almost no children. Everything seemed dry, dead. Sunday attendance had steadily decreased all through the seventies."[3]

Yates went through an agonizing six weeks before concluding that God was calling him from his comfortable position in Sewickley, Pennsylvania, to Falls Church, Virginia. The goal for Falls Church was clear: to become a renewal church. The resources were counted:

Sunday morning worship attendance 300, Members in small groups 0, Children and Youth 5, Outreach budget

$15,000, Full time staff 3.[4]

Plus, there were some vestry members who wanted change, along with Yates's very positive experience as an assistant to John Guest at St. Stephen's in Sewickley. In a sense, the Sewickley church was both the experience base (an invaluable resource) and the standard of measurement for John Yates and for Falls Church as they sought renewal together.

According to Yates, the process went like this:

> Number one, I needed to get to know the church and confirm whether my first impressions were correct.
>
> Number two, I committed myself to getting to know all the leading people of the community—the mayor, and so on—to establish some sort of rapport.
>
> Number three, I saw myself as a fire builder. I had the image of the church as a large ship frozen in the ice. My job was to turn it around and get it going in a new direction. But that couldn't happen until fires were lit all around the perimeter to free it from the ice. I spent the first two or three years kindling small fires throughout the congregation.
>
> I spent a lot of personal time with individuals, primarily evangelizing them. I began discipling a small group of men, all of whom eventually became vestry members. I tried to discern who the spiritually alive people were and put them in positions of leadership.
>
> Another major commitment was to bring as many of the finest biblical preachers and teachers as I could into the church. I didn't want people to think I was alone in what I was saying. Rebecca Pippert, R. C. Sproul, Os Guinness, Richard Halverson, John Stott, Michael Green, and others spoke at church in the first years.
>
> We also needed to organize for renewal. The structure of the congregation needed rethinking. The vestry system had to be reorganized. We had to develop a committee structure.
>
> There was quite a lot of opposition to the changes. I focused on expository preaching, which many people were not used to, and placed an emphasis on personal conversion

and the need for us to be doing personal evangelism. Some fine people disagreed with my perspective.

They wanted evangelism and renewal. When they interviewed me, I told them frankly that changes would have to be made. But hearing it and living through it were two different things.[5]

Yates adds the importance of daily quiet time with God in Scripture and prayer, the support of his wife, and the implementation of various programs. He also admits to mistakes in making some unnecessary changes and moving too quickly.

Success. The numerical measurements are part of the evaluation: 1,000 average worship attendance in 1990, 300 members involved in small sharing and Bible study groups, 350 children and youth involved on a typical Sunday, over $400,000 to outreach in 1990, and 14 full-time staff members. But there are more than numerical measures. Evaluations have been made by persons inside and outside the church who declare that the renewal of Falls Church has taken place.

## Changing to Success

Everyone wants to be successful, at least if they write their own definition of "success." So the place to begin is to define success. What does success mean for me as a person? What is success for me as a pastor? What is success for me as a leader? What is success for us as a church? Take the time and give the energy to write a definition. For those who feel uncomfortable with the word *success*, decide to write out "What God wants our church to be and do" because that is what success really is.

Count the available resources. Make a list of every gift God has given to fulfill his vision for you and your church. The list may include (but is not limited to) prayer, people, plans, money, time, ideas, and more. The best lists of resources are usually made in a group brainstorming together and keeping a record of every idea offered.

Set the standards. What are the values that are most important? Who could serve as an outside "thermometer" to evaluate progress?

1. *Seek success.*

There are two ways to operate in most life situations: instinct and intention. Some people do amazingly well by instinct. They have an ability to know what to do and when to do it. Most of us are not as gifted and do better by intention.

The intentional church thinks through and has a reason for everything possible. There is a reason for the carpet color, times of services, and the name of the church. In the best of situations, the reason is keyed to the purpose of the church. The carpet is red because it communicates warmth to both visitors and regular attenders. The morning worship service is at 10:30 A.M. to be convenient for families who have young children to get ready (so it's not earlier) as well as football fans who want to watch the Sunday NFL game on television (they can make it home in time for the noon kickoff). The name "Christ Community Church" is to establish the importance of Jesus Christ as well as its relationship to the local community—it is a name that seeks to welcome everyone. All of these decisions are to fulfill the church's purpose "to serve Jesus Christ by inviting everyone in our community to know him and fellowship with his church."

There is nothing proud or inappropriate in determining what success should look like and how to achieve it. Just be sure to recognize that success is as individually defined as eyeglasses are prescribed. It is foolhardy, if not self-destructive, to use another's prescription. Often it will produce a headache; sometimes it will mean driving into a tree. Because another church is large or has a certain program does not mean that any other church should do the same.

Once defined, something needs to be done. One of the most effective steps is to analyze whether the church's reward system aligns with stated standards. For example, the church says it wants its members to relate to the unchurched and be evangelistic. Does the same church then honor the members whose involvement with non-Christian neighbors keeps them from the church's evening activities and participation on church committees? Many church leaders increasingly recognize the enormous value of longer-term pastorates—saying the most effective years of a senior pastorate don't begin before the pastor's sixth or seventh anniversary. If that is the standard, does the church reward longevity with salary increases, continuing education time and money, sabbatical leaves, and other encouragements?

## 2. Be faithful.

Does this mean all will succeed? Can a church just define success and then achieve it? Obviously not.

Recently I shared a lunch conversation with the former president of a midwestern Bible college. He rehearsed all that the college had done over the last several tumultuous decades in Christian higher education. He summed it up by saying, "They did everything right but still didn't make it."

If success is reaching the right goal while using our resources according to standards, what is failure? It is simply not reaching the right goal.

God does not guarantee us success, but he does promise his blessing in every circumstance. God does not require us to succeed, but he does tell us to be faithful. Faithfulness is determining what God wants and going for it. If we are faithful but miss, we have done what we should. To not be faithful is to join the ranks of the fired servant in the parable of the talents in Matthew 25.

## Chapter 6

# What's Your Story?

DUBIN'S BAKERY in the New York City borough of Brooklyn was once famous for its challah bread and bagels. But the once Jewish neighborhood changed, and so did the bakery. Today it is called Gig Young's Jamaican Bakery, and it specializes in rum cakes and hard-dough bread. Same place. Different story.

### Every Church Has a Story

During the summer of 1991 I visited a variety of churches across America. I discovered not only that every church has a story of its own but also that I began to hear the story long before I arrived.

Although far from my Minnesota home, I had heard story lines from Saddleback Valley Community Church in Mission Viejo, California, and Coral Ridge Presbyterian Church in Fort Lauderdale, Florida. I knew both were large, successful entrepreneurial-type churches, led by their founding pastors. Both are affiliated with denominations: Saddleback is a Southern Baptist Convention church; Coral Ridge is a Presbyterian Church in America church.

Both have highly defined philosophies of ministry and reputations for being evangelistic. Both are evangelical in theology. They share many similarities, but their stories are quite different.

Saddleback Valley Community Church meets in the gymnasium of a local high school. Someone told me that the church has moved fifty-seven times in its fifteen-year history. The room was well filled for a Saturday evening service. The liturgy was informal, and congregational singing was from words printed in the bulletin. Informal dress ranged from slacks and open-collar shirts to shorts and tank tops—I don't remember seeing a man with a tie. A handful of women wore dresses. There were few symbols of traditional religion. The audience was young—almost all were middle-aged and younger. No effort was made to identify me as a visitor; I just blended in with everyone else. A friend pointed out to me Rick Warren, the senior pastor—otherwise, I might not have figured out who he was, since he maintained a low profile. Once I knew who he was, I watched as he moved around the gym greeting people.

Coral Ridge Presbyterian Church meets in a high-spire edifice, which is an architecturally prominent feature of Federal Highway (US 1) through Fort Lauderdale. The building tells a story of tradition and stability. Before entering the nave, our family was greeted by an older woman who asked whether we were visitors. Inside were fixed pews, large pipe organ, large brass cross, and a number of other religious symbols. Most of the congregation was middle-aged and older. A large majority of the men were dressed in suits, dress shirts and ties, with women wearing dresses. The liturgy was listed in the bulletin and included the Lord's Prayer and Apostles' Creed. Congregational singing was from the hymnal. Senior Pastor D. James Kennedy was on a summer study leave, although present in the service and available to be met in a reception room following the service. Kennedy's name was printed on the bulletin.

So many similarities, yet such different stories. One is not right and the other wrong, any more than Luke's gospel is more right than John's gospel—they're just different stories.

Every church has a story of its own, as unique as an individual's fingerprint. The story is so well known to those on the inside that little thought is ever given to it. Outsiders may never be able to learn the whole story no matter how hard they try, but they have an immediate initial reading of a church's story that influences their evaluation of and relationship to that church.

The story is always complex. It includes history, location, doctrine, relationships, leadership, anecdotes, and even the kinds of cars in the parking lot.

## Sample Stories

The variety of church stories is infinite, but the concept is better understood by looking at some of the more familiar types.

*Family farm* is as much a part of America as George Washington and Fourth of July fireworks. Most of us have good feelings when we think of family farms, which spread across the heartland of the nation. Generation after generation from pioneers to the present have worked the land. It has survived the Indian Wars, dust storms, grasshoppers, and the Great Depression. The "farm policy" has been a significant part of every presidential candidate's platform. But the family farm is now threatened. In some ways it is the victim of progress. Modern agricultural methods have enabled so much to be produced by so few. Large agricultural corporations now own and operate thousands of acres. Children of the farm have gone off to the city, to college, and to other careers and homes in the suburbs. Financially, it is difficult to survive. One thing is sure—outsiders seldom become part of the family farm. Farming is a hard profession to learn if you didn't grow up with it—there is a sense of farming that is learned more in the fields as a child than in the classroom as a collegian or in the office as a businessperson. Those who do become part of the family farm from the outside usually do so through marriage into the family.

There are tens of thousands of family-farm-type churches in America. While many are in rural areas, they can easily be found in cities as well. Although they may not be in agricultural areas, they share the agricultural story. They are small, usually with fewer than seventy-five at Sunday morning worship. They are thought of as the backbone of America with their old buildings on the city corner, town square, or along a country highway. In many ways, it is what the majority of Americans think of when they think of "church" in this country. The reality is that their numbers are shrinking. Nevertheless, they are very durable because they are generally built on family relationships. Even if the building burns, the corporation is bankrupt, and the pastor quits, the family church continues as long as the family continues. Often leadership is limited to those born or married into the same families that have run the church since it was founded. Outsiders are officially welcomed (there may even be a sign outside that says so), but they seldom fully become part of the story. Outsiders almost never make it to top leadership, not even pastors who hold the official calls, titles, and offices. These are challenging days for family-farm churches because of children moving to the city, competition from other churches, and the financial strains of keeping the church going.

*School* is very different from a farm. People aren't usually born into schools. They come to school because they want to learn or because someone makes them attend. In either case, the story of a school is centered on the curriculum, teachers, and students. Even the name may tell part of the school story—Winnie the Pooh Nursery School, Harvard Medical School, United States Air Force Academy, Moody Bible Institute. While most schools claim academic freedom, students who disagree usually end up leaving. How long do you think a practitioner of traditional Chinese medicine would last at Harvard Medical School?

School-type churches make the teaching of their doctrine a prominent part of their story. Sermons are most of the service time. Taking notes may be expected. The pastor's teaching ability and beliefs are high on the list of expectations. Bible may be the church's middle name—or the denominational name may reflect a certain doctrinal position that is central to the church's teaching. You may like the church's building, pastor, and people, but if you greatly disagree with the teaching, you probably won't stay too long in the school-type church.

*Franchise* is a business that is locally owned and operated but controlled and supplied by a central headquarters someplace else. Well-known franchises include Subway, Burger King, Midas Muffler, and major league sports teams. One of the great advantages of franchises is that they are similar and predictable no matter where you go. The Burger King Whopper is pretty much the same in Portland, Oregon, as in Portland, Maine. There are three strikes to an out and four balls to a walk whether attending a major league baseball game in Chicago or Cleveland. However, there is limited flexibility. Midas Muffler stores are not free to sell a competitor's product, and an entrepreneur can't start his or her own American League baseball team in Memphis without league permission.

Most franchise-type churches belong to denominations. You can easily find them in the yellow pages or from the sign in front of the building. They teach the same Sunday school lesson from the same headquarters' curriculum no matter which church you attend. The literature looks alike from the bulletin cover to the missionary listings. All of the pastors have been trained at the denominational seminaries as surely as McDonald's managers have gone to Hamburger U (there really is such a place!). No matter where you go on vacation or move your residence, if you can find your brand of franchise church, there should be great similarity. Some flexibility is allowed to adapt to local culture and needs, but if there is significant variance, central headquarters will move in and either enforce standards or revoke the franchise.

*General store* is not as common as it once was in America's smaller towns, but does serve a very valuable purpose where it continues. It is famous for having a little bit of everything and may really try to accommodate your special need. If you live in the community, you are known to the store owner and personnel. Most often you will be called by name. It is a good place to get the staples—bread and milk, lightbulbs, and paper clips. But, if you need size 13EEE tennis shoes or an air filter for a 1978 Mercedes, you will probably need to shop someplace else. It isn't possible for the general store to stock everything nor to compete with the quality and prices of the big city retailers. General stores are convenient. The problem is competition. Many general stores can't keep their customers from driving to the larger city to do their shopping, and if they can't keep their customers, they can't afford to stay in business. Interestingly, the same people who shop elsewhere are often the most disappointed when the general store closes. They would like it to stay in business just in case they sometime decide to shop there.

The general-store church may be labeled "community church" or "federated church." It may even have a denominational name, but everyone in town knows that the name doesn't mean much because that church tries to serve everyone. Most people really like it and want it to succeed, even if they seldom attend. There is a youth group, but it is too small to sponsor the popular activities promoted and subsidized by the larger church in a town ten miles down the highway. Since there are so few singles in the vicinity of the general-store church, they also go elsewhere. Yet, the same singles who worship in the big city hope the local community church will still be there when they plan a hometown wedding.

*Shopping mall* is a comparatively recent arrival on the American scene. In less than four decades, it has changed the buying pattern of most American shoppers and radically altered the face of many downtown retail districts.

The shopping mall began as a business enterprise. Typically there are two or more "anchor" stores with famous names and large areas of retail space—Sears, JC Penney, Macy's, or Montgomery Ward. Then there are dozens of smaller stores specializing in a wide variety of consumer goods: shoes, men's or women's clothes, furniture, food, flowers, computer software, and much more. Finally, in terms of stores, there are service establishments offering hair care, travel arrangements, exercise activities, movies, dentistry, and still more.

Our description is not complete if the shopping mall is described only in terms of business, because many other social activities give life to the mall. Early in the morning joggers and walkers exercise in the miles of hallways. Teenagers meet one another to hang out. Friends gather for coffee. Business people have lunch appointments at the restaurants to negotiate deals. Families come to play at the amusement parks that are central to some of the newer larger malls. The mall has become "the place to be" for many Americans—the modern equivalent to the old town square. It is the place where a large variety of needs can be met.

There aren't many shopping malls in most cities. Maybe only one. It takes a very large city to support a dozen or more malls. Their influence and significance is far greater than their number.

When a new mall is built, every downtown merchant faces a difficult business decision. It is hard to leave an established location with lower rent to go to the new enclosed shopping center. Besides, if too many businesses pull out, the downtown may die from lack of customers. Every business that leaves hurts everyone who stays. But staying can be a prescription for disaster. The attractiveness, comfort, newness, and convenience of the regional shopping mall is formidable competition.

Shopping-mall churches are nearly as new and not much more numerous than the actual shopping malls. They are large, attractive, convenient, and provide a stunning array of services for a wide diversity of people. The shopping-mall church is a place to meet new acquaintances and fellowship with old friends. It is hard to get a handle on the mall church because no one knows everyone nor fully understands all that is going on. Even after you have been a member for years, you discover programs and people you never knew.

On the one hand, the shopping-mall church has a very simple story told with words like "big," "well-known," "successful," or even "impersonal" and "commercial." On the other hand, the story of the shopping-mall church is so long and complicated with so many substories that only a professional researcher would bother to try to learn the whole story.

*Specialty shop* may be in a mall or stand alone. It offers a product or service that attracts people with very special interests. Those people tend to find the specialty shop no matter where it is located because their interests and needs are not easily met anywhere else. Examples include tropical fish stores, kosher delis, clothiers for big and tall people, and typewriter repair shops.

Specialty-shop churches cater to very special people. Often they meet needs and interests that other churches wouldn't even attempt—services in Vietnamese, ministry to shift workers who work on Sunday mornings, or vacationers who live in their homes only during the summer months. There are specialty-shop churches that are not quite so narrow in their appeal: One focuses on people who have been burned by the legalism of other churches, another appeals to persons who love classical music, and another offers an outstanding program to families that include disabled children.

*Haunted house* is either an unusual abandoned structure in the neighborhood or an attraction at an amusement park. No one really lives there. Those who come seek to satisfy their curiosity rather than become involved. Haunted houses once had life but have become scary places. They are loaded with stories, many of which have been exaggerated far beyond any original truth. There isn't much that can be done to change a haunted house back into a happy family home. Realtors don't like to list them, much less show them. Most haunted houses eventually collapse.

Are there really "haunted-house" churches? Maybe not. But some churches that once had life now are creepy and scary places that others talk about and may visit out of curiosity but never stay. There are intriguing stories that are told and retold many times— and the exaggeration grows with the retelling. Can they be resurrected? Maybe, with a miracle. Most haunted-house churches have had it. They will never be what they once were. Sooner or later they collapse.

Every church has a story. The story is updated and expanded every Sunday. The basic story line is not easily changed. The story not only tells about the past but also helps predict the future. Church stories tend to keep on perpetuating themselves. What are some ways to identify a church's story?

## 1. *What words are used to describe the church?*

Take a simple survey of the congregation. Pass out 3 × 5 cards and request each person to write four or five words that best describe the church. Collate the answers to see the frequency of words listed.

For example, the four most often cited words may be "loving," "caring," "supportive," and "family." These words may indicate that a church has a story of internal connection and compassion. Whether a church is perceived as effective in outreach depends on the frequency of such terms as "outreaching," "evangelistic," and "open."

Like almost all surveys, the interpretation is as important as the collected data. The given answers may reflect reality, perception, or the topic of last Sunday's sermon. The story cannot be fully determined by asking the members of the church, but it is a good place to start.

## 2. *What do others in town say the story is?*

An old textbook on pastoring suggests that a pastoral candidate stop at several service stations and ask directions to the church building. An immediate insight comes from either quick accurate directions or "I've never heard of the place."

Expand on the idea by asking two dozen residents of the community what they know and think about the church. If possible, tape record the conversations. If not, either take notes at the time of the interview or write a detailed report as soon as possible after the interview.

When Wooddale Church was working on determining the perceptions of others, outsiders were recruited to visit the church. A task force of church members each asked a neighbor, co-worker, or friend to visit a worship service once during a six-week period. Most were either unchurched or from a markedly different tradition. They were told that follow-up interviews would seek to learn their impressions. No one at the church knew who these visitors were or when they might come.

The follow-up was a "focus group" held in a rented room at a nearby marketing research company. The visitors gathered with a facilitator while members of the task force listened and watched through a one-way mirror. They were asked what they had experienced, what had impressed them, and what they liked and disliked. Their comments ranged from serious to silly and from affirming to worrisome. A couple with young children were impressed that Sunday school teachers were understanding and helpful when one of their children didn't want to stay in the classroom, but they wondered why their child didn't have any papers to bring home after the hour. Several said they were surprised by how comfortable they felt, because they had perceived the church as much more conservative than they, yet they felt at home. Most commented on the size—some complained that churches are supposed to be smaller, while others said they liked the crowds because they didn't feel singled out as visitors. All affirmed the quality of the music and message. Several felt the ushering should be handled differently. One man who was admittedly unchurched and irreligious said, "That's my kind of church, and I'm going back."

The point is not that they could read the story in a single visit, but that they could see the story from an outsider's perspective. It is one more piece to putting together the puzzle that gives a picture of the story.

### 3. What is important to the church?

A few highly observant insiders may be able to research the church's priorities. If not, an outsider may be needed. There are several places to look.

Where does the church spend money? This is the most measurable piece of the story. Read the budget or review the canceled checks. What percentages of expenditures go to the care of the facility, to programs, to the denomination, to social ministries, to missions, to salaries and benefits, to advertising and outreach? Some may believe evangelism is the church's priority, but discover that less than 1% of the budget goes to outreach. The church may say it wants to slow down the parade of short-term pastors, but the salary says otherwise. When reasons, excuses, or explanations are given on why the money is received and disbursed as it is, that is an important part of the story as well.

What do people fight about? Few fight about matters of low importance. Are hallway conversations and board meeting discussions about doctrine, discipline, or decorations?

What can't be changed? In some churches it is the platform furniture. In others it is the memorial plaques. In many it is the person in charge of important programs.

What are the symbols? The cross? Flags? Baptistery? Hymnals? Overhead projector? Organ? Piano? Tape deck? Almost every symbol has a story of its own and is as important to the church family as the old picture album is to your parents' family.

### 4. What shows?

Just looking around and noticing whatever shows will help you understand the story. Are the cars in the parking lot new or old, shiny or rusty, sedans or pick-ups?

Is the outside of the building shabby or sharp? Look at the paint, shrubs, sign, lighting, and entrances. Often I have visited

churches where the buildings seem to say, "This is the front entrance," but there are no people or cars around. The old-timers
all park in the back and use the shortcut to the coatroom or classroom. It has become a "back door church," which is comfortable
to the regulars but deceptive to the visitors.

How are people dressed? Almost all churches have unwritten
dress codes, which range from formal to casual and are enforced
by stares and comments. Interestingly, informal dress codes are
more and more replacing formal dress codes, being dressed up is
more of an offense in the casual church than casual dress is in the
formal church.

How well do visitors fit in? Churches with strong insider stories
tend to make visitors feel out of place, while churches with strong
outsider stories tend to make visitors feel more comfortable.

During the late 1970s our family was vacationing on Cape Cod.
Charleen and I visited a Saturday night mass at St. Francis Xavier
Roman Catholic Church in Hyannis, Massachusetts. It is most
famous to outsiders as the home church of the Kennedy family (a
significant part of that church's story!). The building looks much
smaller than the actual seating capacity of its three naves coming
off the altar area in a cross-shaped building. A capacity crowd
filled every seat. The liturgy included more recitations with standing and sitting than our church background taught us. We both
know the Lord's Prayer and the Apostles' Creed by memory, but
were not as quick as the others at that service. Thus, we had
trouble sitting and standing at the right times and couldn't quite
keep up with the congregational recitations. About halfway
through the service, a man seated near us leaned over to Charleen
and said, "You're not Catholic, are you?" He could tell we didn't
know that church's story. He knew we were outsiders. It showed.

5. *How does it all fit together?*

Combine key answers to these questions into a composite description of a specific church. Tell its story from past to present.
Be complete to the point that the story is detailed enough. Be brief
enough that the main point isn't lost in trivia.

The indications that the story has been captured are tied to the
responses of others. If insiders hear it and say, "Sure, that's us!"

and outsiders say, "I've never been there, but I feel as if I know your church," and visitors observe, "That fits with what I experienced," then you've got it!

Although capturing the story of a church is not an exact science, there is enormous value in the research and in the attempt to state the story. More important, knowing the story is an invaluable prerequisite to changing a church, because changing a church requires changing its story.

## Every Person Has a Story

Shortly after Charleen and I were married, we lived in Peoria, Illinois. We moved there without jobs in order for me to attend the university. She quickly found employment with the *Peoria Journal Star*, but I didn't do as well. I looked hard without success. After I was sick for a week, which interrupted my job search, more unsuccessful looking followed. Money was running out, and I was discouraged. At the same time, we were looking for a church and visited one that met many of our expectations. Each Sunday the pastor prayed for the congregation and included a line that so grabbed my attention that all else was forgotten. He prayed, "Thank you, God, for our jobs." I doubt most of the large audience paid much attention to his words because they had jobs. Employment was part of their personal stories. But it was not a part of mine. We went to a different church.

It is easier to learn a person's individual story than a church's corporate story. Most people are glad to tell it if they're asked, and many tell their stories even when we don't ask. Of course, the story we know the best is our own.

Our own stories are the composite of all the history, symbols, experiences, and relationships that make our individual biographies: gender, race, year of birth, family of origin, education, vocation, religious faith, marriage, children, socioeconomic status, preferences in music, colors, entertainment, and politics. Some of our stories have very powerful symbols around which almost everything else revolves: physical disability, divorce of parents, winning the lottery, conviction of a crime, being raped, parenting triplets, musical talent, and so on.

Part of my story is my name. Leith is the seaport of Edinburgh,

Scotland. My mother was born and raised in the north of England, and because she liked the name, she gave it to me. While there are a few others with my name, it is relatively unusual. When making motel or travel reservations, I sometimes wish I had a name like Bob or Bill. Almost always I must spell my name to strangers. (I sometimes say, "It's like Keith only with an L instead of a K." Once one person missed the explanation and started calling me Kleith.) While other people think nothing of calling another person by their name (Jane, John, Barb, or Bill), I have never called anyone else by my name. There is a sense in which I think of it as uniquely my own, never to be shared with another. (Although I did meet another Leith when I was in college, I never spoke that person's name and still somewhat resent some other parents having given *my* name to . . . her.)

Jesus understood the power of personal story when he interacted with the woman at the well. He knew her story and used its primary facts and symbols to win her. She was a Samaritan woman, and Jesus said to her, "You are right when you say you have no husband. The fact is, you have had five husbands, and the man you now have is not your husband" (John 4:17–18). The reason he was able to quickly build a rapport and win the hearing and faith of this stranger was his knowledge and use of her personal story. A less effective approach would have started and finished with Jesus' own story of who he was. Of course, he did tell his own story, but when he did, it was woven in with hers.

Examples go into the billions. Every person in the world has her or his unique story. It is a very personal and strongly felt possession. For most of us it is impossible to distinguish between our stories and ourselves as persons.

The question is not our ability to tell our story but the ability to learn another's story. To assume that others share our story is not only egocentric but also ineffective.

Critical to the art and discipline of learning others' stories is the ability to ask and then listen. Effective church-change agents frequently encourage others to talk about themselves. We try to understand who they are to the point that we could almost tell their stories for them. We understand what makes them laugh and cry. We know what they count important. We are sensitive to their needs and wants. Others' stories have been adequately learned when we can not only describe them to their satisfaction but also predict their future behavior on the basis of their story lines.

The obvious impossibility is to learn all of the stories in a church or community. The numbers would quickly expand from hundreds into thousands or millions. The alternative is to discover the story similarities among groups of persons. For example, persons born in the same year and growing up in the same country have many similar symbols. Baby boomers were influenced by Elvis Presley, John Kennedy, Woodstock, and Vietnam. Another example are those who have experienced divorce and thus share many story similarities—they know the pain of broken relationships and the economic cost of breaking up a family. Other examples of people who share story similarities are single parents, retired men, and self-employed business people.

Alcoholics Anonymous is composed of men and women whose stories have been significantly shaped by addiction. Their pain and problems have drawn them together into thousands of support groups, which have melded the Twelve Steps and interpersonal associations. One of the binding features of AA meetings is the telling of individual stories. Each one is different, beginning with the words, "My name is. . . . I'm an alcoholic." All other alcoholics in the group identify with the central theme of the story because it is their story as well.

Churches that are effective in outreach and evangelism excel in knowing and articulating the stories of the people they reach. Some do it intuitively, while others do it intentionally. They are able to describe the stories of others so well that those persons say, "Hey, that's me you're talking about." Bill Hybels at Willowcreek Community Church has described Unchurched Harry, and Rick Warren at Saddleback Valley Community Church tells about Saddleback Sam—both are telling the personal stories of the type of people their churches are out to reach.

## Matching Stories

Dr. John Webb, communications professor at Pacific Christian College in Fullerton, California, has carefully studied how people choose churches based on their symbols and symbol systems:

Church growth leaders believe that people are no longer

as tied to denominational traditions as they once were. They tend to look for congregations which appeal to their personal tastes in worship, ministry, and lifestyle. A part of the explanation for this can be found in the study of symbols. People look for symbols which match those they already possess. If they visit a congregation whose only connecting symbol is the denominational name, it may not be strong enough to hold them. Consequently, they look for another church where more symbols fit into their present symbol system. The general principle could be stated as follows: *people will seek out a congregation whose symbols and symbol system cause them the least amount of trauma.*[1]

We all intuitively seek to match our story with others. We feel most comfortable when the story being told parallels our own experience. When the stories don't match, we want to get out.

Recall the last time you were visiting an unfamiliar shopping mall. You saw a clothing store you had never heard of before, so you stepped inside to check it out. Within less than a minute you made a preliminary decision on the compatibility of that store's story with your own. On the one hand, if you are petite and it was a store for large and tall people, you didn't stay long. On the other hand, if the design of the clothes, prices on the tags, and style of the salespeople *fit* your wardrobe, income, and style, you probably stayed to buy.

A few weeks after Wooddale Church moved into a new Worship Center, I rushed to the rest room less than two minutes before the start of the second service. In my hurry I neglected to notice the sign on the door. You guessed it—I walked into the ladies' room. It took me less than a second to realize: "This is not my story," and I got out of there as fast as I could.

Churches attract people whose stories match the church story. They fit. They feel comfortable. They are at home. Otherwise they leave.

The best possible combination for growth is the alignment of the stories of the pastor, the church, and the community, which is a dynamic combination for attracting and retaining significant numbers of new people.

The practical question becomes: "Who fits our church's

story?'' If there is a good match with most of the people the church seeks to reach, the next task is to get them to give the church a try. If the match is poor or there is no match at all, getting people to try won't help.

Unfortunately, some churches have stories that only match with insiders. All outsiders feel uncomfortable. Those churches must decide to either limit themselves to insiders or change their story to attract outsiders.

Remember that we are not talking about changing essential doctrine or compromising biblical truth in order to accommodate unbelievers. Rather, changing the story refers to the system of symbols that make up the social appearance and style of the congregation.

Steak is steak. Bread is bread. Coffee is coffee. But there is a big difference between the way these foods are served in a home and in a restaurant. It is wonderful to have a home-cooked meal— but you would never go to another person's house to eat it unless first invited. Even if you had a good time, you can't forget that you are an outsider—all the family members know one another very well; they have regular places to sit; they have an inside humor you don't always catch; and when the meal is over, they stay and you leave. Everything is on their terms, not yours. A restaurant is different. Restaurants cater to outsiders. They exist for outsiders. Customers get the best tables, set their own schedule, and leave when they choose. Same food, but different stories.

Inward churches are like families serving home-cooked meals. Visitors may be invited and have a good visit, but the story tells them they don't belong. Outward churches are more like restaurants that are designed in every detail to attract customers and match their stories.

Wooddale Church has many intentional designs to be outreaching, including the weekly FaithStory. This is a five-minute presentation given on Sunday mornings by different people from the church family. They tell their own story of either coming to faith in Jesus Christ or sharing their faith with someone else. These personal stories vary widely—going through a divorce, making a business deal, moving into a new community, riding the bus to work every day, marrying again to create a blended family with two sets of children. Those who listen silently say, "That's my story too!'' They realize that this church is made up of ordinary people struggling with modern problems. It is not only a powerful tool for evangelism, but it is very effective at matching stories as well.

## Changing Stories

Churches change stories whether they want to or not. It is a normal part of life.

One pastor fit in well with the congregation. His preaching focused on Bible teaching with parallel-point outlines—usually three main points all starting with the letter P. The subpoints all started with the same letter and sometimes even the sub-subpoints. He studied hard. He related well to people. His illustrations were a mix of history, current events, and everyday life. He was predictable.

Then his wife suffered a stroke. At first there was doubt she would survive. The pastor not only cared for his wife but also never missed a Sunday in the pulpit. The congregation loved him all the more because of his strong demonstration of faithfulness. It added to his story. They liked what they saw and heard. One memorable Sunday morning he digressed from his outline to talk about his wife, her suffering, and the personal cost to him. It touched the hearts of the people. The next Sunday he mentioned her again, and cried again. She made it into the sermon week after week—always with emotion and regardless of text or topic. After a few months attendance began dropping as parishioners drifted to other churches. His story had changed, and now it wasn't their story.

A similar thing happens when a new pastor comes to a church. The former pastor had a story people had identified with, and some will never identify with the new pastor's story. So they leave.

There are churches where the people change their story and force the pastor out because the stories don't match. That has happened on the issue of divorce and remarriage. The strict position from the pulpit hasn't varied in thirty years, but the people in the pews have had their divorces and no longer like what they hear. Or, perhaps, the pastor has always been something of a male chauvinist in his sermon terminology—usually using "he" and "him" to refer to almost everyone, while speaking of adult women as "girls." The congregation lives and works all week in a context where sexist language is considered inappropriate. Their story has changed, but the pastor's story hasn't. They either leave the church, or they get rid of the pastor.

Fortunately, there are hundreds of churches that have changed their stories for good reasons. Pastor Leon Thompson of Thomasville, North Carolina, tells how the Mt. Zion Wesleyan Church changed its story:

> I began to feel God preparing Mt. Zion Wesleyan for a new direction in carrying out the Great Commission in October 1990. For the past twelve months there had been some tremendous revival thrusts by the Holy Spirit within the church and community. Many in the congregation felt the "spiritual temperature" rising. People were being converted, were joining the church, and were bringing their friends and families to Sunday School and worship. Our sanctuary was eighty to ninety percent full each week and the parking lot was full.
>
> Checking the church records, I found that this had happened at least three times before in the church's history. Each time, the records showed, there had been a "falling away" after about a year of growth. The 300 attendance level was our "comfort zone" and we liked it! After all, Mt. Zion was the second largest Wesleyan church in the state and in the top percentages of the denomination.
>
> I began to gather information from various sources on the "how to" of going to two services. In January of 1991 we surveyed the congregation, began planning with staff, and showed videos to the members of the Local Board of Administration and other congregational leaders. At the same time, many of us began praying earnestly for God's will to be made clear in this proposed leap of faith. After all, we had never done it like this before!
>
> That same month I proposed to the church board and staff, "Let's try two morning services for the spring quarter (13 weeks) as an experiment." Ninety percent said, "Let's do it!"

The first Sunday in March was the worst weather Sunday of the year! Rain and a cold wind began Saturday and continued into the night and through most of Sunday. I had hoped for 150 in the early service which began at 9:00 A.M., but was elated when 117 "waded in!" There were 247 in the second service at 10:50 A.M. The next Sunday, 168 attended the early service and 268 the second service. Palm Sunday we had 480 total in our services and Easter Sunday 512. Overall, our March average morning worship attendance was 143 more persons than the previous March.[2]

Mt. Zion Wesleyan Church changed its story. The old story was smaller, single service, and retrenching. The new story is larger, multiple service, and advancing.

Changing stories relates to both outsiders and insiders. The church that wants to reach out and evangelize gives high value to identifying the stories and symbols of its target audience.

When Wooddale Church considered designs for a new Worship Center, outsiders were asked, "What do you think a church's building should look like?" The overwhelming answer was "a church should look like a church." This called for traditional architecture with a high steeple, tall windows, and the assurance that passersby would not mistake the building for a shopping center. This view ran against the popular wisdom of many who design church-meeting places to look as little like a church building as possible. Could both be right? Certainly, in different places or with different target audiences. In the Minneapolis suburb where Wooddale seeks to reach people, there are large numbers who don't go to church but want it to look like a church if they ever do go.

At the same time, Wooddale Church sought to incorporate many of the architectural features people experience in schools, office buildings, and shopping centers. The building must seem comfortable to those who have never gone to church before. There are large halls, shopping-center-type parking lots, contemporary interior decorating, disabled access, user-friendly signage, Coke machines, gymnasium, commercial kitchens, and modern offices. The symbols and story match the people of the community.

Changing stories can be tricky business. It is difficult to attract newcomers without losing old-timers. The age of the average purchaser of a 1990 Chevrolet Caprice was 64—too old to keep the car's market share. The Caprice is one of the largest cars sold in America. It is rear-wheel drive, plush inside, and has a soft "living room" type of ride. Younger buyers, however, like smaller cars with front-wheel drive and a hard European "sports car" type of ride. Thus, younger buyers don't often purchase Caprices. The challenge for the Chevrolet division of General Motors was to change the car's story and symbols in a way that would keep the old buyer and attract the young buyer. That is not easy to do, but the same challenge faces many churches. Old-timers (who control the money, power, and votes in many churches) like the way things were. Younger newcomers (or potential newcomers) want things to change. Keep the church the old way and the church dies with the older generation; change the church to the new way, and you risk losing the old without gaining the new. Tricky business.

There are too many sad stories of unsuccessful attempts at story changing. Pastors have traveled across country to conferences that show and tell how to do it—worship choruses and a drama; busing children from every subdivision; preaching 45–60 minute academic exegetical sermons; incorporating the charismatic renewal elements of signs, wonders, healings, and tongues. The pastor returns greatly excited with an entirely new story for the church. There may be little groundwork and no knowledge that the new story fits either the church or the community. But the pastor charges ahead toward implementation. Even if the new plans and programs are very good, the church resists and rejects the new story. Within twelve months the pastor is out looking for a new job or starting a split-off of the old church. Worst of all, the church has been turned against change.

It is far better to begin with a mission statement of why the church exists and what the church is to do. Then get to know the stories and symbols of those people the church has agreed to reach and determine how the church must change its story to fulfill its mission.

Take the example of a church that determined to reach adults in their thirties and forties. Careful research convinced the leaders to alter significantly the style of worship, incorporating informality and modern musical instruments like drums and synthesizers. Even though the new approach included an additional worship service while keeping the traditional service, it was still more of a story change than many old-timers could accept. Consequently, the pastor and leaders of the church met with each opponent and explained, "We are really concerned about reaching these people for Jesus Christ. We know the changes are hard for you. But suppose there were a church like ours in the area where your children live—aren't they also in their thirties and forties? And suppose that church could make some changes that would bring your children and their families back to the Lord and into the church. What would you think?" The old-timers not only agreed to the changes but gave strong support as well.

What happened is simple but powerful. Certain strong symbols and stories were elevated—the evangelistic mission of the church with the desire of parents to see their children connected to the church and living Christian lives. When these were reinforced, the old-timers accepted the changes in the church's story.

It doesn't always work this way. Sometimes church leaders are not as skilled in story change. Sometimes insiders will not accept story change under any rationale. Because society is dynamic, those churches that refuse to change their story will die. The only question is how long it will take.

## Strengthening Stories

Beware of changing stories just to change. Yours may be a church that has a story that is very much in tune with God's truth and the people you want to reach. When the story does need to be changed, one of the most effective ways is to find a current substory and elevate it to greater importance within the church.

Peter Drucker, the senior dean of American management consultants, wrote insightfully in the *Wall Street Journal*:

> Changing the corporate culture has become the latest management fad. Every business magazine carries articles about it.
>
> There is indeed a need to change deeply ingrained habits in a good many organizations.
>
> What these needs require are changes in behavior. But

"changing the culture" is not going to produce them. Culture—no matter how defined—is singularly persistent.[3]

Drucker explains that behavior and habits need to change in order to become effective. He then proposes four steps for changing habits:

1. *Define what results are needed.*
2. *Ask, "Where within our own system is this done already?"*
3. *Leaders need to promote the practice of what is already being done well.*
4. *Change recognitions and rewards to change habits.*

He gives examples of changing habits without changing culture. One deals with railroads:

> The American railroads began their turnaround in 1948 or 1949 when executives at the Union Pacific, the Chesapeake & Ohio and the Norfolk & Western first asked: "What is the most important result we need?" They all answered, "To get back on the railroad the shipment of finished automobiles from factory to dealer." Then they asked: "Is anyone on any railroad actually doing this?"
>
> The moment the question was asked they all realized that one subsidiary of the Chesapeake & Ohio—the one serving Flint, Mich., home of the Buick Division of General Motors—was actually increasing its share of finished automobile shipments while every other railroad in the country was losing automobile business. Yet all these people in Flint had done was to find out what traditional railroad services Buick needed and was willing to pay for—and then to provide the service with true excellence.[4]

It is not difficult to apply Drucker's principles and this story to the twenty-first-century church. Each church needs to answer the question: "What are the results we need?" and then find out where those results are being attained in that church or a similar church.

For example, many churches with declining Sunday attendance have weeknight children's club programs that are very successful. The typical approach is to try to recruit the weekday children for Sunday school, or try to attract their parents for Sunday worship and church membership. Perhaps a better approach is to find out what causes the weeknight success. Bring the workers and some of the children together. Ask them what they are doing. Find out how they would change the rest of the church life and program to do some of the same things. The genius may be informality, casual dress, athletic competition, convenient schedule, or understandable Bible stories. Next, determine how to bring the genius of the weekday program with children into the rest of the church program with adults.

If there really are no effective areas within the present church, the best place to look is another similar but successful church. Churches are more likely to change when they can see the change somewhere else. If the other church is similar enough, the response often is, "We can do that too!"

The situation is different when starting a new church. The culture is being created. The advantage may be fewer bad habits, but the disadvantage is no good habits to monopolize on.

A second Drucker story illustrates a change in behavior and habits by changing recognitions and rewards:

> The best example is the way the American military services worked together in the recent Iraq campaign. In the invasion of Grenada in 1983 there was no cooperation at all between the services—if there had been the slightest opposition, the invasion would have been a disaster. The military immediately organized all kinds of conferences, pep sessions, lectures and so on, to preach cooperation. Still, less than a year and a half ago, the Panama invasion almost foundered because the services still did not cooperate.
>
> Only a year later, in Iraq, cooperation worked as no service cooperation ever worked before. The reason: Word got around, I am told, that henceforth the appraisal of an officer's cooperation with other services—as judged by those other services—would be a material factor in promotion decisions.[5]

Some may think that changing recognition and rewards in a church is harder to do. But it has been done and can be done.

A friend told me about an old New England church that wanted to recruit new members. The search committee offered a contract to the senior pastor candidate, which tied salary increases to the number of new members added. It turned out that the new pastor was a fantastic recruiter. Membership soared, and with it his salary, which multiplied several times over until the church leaders decided that this was not an appropriate standard for remuneration and canceled the contract.

I'm not convinced that pastors should be paid on a commission or quota system, but the search committee members had the right idea in that they connected the changes they wanted to the rewards they offered.

Consider another possibility. The story of many churches is that positions are more important than ministry. It is not unusual for a church to have boards and committees totaling 75 to 100 different positions. Some larger churches have hundreds. Some have so many positions that members must serve on several different committees in order for every office to be filled.

The problem is that churches have set up reward and recognition systems tied to positions rather than to ministry. The better approach could be to increasingly give recognition to those who teach, evangelize, help, give, pray, visit, and otherwise minister. At the same time, decrease visibility and recognition for those who hold the traditional positions in the church. Stop publishing lists of officers. Leave unfilled positions vacant. Disband committees. Let fewer people make the decisions and more people do the ministry. This approach changes the focus from position to ministry through incrementally changing the story—by altering the system of recognition and rewards.

Peter Drucker suggests that the work begins when the committee adjourns. In church terms, maybe we should say ministry begins when the committee adjourns.

# Chapter 7

# *Is This Body Healthy?*

WE BOUGHT OUR SUBURBAN Minneapolis house during December. The temperature was below zero and the ground was covered with snow. While we checked to see if the furnace worked, we never gave a moment's thought to the lawn. When the spring thaw came and the neighbors' lawns turned green and lush, our yard looked lousy. Not only were there more weeds than grass, but someone also told us that guests of the previous owners used to park their cars on the front lawn.

I called ChemLawn to sign up for lawn-care services. Even though it would be expensive, I figured it was necessary to make the grass look good. The ChemLawn representative came over, measured, evaluated, and gave me the verdict: "Rejection." Our lawn was so bad that ChemLawn didn't want anything to do with us.

Meanwhile, a member of our church offered to scrape off the old lawn and start over again. I wasn't ready for such radical surgery.

Then a former farmer gave me some interesting advice. He said, "Don't worry so much about getting rid of the weeds. Just grow the grass, and the grass will take care of the weeds." We followed his plan—watering, nurturing, reseeding, and otherwise growing the good stuff. After a couple of years, our lawn looked as good as the neighbors'.

## Grow Grass or Kill Weeds?

The same decision must be made for churches. Will the primary focus be on getting rid of the problems or growing the blessings?

Let there be no doubt that every church has its own set of problems. Not one is weed free. But there is an enormous negative danger in making the problems the self-description of the congregation.

During a retreat of church leaders, a pastor gave an impassioned speech for ministering to the problem people in our churches. He presented a long list of the maladies faced by individuals and families in his congregation. He encouraged others to take a closer look at the problems in their churches and to address them more assertively.

He was taken aback when I asked him what the health of his church was. I feared that the integrating motif of his church's life was illness rather than health.

Please don't misunderstand. Churches must be hospitals for hurting people. But the best hospitals see themselves as places for health rather than places for sickness.

I would go so far as to say that those churches that elevate problems as central become ineffective in solving problems. By contrast, those churches that elevate health as central become the most effective communities for healing.

## "Do You Want to Get Well?"

One of Jesus' most surprising questions was when he spoke to a man who had been an invalid for 38 years. Jesus asked him, "Do you want to get well?" (John 5:6). At first hearing, his question sounds offensive. What could a lifelong invalid want more than to get well? Since he was waiting at the Pool of Bethesda where the waters were supposed to heal, the answer seems obvious.

Some sick people don't want to get well. They enjoy the attention their illness brings. The possibility of functioning competitively in a world they don't really understand frightens them. Much of their self-identity is tied to their disease. They would really rather stay sick.

Since Jesus never did get a straight answer from the man, he simply told him to act healthy. "Get up!" Jesus said. "Pick up your mat and walk" (John 5:8). The man's answer to Jesus' question came in his response to Jesus' orders. When he obeyed Jesus' command to act healthy, he was really saying he wanted to be well, and so Jesus healed him.

The same question can be asked of sick churches. They are sick from sin, lethargy, infighting, heresy, undernourishment, incompetence, irrelevance, or any one of a thousand other ecclesiastical diseases. The people of the church may actually enjoy discussing the symptoms—lack of growth, insufficient finances, too few leaders, successive short-term pastorates, and so on. Some go so far as to wear their problems like a hero's medal: "We have so few people because we are the only church still faithful to the true gospel of Jesus Christ."

When the Lord asks a sick church, "Do you want to get well?" the answer is not always obvious. Getting well may require exercise of spiritual gifts, stepping forward on faith, incorporating newcomers who are unlike the old-timers. Comfort zones will be invaded. A new identity may have to be forged. While few churches will ever actually say no either to Jesus or to his question, their real answer is, "We would rather not!"

Getting well always requires change. It always calls for action. Getting well means we must pick up our beds and walk. We must act healthy.

## What Is Health?

The quickest answer to this question is that health is "lack of sickness." But there must be more to it than that. For the theologically inquisitive, what was the ordinary physical condition of Adam and Eve in the Garden of Eden? They were healthy before sickness began. How would they define health when they had no vocabulary for disease? After all, if we don't know what health is, we're not likely to experience it. And if we insist on defining health in terms of illness, we will be malady-centered.

The dictionary definition of health includes "the condition of being sound in body, mind, or spirit" and "flourishing condition." The thesaurus adds such synonyms as "well-being, hardiness, robustness, vigor, strength, vitality, stamina, hardihood."

Personal health is a function of design, individuality, and setting. Design refers to the purpose of any particular part of the body. For example, a healthy eye can see and a healthy ear can hear as they are designed. Individuality varies so that a healthy nine-month-old crawls, but a healthy nine-year-old walks. Setting acknowledges that health may vary because of circumstances. The same healthy man who runs without panting at sea level may be out of breath going up a flight of stairs in the high altitude of Leadville, Colorado.

When you ask a physician what is healthy blood pressure, the doctor will probably answer with a few questions: "How old is the patient? Resting or exercising? Medicated or unmedicated?"

All of these principles apply to churches. What is healthy for one may be different from what is healthy for another. Healthy for a young church in a booming suburb of Orlando includes a growth rate of 50% per year. Health for an old church in a declining inner city of the Rust Belt may be staying the same size.

Each church needs to define health for itself. That comes through a process of comparison, consultation, and self-evaluation. Comparison is made with other churches, especially healthy ones. Consultation with outsiders helps us see ourselves as others see us. Self-evaluation is applying insider's insights to the comparisons and consultations. An individual might conclude that health for me at my age and with my setting is that I should weigh 175 pounds, have a normal body temperature of 98.4, a pulse of 72, 20/20 vision with contact lenses, and run a mile in 7 minutes. For a church it might be that health for us is an annual growth rate of 5%, with half of that growth coming through evangelism, annual offerings of $1,000 per person (based on average Sunday morning worship attendance), 40% of adults in small-group Bible studies, and average pastoral tenure of at least nine years.

## Health Signs

While not exhaustive, consider an initial list of healthy church characteristics:

*Glorify God* is what the church is supposed to do. "The chief end of man is to glorify God and to enjoy him forever" (Westminster Shorter Catechism).

Unfortunately, "glorify" has become religious jargon so that few people have a meaningful understanding of the term. In the New Testament "glorify" comes from the Greek word *doxa* (from which comes the name of the historic praise hymn *The Doxology*). In its earlier history *doxa* referred to a person's reputation. When applied to God, glorify means "to enhance the reputation of God."

No one can improve on who God is. He is great and good and perfect. But his reputation often does not measure up to reality. God has a very poor reputation among some people. He is perceived as arbitrary, inconsiderate, unkind, and unfair. When a Christian lives a godly life and represents God well, the reputation of God is improved, and God has been glorified.

The healthy church improves God's reputation in its community, among believers and unbelievers, and to the broader world. It is like the description of the maturing Jesus in Luke 2:52, "Jesus grew in wisdom and stature, and in favor with God and men." Jesus made God look good.

In many communities the reputation of God is directly tied to the reputations of churches. Churches that are kind to people, pay their bills to vendors on time, seek to serve rather than be served, and handle difficulties in a Christian manner are those churches that glorify God.

An extreme case is one where the long-term senior pastor of a church is charged and later convicted of sexually assaulting children in the parish. God's reputation is dealt a severe blow. That church wonders whether it will ever be able to contribute positively to the reputation of God again. If not, it should shut down. The better (although more difficult) approach would be to demonstrate the attributes of God by handling such a devastating situation in a manner that will make God look good.

The point is that the healthy church is more concerned about glorifying God than about perpetuating an organization, representing a denomination, or maintaining social relationships.

*Producing disciples* is what a healthy church seeks to do. It is an "outcome" approach to church life and ministry. The opposite is to define a church in terms of the number of people it brings in and keeps. Size means more than quality.

In Matthew 28:20 Jesus defined a disciple as someone who obeys all that he commanded. It is not someone who knows all that Christ commanded, although some knowledge is a necessary prerequisite to obedience.

Frankly, evangelical American churches have heavily tilted toward counting bodies and teaching truth as expressions of health. Both are part of health, but the outcome is more important than the process.

Without being legalistic, define what a Christian should be like after five, ten, and fifteen years in your church. What will mark her life in terms of prayer, relationships, exercise of spiritual gifts, and handling of problems? The healthy church is continually striving to shape and send out people who are disciples.

One of the spin-offs to this aspect of health is that the healthy church is more concerned about an individual's discipleship than about keeping that individual in the same church. As a pastor, it is important for me to recognize that our church is not always the best place for every believer to grow and mature. Just as a competent physician refers a patient to another doctor, I must be willing to let go and send a church member elsewhere in order for God's best to happen in his or her life.

There has been so much said and written about dysfunctional families in recent years that one wonders whether there is such a thing as a "functional family." Indeed there is. A functional family handles problems in a way that will move itself toward health and maturity rather than in a dysfunctional way that will move to hide its problems and perpetuate illness and immaturity.

Dysfunctional people exist in every church. Some are simply carnal. Others are victims. Others are mentally, emotionally, or socially sick. Does the church act in a healthy way to confront those who are dysfunctional and move them toward health, maturity, and discipleship? Or does the church perpetuate and increase their dysfunction?

Take the case of the church bully. Let's say that this person happens to be a woman. She intimidates and seeks to control. Her opinions are expressed and imposed on aspects of church life from the mowing of the lawn to the picking of the new pastor. She chases newcomers out of the church and damages old-timers who stay in the church. Often she focuses most of the church's energies and resources on things that really don't matter. Here is the question: Is this church making her a disciple by allowing her to behave in this way? Obviously not. The unhealthy church allows her to continue and even establishes systems of protection for her. The healthy church loves, confronts, disciplines, and directs the church bully in order to change her into a healthy biblical believer.

On the very practical side, healthy churches are always reviewing their programs and style to see whether they are outcome and disciple-making oriented. The Sunday school class that produces disciples is promoted and encouraged. The class that produces sickness or effects no change is shut down.

*Exercise of spiritual gifts* is one of the clearest New Testament characteristics of church health. Interestingly, much of the biblical teaching about spiritual gifts is directed to an unhealthy church (1 Cor. 12—14).

At Woodddale Church we started to offer a "Spiritual Gifts Seminar" over a decade ago. During the first round we used a course that came as a complete package. It didn't work well. Instead, an original course was written with nineteen study guides for inductive Bible study of the New Testament spiritual gifts. We invited a dozen from the church to join a second pilot project. The second time went much better.

We now have a six-week course with a limited enrollment, meeting ninety minutes each Wednesday evening. Homework is prepared in advance, including readings from *19 Gifts of the Spirit* by Leslie Flynn, which is used as a background resource book. There are lectures, discussions, and even written tests.

In this class students are taught that every Christian has at least one spiritual gift, that a spiritual gift is a job somewhat similar to a secular occupation, that ministry is more important than office, and that gifts are primarily given to the body (church) rather than to the individual. Slowly, week by week, the concepts are grasped and owned. It is only the beginning of the gift discovery process.

Perhaps most important is the realization that we are called to serve God through the exercise of gifts like faith, leadership, mercy, helping, teaching, evangelism, giving, and others. They are told that the church has few boards, committees, or offices. The organization is kept as lean as possible so that as many as possible can be in ministry. One of the stories that "turns the light on" for those in the class is about a young executive at Wooddale Church who has the gift of evangelism. She regularly introduced others to personal faith in Jesus Christ. She would often go by the pool of her apartment complex to meet strangers with whom she shared her faith. Because she was so good at evangelism, someone asked her to serve on the evangelism board of the church. She came to ask my advice. I said, "Kathy, it's kind of crazy putting someone with the gift of evangelism into a boardroom filled with other Christians. I would much rather that you spend your time out by the swimming pool."

In other words, the healthy church pushes people into ministry where the Holy Spirit has gifted them rather than where the church organization needs them. To do otherwise would be like using a nose for feeling and a hand for walking—it can be done, but it's not in keeping with the original design.

*Relating positively to one's environment* normally accompanies good health. Healthy people do not live in isolation.

Historically, the United States went through a highly isolationist period during most of the first half of the twentieth century. The country reluctantly and limitedly participated in World War I and failed to give adequate support to the League of Nations. As World War II approached, an even stronger voice for isolation was saying, "Let Europeans fight a European war."

Everything changed when Japanese bombs sank ships in Pearl Harbor on December 7, 1941. America quickly joined the Allied war efforts in the Pacific and the Atlantic with a will to win. The nation changed its relationship to the global environment.

Relating to one's environment does not mean agreeing or condoning. In fact, Christians are necessarily counterculture by their spiritual nature.

Healthy Christians pursue an incarnational ministry modeled after Jesus Christ. As the eternal Son of God, he came to earth, became fully human, and engaged himself in the environment of our sinful world. He proved that relationship with sinners does not require sinning. Jesus often got along better with those labeled "sinners" than those labeled "religious." In fact, Jesus spent so much time with the socially unacceptable that he was called a glutton and a drunkard (Matt. 11:19). Interestingly, Jesus did not consider these slanderous accusations as tarnishing the glory (reputation) of God. In other words, incarnational ministry that was misunderstood by the religious was one of the ways in which Jesus enhanced God's reputation on earth.

Healthy churches are also incarnational. They are well informed and involved in the world. This means knowing what is going on, spending time with people unlike ourselves, finding ways to serve others, risking accusations and misunderstanding in order to be with those who are sinners.

Bear Valley Baptist Church in Denver has established a national reputation for freeing parishioners so they can relate to their environment and undertake ministries outside of the church building. The approach has been to encourage anyone in the church who has an interest or a call to a type of ministry to "go for it." That does not mean the church routinely endorses every undertaking without discretion. Proposals are reviewed before they are endorsed. Nevertheless, the church has ventured into medical ministry for the poor, revitalized troubled churches, engaged in a myriad of social programs while maintaining direct evangelism.

Another aspect of relating to the environment is use of the church building. Wooddale Church decided as part of its outreach strategy to give priority for use of the church facilities to secular rather than other religious organizations. The church building has been used for hospital-sponsored birthing classes, blood mobile visits, staff parties for local restaurant staffs, practice for NFL cheerleaders, city council and neighborhood meetings, out-processing of laid-off manufacturing employees, professional athletes' meetings, executive planning retreats for local businesses, secular music concerts, and many Alcoholics Anonymous meetings. Between regular church activities and these outside secular events, there isn't much time or space left. Thus, most Christian organizations are not able to use the facility—they must go elsewhere.

Different churches will adopt different approaches, but healthy churches aren't ostrichlike with their heads in the sand. Healthy churches are incarnational, knowing what's going on in their world and relating positively to it.

*Reproduction* is an evidence of health in animal life *and* in church life. God designed the perpetuation of species through having babies. At least for the typical reproductive years, healthy humans have healthy reproductive organs that will produce new offspring.

Most people would agree that churches should reproduce through evangelism. We all recognize that the threat of extinction is only one spiritual generation away.

Too many churches are evangelistically ineffective. They seldom or never reproduce. Most converts are children of Christians, and most church growth is transfers from other churches.

A *Christianity Today* analysis claims, "Among evangelicals, no single topic beats evangelism at capturing interest—or creating guilt."[1] As a result, evangelicals have experienced waves of methods over the past five decades that include altar calls, tracts, crusades, radio preaching, TV shows, door-to-door witnessing, personal conversation (and confrontation), investigative Bible studies, and many others. All have worked well in specific times and places. Most are either very individual (like the Four Spiritual Laws presentations) or very institutional (like televised Billy Graham Crusades.)

Consider the "body evangelism" model. It is based on an analogy to human reproduction. While the uterus is the primary reproductive organ of the female body, it cannot reproduce alone. Most of the other parts of the body contribute to and are essential for the conception, development, and birth of a baby. The lungs provide oxygen; the heart pumps blood to the fetus; the digestive system gives nutrition; the skeleton and muscles provide protection. The whole body participates in healthy reproduction.

With "body evangelism" the whole church participates in reproduction. Not everyone is involved in direct evangelism, but everyone is encouraged to function evangelistically. For example, John uses his gift of hospitality to the Hendersons, who have just moved into the neighborhood. He introduces his new friends to some Christians, who help connect them to the schools and civic associations of the town, and also to a Tuesday evening Bible study group. Jeff and Jan Kimo, a couple in the Bible study, bring the Hendersons to church. Pastor Hank Rutledge helps answer some tough religious questions that always blocked Larry Henderson's consideration of the gospel. After a church service Larry sees Ralph Duggan, a co-worker with whom he connects for lunch every Friday. At one of those lunches Larry accepts Jesus Christ as his Savior and Lord. He grows spiritually through a discipleship group Ralph introduces him to. Larry learns quickly, shares what he learns with his wife and children, and they come to faith three months later. Now they are all actively involved in the life of the church. Here is the question: "Who gets the credit for winning this family?" The answer is no one person. It is the body, the church. More important, God receives the glory.

Healthy churches are permeated with the desire to reproduce. It is not so much a program as a way of life. Some even contend that the most evangelistic churches don't have formal evangelistic programs.

In defining health we must be careful not to play a numbers game. Healthy humans have different numbers of babies. Some have a dozen, and some have none. Most have some. Reproduction is normal. Likewise, churches have more or less converts to Jesus Christ. Most normal healthy churches, however, have some.

*Incorporation of newcomers* may be one of the most identifiable and measurable signs of health in a church. Healthy churches assimilate new people into the life and leadership of the congregation.

One of the more common criticisms of established churches comes from those who feel the fellowship is tough to penetrate: "When I first visited Community Church, people were so friendly. I was greeted by almost everyone. I thought it was the friendliest church I had ever seen. But then I ran into a brick wall after just a few weeks. They were too busy to become friends. Now, after being a member for a full year, I still feel like an outsider."

When pastors hear such criticism, they intuitively turn up the heat for hospitality. You can almost hear the words from the pulpit: "We've got to make friends with new people. We used to. I don't know what has changed. Here's what I propose—everyone should plan to have guests for Sunday dinner. Before you come to church, put a bigger roast in the oven and set some extra plates at the dining room table. When you meet visitors at church, immediately invite the whole family to come home with you for a Sunday dinner."

Often that same pastor invites a gathering of old-timers and newcomers over to the parsonage on a Sunday evening—to get the two groups to meet each other and become friends.

Neither approach works well in most modern churches. Many people aren't going home for Sunday dinner, they are going to Arby's or Burger King. They can't afford a big roast, and they may not have a dining room. Their lives are already too busy, and their budgets are already too stretched. They are not looking for anyone else to know or anywhere else to spend money. Pastoral pressure may get temporary results, but they don't give busy people any more time to be friendly.

A colleague gave me some helpful insight into the dilemma when she said, "The church is initially friendly, but then I discover that everyone has a relational waiting list." It's almost as if newcomers have to sign up for future friends and wait for an opening.

Do you know what Legos look like? They are pieces of plastic that can be snapped together into creatively designed toys. Children love them. Legos can be made into cars, stores, bridges, houses, schools, or church buildings. Most Legos have about six snap-on points. Some have many more, and a few have only two or four. When a Lego is all snapped up, you simply can't attach anything more to it. The only way to snap on something new is to unsnap something old.

The social structure of churches is made up of people like Legos. They have a limited number of snap-on points—few have more than six. After people have been in a church for a couple of years, they are all snapped up. They have all the friends and relationships there is time and energy to service. Telling them to invite others over for dinner may work for one meal, but they won't become attached to the newcomers if there is no place to attach. An invitation to the parsonage is nice, but rarely will that snap the old-timers together with the newcomers.

So what should a church do? Seek to snap newcomers to newcomers. Most of them have several snap-on points available and are looking for relationships. Rather than seeking to assimilate large numbers of newcomers into existing Sunday school classes, start a new class. Begin new groups, new ministries, new worship services, new choirs. This will not only attach newcomers, but it will also draw out the established church members who are seeking new relationships and those who want to break from existing networks into new networks.

Won't this make for a polarized church with seniors, juniors, sophomores, and freshmen who hardly know one another? It could, which raises another health issue. Are leadership and ministry positions in the church open to new people? How long does it take for someone to make it to a committee, board, or other position of influence in the church. In healthy churches the answer will typically be one to four years. The newcomer should be able to experience initial assimilation and take a first position of leadership, ministry, or influence within the first year. At most, that person should be able to learn the system and prove oneself in a maximum of three more years.

Like taking the temperature of a patient, list the leadership and ministry positions of a church and write down the number of years each person holding a position has been part of that fellowship. If the majority of the leaders have been in the church a long time, it usually means the old-timers will not allow others into "their church." When checking, watch out for excuses. Explanations like, "Those new people just don't understand how the church works," or "They're not spiritually mature" may be either a cover-up for unwillingness to share power or an admission that the present leaders are incapable of preparing newcomers for leadership roles. Both are unhealthy.

One way to check the health of the assimilation process is to listen to how long it takes newcomers to switch their pronouns from *your* church and *their* church to *our* church and *my* church.

William Ramsden recommends tracking church visitors. Rate the welcome factor of the church by how many first-time visitors (excluding out-of-town guests) come a second time and by how many third-time visitors eventually join the congregation. He measures the incorporation factor by how many church positions are filled by volunteers who have joined the church in the past three years.[2]

Healthy churches incorporate new people as equal members in a short enough period of time that those people do not become discouraged and go elsewhere.

But does membership really measure incorporation? Increasingly no. The trend toward non-affiliation means that more people feel they belong, yet will never officially appear on a church's membership role.

Church membership is not biblical terminology. Unfortunately, it is difficult to find a good alternative. Some churches have a small board of directors for purposes of legal incorporation, but no one else is a member. Parishioners become like customers at a privately owned retail store. The downside is seen in such churches when they face catastrophe with mismanagement at the top and no formal accountability to their constituents. Other churches avoid official membership but have a very clear mental picture of "who's in and who isn't." They have membership without a written list. One church has switched to the term "belongers" to encourage people to join who don't want to become members.

A common solution is not to worry about it—let the old-timers who like membership join and let the newcomers who don't like membership stay off the list. The problem with this approach comes when votes for structural change are required—the only ones with votes are those least likely to change.

I don't have a proposal to fit the times, solve all the problems, and keep everyone happy. It's like the recent observation about the aging 77 million baby boomers: "Whoever invents a comfortable wheelchair will become a very rich person." Whoever invents a way for nonmembers to be church members may not become rich but certainly will be creative.

*Openness to change* is more difficult to measure. Usually we should assume that most institutions, and especially churches, are resistant to change. Indeed, too much resistance to change causes petrification. If we don't exercise, we eventually can't exercise.

We often hear the axiom: "Don't change just for change sake." I'm not sure that is good advice. We have encouraged some change in the constitution of Wooddale Church almost every year since I became the pastor. Recently, after the church's annual meeting, I commented to my secretary, "I feel badly that we didn't make any changes in the constitution this year." She replied, "That's because there is nothing left to change!" That's when I said, "Maybe we should start putting it back the way it used to be."

Of course I'm not endorsing frivolous or unproductive changes. However, I am convinced that healthy churches are changing churches. They are willing to take risks, to undertake new projects and programs that may fail.

An executive recruiter once told me about one of his interviewing techniques. He explained that he asks prospective employees to list some of their biggest failures in previous jobs. He always preferred to hire those who had failed and still had their jobs. He shied away from prospects who couldn't think of significant failures because he knew they weren't risk takers.

It is risky to reach out to unbelievers. It changes a church when newcomers are unlike old-timers. God's work is seldom neat, clean, and free of problems. Our world is changing around us. All healthy organisms adapt or die. The same goes for churches.

In George Barna's *User Friendly Churches*, he explains that successful churches "subscribe to a common philosophy: the ministry is not called to fit the church's structure; the structure exists to further effective ministry."[3] That means that when the structure doesn't work, it is changed. Barna adds:

> These churches had a keen sense of direction and purpose (i.e., vision and plans). Their top priority was to achieve their ministry goals. If the organizational charts and structural procedures inhibited such ministry, they would cautiously but willingly work around the barriers. They were not about to let a man-made system hinder their ability to take advantage of a God-given opportunity to change lives for the Kingdom.
>
> Structure, in fact, was not an issue in these churches. Certainly, these congregations were led by individuals who see the wisdom of developing and maintaining orderly processes. They recognized the importance of formal hierarchy of authority, and the importance of avoiding anarchy (even if the intentions of the anarchists are good). But structure was viewed as a support system, a means to an end, rather than an end in itself. The structures they used had been developed, accepted, implemented, reevaluated and upgraded. At all times, the focus was upon ministry, not structure.[4]

The constants must be the Bible and the mission of the church. Everything else is negotiable.

One of the ways to test for healthy changeability is to invite leaders to study other churches. In fact, one of the best approaches is to go as a team to visit a successful church that is different. Then discuss what ideas could be adapted to your church. I serve on a church staff that spends at least one day every year visiting other churches. We have lay leaders travel to study other congregations. Periodic luncheons are hosted for other church staffs. In our leadership course, students are assigned to visit and research other congregations and compare them to our congregation.

If such studies generally produce responses like "That's a good idea," "Let's try that," "I would like to see that happen here," you have a healthy church—well, almost. There needs to be more than research and talk. Ideas must be implemented or at least tried. Blessed is the church that tries a different style of music, a new approach to evangelism, or adds a Saturday evening service— even if it doesn't work. And blessed is the church that celebrates the risk taking and openness even if the success that was anticipated does not happen.

## Healthy Churches Trust God

Don't all churches trust God? Unfortunately, no. The unhealthy extremes are self-dependence and corporate pessimism. Self-dependent churches often have highly motivated, capable people with large resources and a history of success. They may give lip service to God but really believe and behave as if they can do anything themselves. There is a "can-do" attitude that is contagiously exciting. Often prayers for God's blessing follow the making of excellent plans. The other extreme is a corporate pessimism that permeates a church to the point that a "can't-do" attitude prevails. There is little point in trying anything because it probably won't work anyway. Even the prayers are depressing because they evidence little faith. Both extremes are spiritually sick.

Healthy churches believe they belong to God and that Jesus Christ is the head. You can pick it up in hallway conversations and boardroom deliberations. There is minimal concern about denominational priorities, institutional preservation, individual status, or ecclesiastical politics. The big issue is what God wants and how to get it done. Faith is not reckless, but it does take risks—assuming that the final outcome is God's to determine. Failure is most often defined in terms of unfaithfulness rather than in terms of dollars, numbers, or unhappy people.

Prayer is a natural part of the proceedings of healthy churches. The prayer is balanced between individual and institutional needs—asking for God's help in "Jane's job situation" and "figuring out how to reach this community for Jesus Christ." While prayers may routinely begin and conclude formal meetings, leaders also feel comfortable, if not compelled, to stop for prayer in the middle of a discussion or call a meeting just to pray about a major decision.

Churches with healthy faith don't worry about committee unanimity as much as discovering the mind of Christ. Often they will interpret a split vote as a means for discovering the mind of Christ, and those voting with the minority will be quick to join in the implementation of that which they initially opposed.

Sincere consideration of the Bible as God's Word is woven into decisions and actions. The healthy church welcomes quotations and examples from the Bible that apply to their church life. There is a positive excitement over comparing one part of the Bible to another in the process of figuring out what to do. The Bible is seen as a source of direction and inspiration rather than as a political weapon to get one's own way.

Back to "glorifying God": The healthy church that trusts God readily gives him credit for their victories. When outsiders ask the secret of success, the answer always includes God. Not that these churches are unwilling to mention the programs, procedures, policies, pastors, or other human pluses, but they are always a little uncomfortable with these answers because they know that the listener may get the wrong impression. The healthy church really believes it lives and breathes because it is the church of Jesus Christ.

## Looking Good on the Outside

We have all known people who look good on the outside but are dying of some terrible disease on the inside. They look healthy but are really sick. And we have all known those people who look terrible on the outside but have healthy hearts, normal blood chemistry, and will probably live to be 100. Outward appearance can be deceiving. That's why patients have CT scans, blood work-ups, and all the other battery of tests to find out about internal health. That's also why churches should consider the signs of internal health listed previously.

However, don't discount external appearance. When a surgical patient goes through a major operation, her appearance often isn't good. You visit your friend in the Intensive Care Unit and are taken aback by the poor skin color, messy hair, bad breath, and unkempt appearance. You tell family members, "I'm really worried. She just didn't look good." A few days later that same patient is sitting up in bed, her color looks better, and she says, "Could you bring me my mirror, brush, and hair spray from home?" You are elated! Not only does she look better, but also she cares about how she looks. That is an encouraging sign of improved health.

The external appearance of churches isn't everything, but it is a sign of health. Those superficial appearances of health include the upkeep of the church building, invitations to the unchurched by church members, excitement in the hallways before and after services, and the sense that this church is alive and going somewhere. Just looking and listening goes a long way in concluding, "This is a healthy church!"

# Chapter 8

# *What Is Contemporary?*

IT'S TIME to take a test. Here are the instructions:

1. Read each of the following examples, and decide whether it is best described as "traditional" or "contemporary."
2. Don't look ahead for the answers.
3. Remember your answers.

Example #1 Robed Choir

The choir numbers 100, each wearing a scarlet robe with a white stole. Choral music is a central and seldom omitted part of the Sunday worship experience. The choir is led by a music director and accompanied by an organist playing an electronic organ. Traditional? Contemporary?

Example #2 Uniformity & Fixed Seating

Almost all of the people on the program are dressed alike, in uniforms. Spectators are kept separated from program participants. The program begins with singing a congregational hymn written in 1814, with organ accompaniment. Strict rules of behavior are enforced, and those breaking the rules are immediately disciplined. Traditional? Contemporary?

## Example #3 Drama

Powerful drama is the central feature of this religious event. Expensive props and costumes have been prepared. The actors and actresses are all volunteers, although they are so good you would guess them to be professionals. There is no sermon. Visitors come from great distances to experience the drama but often leave saying they had a profound spiritual experience. Traditional? Contemporary?

## After the Answers

Most of us don't find that to be a very hard test. We quickly and easily conclude what is traditional and what is contemporary and add our judgment about whether we like it or not. To some people anything "traditional" is good because they like the patterns of the past and are skeptical about the styles of the present. Others are the opposite, liking the new and disdaining the old— "traditional" is a sure turnoff and "contemporary" is always attractive.

Is it really that simple? Let's review the examples. *Example #1* describes a typical church in one of the fastest growing segments of American religion, the African-American churches. The robed choir is standard fare in most of the larger and more successful congregations. Nationally, African-American churches are increasing at the rate of 13.5% annually.

*Example #2* is a World Series baseball game, which starts with the hymn "The Star Spangled Banner"—the words were written by Francis Scott Key during the War of 1812, and the tune came from a British drinking song from the 1700s. The baseball players and umpires wear uniforms and are the only ones allowed on the playing field. The spectators are limited to the stands, which have fixed seating in rows that are numbered. Baseball is often referred to as "the national pastime" and is considered to be quintessentially American.

*Example #3* is a description of the Oberammergau Passion Play performed in Bavaria, Germany, since 1633. Normally the presentations are every ten years. The play lasts eight hours and involves 1,200 performers. Tickets are expensive and are often purchased long in advance. Tens of thousands attend.

The point of these examples is that "contemporary" and "traditional" are not always what they may first appear to be. Sometimes the contemporary can be very old and the traditional can be up to date. It is a subjective judgment combining numerous factors.

## Tradition Happens

The outsider watched with fascination as the Danish village people filed into the Lutheran church building for worship. Each one walked up the center aisle to the place where there was a break between the pews and a plain white wall. Every worshiper paused, turned, and genuflected with bowed head and knee facing the blank wall, and then went to sit in their usual pews.

Since the observer couldn't figure out the meaning of this ritual, he asked both the clergy and laity for an explanation, but no one knew. "We've always done it that way" was the sincere but uninformed answer. Further research revealed that there was an elaborate painting of the Virgin Mary behind the white paint on the blank wall. The painting dated back hundreds of years, before the Protestant Reformation when the church was Roman Catholic.

The village people had bowed to the Virgin for generations as Catholics. When the church became Protestant and the Virgin was painted over, the worshipers just kept on bowing. Generations later the bows continued, even though the reason had long since been forgotten. It was tradition.

Traditions begin when someone does something new that others like and imitate. It has meaning, often a powerful and significant meaning. Those who value the meaning join in the practice. When the practice is passed down to the following generation, it becomes a tradition. The root meaning of the word is "action of handing over," and the dictionary definition of tradition is "the handing down of information, beliefs, and customs by word of mouth or by example from one generation to another."

Difference in the meaning of the tradition occurs because seldom does the tradition *mean* the same thing to the subsequent
generation as it did to the previous generation. The Danish village
worshipers kept the tradition but changed the meaning. Christmas
traditions go back hundreds of years but mean something very
different to modern secularists than to earlier Christians. Sunday
as a "day of rest" meant going to church for the Puritans of yesterday and staying in bed for the party-types of today.

We all need traditions. Life would be frighteningly unstable if
there were not some practices and information anchoring us to the
past and the present. Any one of us who takes the time to do a
"tradition inventory" will find most of life operates by traditions.

Tradition determines our schedules (almost everyone is awake
days and sleeps at night), our transportation (we drive cars the
way our parents drove cars; the nontraditionalists were our grandparents who switched from horses), our dress (shoes, underwear,
and jewelry are all traditional), and most of everything else that
we do. A conservative guess is that 98% of our behavior is rooted
in one tradition or another. Those who operate at the 99% level
are considered to be old-fashioned traditionalists, and those who
operate at the 97% level are called avant-garde nontraditionalists.
It is mostly a matter of degree.

The critical question is *meaning*. What do the traditions mean
to the persons who practice the traditions. Communication theory
teaches us that meaning is in the mind of the person, not in the
words or deeds. Examples abound. The action of plunging a knife
into another person may mean homicide, self-defense, or abdom-
inal surgery. The symbol of a cross may mean criminal execution
to an ancient Roman, salvation to a Christian, and jewelry to a
fashion model. The tradition of singing the national anthem before
sports events means patriotism to some, nationalism to others, and
"it's almost time to play ball" to others.

A foolish but common assumption is that traditions mean the
same thing to others as they mean to us.

Ash Wednesday is the first day of Lent. Ashes from the burned
palms of the previous year's Palm Sunday are used by the Catholic
priest to mark a cross on the parishioners' forehead. The priest
says, "Remember, man, that dust thou art, and unto dust thou
shalt return." It is a tradition symbolizing penitence and prepa-

ration for a holy death. Imagine a sincere Roman Catholic leaving the ceremony and meeting a friend on the street who says, "You've got some dirt on your forehead," as he reaches up to wipe the spot away. The tradition may mean much to one and nothing to another.

It is very difficult for many Christians to comprehend that their meaningful traditions mean little or nothing to another person—Sunday worship, hymn singing, baptism, communion, church membership, altar calls, recitation of the Lord's Prayer, or singing of praise choruses.

Traditions can be learned until they are practiced with precision but have no meaning or a different meaning to our children. Naively, each generation tends to think that its creative new ideas are tradition-proof. Today's innovation becomes tomorrow's tradition.

Ongoing efforts must be made to determine the *meaning* words and actions have. Traditions must be revitalized with new meaning in every new generation. New traditions must and will be established. Old traditions must be abandoned. The essential issue is not the tradition but the meaning.

A good place to begin bridging the gap between generations is to ask openly what each tradition means to each generation. Seek to come to primary agreement on meaning and then deal with tradition.

All of this is more than theoretical to the twenty-first-century church. The dominant baby boomers have been slow to accept the traditions of their parents and strong to establish their own new traditions. They have repeatedly asked for the meaning to yesterday's traditions and abandoned those traditions that seemed to have inadequate or inappropriate meanings. But the changing of the times and the ticking of the biological clock may adjust the baby boomer perspective. When society is destabilized, we tend to return to old traditions whether they are rational or not. Look for traditional baby boomers to struggle with their baby buster children, who are now questioning the boomer's traditions, putting many boomers ironically in the new and uncomfortable position of defending traditions rather than challenging them.

With all of this background, let's define the traditional church as the one that has information, beliefs, and customs that have been handed down from a previous generation. In order to be Christian, a church must be traditional—because the gospel message itself has been handed down. More practically, the popular notion of a traditional church is one where the symbols and stories were inherited rather than created. The list can be very long but includes order of service, role of clergy, leadership of laity, music, governance, style of prayer, symbols, collection and distribution of money, dress, and practices of baptism and communion.

Critics of changing churches accuse them of abandoning the traditional. That accusation has less validity than it seems. Suppose aliens were to visit different style Protestant churches in America and contrast cultures and activities. Would they not find more similarities than differences? Don't all read the Bible, celebrate Easter, have pastors, and take offerings?

## Contemporary Is Cultural

To many older Christians "contemporary" means new, and they don't like it. To many younger Christians "contemporary" means new, and they do like it.

Contemporary, however, is merely a contrast to traditional. It means that it originated during the present generation rather than inherited from a previous generation. It is not better or worse; it is just later.

Contemporary is culturally defined. Some of the hottest interests of late twentieth-century Americans are New Age practices, which are very old and traditional in other parts of the world. They are just being discovered by Americans and are therefore considered contemporary.

We learn and change by bridging from the familiar to the unfamiliar. In order for persons born in the 1950s and 1960s to relate to the absolute truths of the Christian faith, they must begin with their own culture and ways of thinking. You might compare current culture to language. The only way English-speaking Americans can understand the Bible is through their contemporary language, not through the traditional Hebrew and Greek of the original Bible. It would be futile to insist that people must first learn ancient languages in order to become believers. Instead, we have all had the ancient and traditional translated into our contemporary idiom.

Making the gospel message and the church contemporary is necessary in every generation. Otherwise both will be lost.

Once again, the emphasis must be on meaning, not form. If the true meaning of the Bible is present in ancient Greek, King James English, or twentieth-century paraphrase, that is what really matters. Those who inflexibly insist that their traditional version or modern translation is superior have fallen into the tragic trap of idolizing the form over the substance.

The essential exercise for every church leader is to first understand the culture and then translate the meaning of the message into that culture. It is much like a missionary going to a country and learning a new language and culture. We too often think that learning the language is all that is necessary. Language and culture cannot be separated. Learning and relating to the culture are absolutely essential if the gospel is to be effectively understood.

In a 1990s American church, the generations and the cultures often mix. Each year nearly one in five American households moves. This puts people into churches who are unconnected to the traditions of the new church but bring their own traditions from their previous location. Consequently, here's what can happen. Evelyn comes into a church service where the music is loud and the dress is casual. The pace is fast with never a moment for meditation. The singing is from a projection screen using unfamiliar and often repeated words. The sermon is full of stories and punctuated with a range of emotions that runs from tears to laughter. She walks out saying to herself, "That wasn't church!" Her traditions call for hymns from a book, quieter music, linear logic, opportunity for meditation, and more formality. Melody, who is younger and newer in the faith, experiences the same service with a totally different conclusion: "That was great! I really felt God!"

Thoughtful Christians will recognize that the differences are not right or wrong. They will also recognize that both Evelyn and Melody have a right to experience God and gain meaning in the ways that best fit each of them—and that is tough to do in the same church.

## Describing Differences

In the *Win Arn Growth Report* there appeared a helpful list of contrasting styles, which he calls "old paradigms" and "new paradigms." The same list could also be called "old traditions" and "new traditions."[1]

|                    OLD                    |                    NEW                    |
| ----------------------------------------- | ----------------------------------------- |

### Effective Evangelism

| OLD | NEW |
| --- | --- |
| Confrontational | Relational |
| Mass | Personal |
| General population | Specific "people groups" |
| Single presentation | Multiple exposure |
| Single method | Multiple methods |
| Goal: a decision | Goal: a disciple |
| America: a Christian nation | America: a secular mission field |
| Church membership | Church discipleship |
| Motive: guilt | Motive: value & love |

### Pastor & Staff

| OLD | NEW |
| --- | --- |
| Enabler | Initiator |
| Activity-oriented | Achievement-oriented |
| Teaching style: propositional | Teaching: experiential |
| Selection based on credentials & denominational history | Selection based on performance |
| Church staff drawn from seminary | Church staff drawn from congregation |

### Christian Education

| OLD | NEW |
| --- | --- |
| Sunday school | Small groups |
| Age-graded | Lifestyle-graded |
| One weekly meeting time & place | Numerous meeting times & places |
| Verbal-oriented | Visual-oriented |
| Paid youth director | Staff with youth & other tasks |

### Senior Adults

| OLD | NEW |
| --- | --- |
| Requires volunteers | Source of volunteers |
| Care-takers | Care-givers |
| Apathetic outreach to seniors | Intentional outreach to seniors |

| One senior adult group & program | Multiple senior adult groups & progams |
| Retirement motive: play | Retirement motive: work, learn, serve, play |

### Facilities

| Considered adequate | Regularly upgraded |

### Worship

| Presentation | Participation |
| Intellectual | Experiential |
| Focus on Christians | Focus also on non-Christians |

### Volunteers

| Sacrifice self | Maximize self |
| Members serve institution | Institution serves members |
| Volunteers | Paid employees |

### The Denominational "System"

| Resists change | Insists on change |
| Centralized | Regionalized |
| Bureaucracy | Accountability |
| Served by churches | Serves churches |

This list gives a fair picture of the perceived differences between the traditional church and the contemporary church. It also raises a number of questions that every church should answer.

What are the underlying meanings and values of each item? For example, is intellectual worship better or worse than experiential worship? Theologically we believe God is a Trinity of three Persons. Personhood is defined in terms of intellect, emotion, and will. We are persons; we also have intellect, emotion, and will. Jesus commanded us to "love the Lord your God with all your heart and with all your soul and with all your strength and with all your mind" (Luke 10:27). The value is worshiping God. The meaning is that we are to worship him as whole persons, acknowledging that different individuals may place greater emphasis on intellect or emotion. In other words, neither an intellectual nor an emotional approach to worship is inappropriate or unbiblical.

What are the meanings to the traditional, and how can those

meanings be housed in the new? In the comparison between age-graded and lifestyle-graded, the meanings both address learning in segmented groups. Some Christians feel more comfortable in groups of the same gender while others prefer co-ed. Some learn better with people their own age. Others don't care about age but want to be with Christians who value an educated lifestyle. The compromise is to offer age-graded and lifestyle-graded groups.

The comparisons go on. A far more basic question, however, has gone begging. There are thousands of churches steeped in tradition who want to change but are afraid of the traditionalists. There are traditionalists who are afraid of the innovators, worrying that absolute core values will be forsaken. There are thousands of churches being polarized over the style of worship services—with no acceptable compromise. I do not underestimate the seriousness of the issue for those facing it. In some cases there is no common ground, and the only compromise may be to divide into two churches or at least have two different style services in the same church.

Anyone, however, who thinks that a different style of worship service makes a contemporary church has missed the mark. That would be like installing a hot tub in an outhouse and calling it modern plumbing. It's a lot more complicated.

Contemporary churches are those that relate to people in terms of today's culture rather than in terms of yesterday's traditions. Neither today's culture nor yesterday's traditions are necessarily right or wrong. It is possible to have a liturgical worship service with clergy vestments, classical music, and a sermon from the lectionary—and be a very contemporary church. It would be contemporary if the rest of the church relates well to today's culture, if the vocabulary and style of the sermon are easy for today's visitors to understand, and if the programs and principles of the church are a good fit with the local culture. On the other hand, a church across the street with drums, synthesizer, drama, worship choruses, and casual dress may be very traditional—using stories, styles, and systems that are carry-overs from an earlier generation and don't make sense to the twenty-first-century American.

The changing of a traditional church must happen over time. It often will end with changes in the public services rather than begin there. The beginning is an understanding of the culture on the outside and the traditions on the inside. The next step is to change the church in ways that retain the biblical values and traditions, while adopting styles and communications appropriate to the culture.

One of the strongest and highest traditions of the church has been a desire to effectively reach people for Jesus Christ. The effective change agent will call all parties to that elementary Christian norm by taking advantage of the deep values that underlie their traditions, instead of attacking them.

## Current Concerns

In simplest terms, the contemporary church is one that recognizes the needs in our culture and structures itself and its programs to meet those needs effectively. The contemporary church will use those needs as a means to bring people into a personal relationship with Jesus Christ as his disciples.

By contrast, the contemporary church does not seek to perpetuate traditions just because they were effective in meeting the needs of an earlier generation. Traditions for themselves are not valued, but traditions that meet current needs are valued.

Does your church have a "feeling" about it that communicates a concern for people and their current concerns? That feeling is probably more important than any other single factor in defining a contemporary church. Experience is certainly a key factor in judgment for baby boomers and baby busters, but it is also important to older generations as well.

Clark Morphew, nationally syndicated religion writer, undertook a study of megachurches and found some overarching characteristics that contributed to success. He prefaced his list by writing, "The techniques that drove these congregations into explosive periods of growth vary, depending on members and the personalities of the chief pastors. But there are some factors that seem to be a part of every megachurch plan."[2] His list is short and simple.

*BICKERING IS OUT.* The emphasis is on the positive. Staff and congregational leaders spend little time trying to placate hurt feelings or referee petty squabbles.
*PREACHING AND MUSIC; QUEST FOR EXCELLENCE.* Megachurch leaders make the assumption

that people are tired of coming to church and suffering through a boring sermon and poorly executed music.

Megachurches tend to offer a variety of musical styles—classical, traditional hymns, contemporary Christian tunes, jazz and bluegrass. Some have even rocked to the sounds of polka music.

In both preaching and music the emphasis is always on excellence. If quality volunteer musicians can't be found within the congregation, for instance, megachurches will likely reach outside the church walls for talent.

*USER FRIENDLY.* Megachurches strive to make people feel comfortable the minute they enter the building. Confusion about programs, embarrassment during worship, being out of touch with church activities, all of those feelings will encourage people to stay home next Sunday.

Most megachurches also have extended educational and recreational programs for all ages. And the educational offerings run the gamut from parenting classes to intensive Bible studies. And megachurches can mobilize large numbers of people for social-action projects, such as feeding the hungry at shelters or building homes for the poor.

*CONSTANTLY IN FLUX.* Megachurches don't count on past victories and successes to carry them through the tough times. Long-range planning is constant, and leaders must be willing to take risks to solve difficult problems.

The secret to continual growth, say the experts, is to always be building on past success and never allowing the congregation to become satisfied with the status quo.[3]

Morphew concludes that "above everything else—the techniques, the long-range plans, the magnificent buildings—megachurch pastors say the most important element of a great church is ministry."[4] He also quotes David Johnson, senior pastor of Church of the Open Door (meeting in Robbinsdale [Minnesota] High School gym with an average worship service attendance of 4,500): "The church is for broken people. The mark of a church is when you see the kind of people that Jesus ministered to, and they're being healed."[5]

Forget the "megachurch" and substitute "contemporary church" to Morphew's words, because the issue isn't size but relevance. Most of these churches became large because they understand the culture and the current concerns of people and do what they need to do. The dozen churches studied range from charismatic to non-charismatic, from traditional liturgies to modern nontraditional freestyle worship, from classical music to jazz music, from Presbyterian and Lutheran to Assembly of God, Christian and Missionary Alliance, and independent. The point is made one more time: contemporary is much more than worship service style and encompasses far more than is typically characterized as contemporary.

The contemporary church is ministry-driven, addressing human needs in relevant and effective ways.

## Regional Religion

One myth identifies "contemporary" as "reaching the unchurched." That myth assumes that most of those who need to be reached in America assume themselves to be unchurched and that they are totally turned off by anything religious. That is a dangerous oversimplification.

Think of the American population in terms of four quadrants: Christians who go to church; non-Christians who go to church; Christians who don't go to church; non-Christians who don't go to church. The next chart assumes some definitions. I define a Christian as someone who has a personal relationship with God through Jesus Christ as Savior and Lord. I define churched as a person who has a meaningful relationship with a local church and participates on a regular basis.

Those are definitions from someone at the center of church life. Those closer to the periphery or outside of church life may use very different definitions. How they see themselves is very important to how a church reaches them.

A survey of 113,000 households in the forty-eight contiguous states was conducted from April 1989 through April 1990 by ICR Survey Research Group based in Media, Pennsylvania, and summarized in a *USA Today* article by Desda Moss:

Most Americans are religious and aren't afraid to say

so, a sweeping new survey on religious affiliation shows.

The survey, commissioned by the Graduate School of the City University of New York, found 86.5% of Americans identified themselves as Christians, 2% as Jewish and 0.5% as Muslim.

Only 7.5% of the respondents said they had no religion.[6]

Most Americans consider themselves religious. Seymour Lachman, dean of community development at City University of New York, said, "For many Americans, religious identity is important, perhaps as important as their ethnic or racial identity."[7]

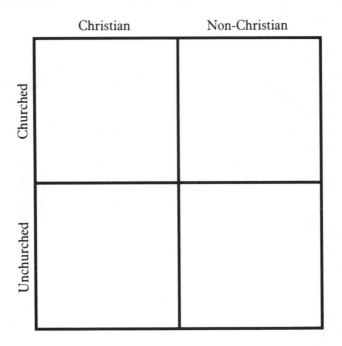

When the church reaches people on the outside, those people do not have blank religious slates. They already see themselves as religious people with beliefs, traditions, and deep convictions. Of course, their self-perceptions do not mean that they have a personal relationship with God through Jesus Christ or that they have any meaningful relationship with any local church. But they must be approached as the religious people they perceive themselves to be.

The statistics indicate that the unchurched/non-Christian quadrant is relatively unpopulated, at least as far as Americans think of themselves. This refers to the nation as a whole. When regional statistics are analyzed the picture changes.

Five states lead the nation in the percentage of persons who say they have no religion. While the national percentage of "no religion" Americans is 7.5%, it is 14% in Washington, 17% in Oregon, 13% in California, and 14% in Wyoming. Logic says these are the states where churches should design ministries targeting the unchurched/non-Christian quadrant. Even then, care must be given, since 87% of Californians count themselves as religious.

What if your church is in Rhode Island, Georgia, or North Dakota? Rule #1 is to "go slow" if considering copying a successful California or Oregon church. In Rhode Island 62% of the residents say they are Roman Catholic. In Georgia 51% identify themselves as Baptists. Up in North Dakota the population is 37% Lutheran. The regional religions have a great influence on the culture as well as the notion of "contemporary." In Rhode Island and other strongly Roman Catholic states (Massachusetts = 54%; Connecticut = 50%; New Jersey = 46%; Louisiana = 47%), Catholic traditions and ideas even influence Protestant churches. "Informal," "casual," and "contemporary" to someone who grew up in the Catholic church may seem very formal and traditional to the totally unchurched Californian. Altar calls may not make much sense to those influenced by the Lutheran heritage of Minnesota (34% Lutheran), but even the unchurched of Mississippi may see altar calls as a normal part of church in a state where Baptists hold a 55% majority.

It may seem like the plainest of common sense that effective churches must understand their culture and relate to it. It seems so obvious that different regions will require different approaches. Unfortunately, many have missed the obvious. Eighteenth-century missionaries to Hawaii built New England-style clapboard church buildings, which must have been a cultural novelty to the

Hawaiians (although a contemporary architectural style to the New Englanders). We may chuckle at how out-of-tune that was with the culture. But even during our times, pastors of Snow-Belt churches have been known to mimic some of the drive-in churches of southern California, which don't quite fit during sub-zero temperatures.

## Generational Generalities

Just as contemporary and traditional are defined by culture and region, they are also defined by generation.

Two West Coast examples provide interesting contrasts. One Southern California church has moved most of its programs into evening hours because of the schedules of the families in their area. Typically both parents work, and children are in school during the day. During many weekends they are away. The most convenient and convincing time for support groups, parenting classes, children's clubs, and committee meetings is early evening. Dinner is provided for those who come directly from work. Another church in neighboring Arizona is located in a retirement community where everyone is over 55 and children come only as short-term visitors. The nearest school is more than a town away. When this growing church called a new pastor, one of the requirements was that he agree to a "no-night meetings" policy. The generation of that church wants all daytime activities and prefers not to drive after dark.

Contemporary in the California church is evening activities. Contemporary in the Arizona church is no evening activities. Both churches have recognized and adapted to their generational cultures.

Not everyone fits the generalizations, but it is helpful to consider characteristics of pre-boomers (born before 1946), baby boomers (born 1946–1964), and baby busters (born after 1964). The Great Depression and World War II greatly influenced the pre-boomers. The postwar prosperity, television, rock and roll music, mobility, the sexual revolution, and the Vietnam War made a significant impact on the boomers. Economic woes, information explosion, high-tech advances, and the Persian Gulf War are shaping the lives of baby busters. Just as they see the economy and politics differently, they see church differently.

Gary L. McIntosh, director of the Doctor of Ministry program at Talbot School of Theology and publisher of *The McIntosh Church Growth Network* newsletter profiled these generations in terms of their characteristics. Consider the contrasts in church-related areas:[8]

| Pre-Boomers | Baby Boomers | Baby Busters |
|---|---|---|
| **Religious Factors** | | |
| Commitment to Christ = commitment to church | Commitment to Christ = commitment to relationships | Commitment to Christ = commitment to community |
| Program-oriented | People-oriented | Community-oriented |
| Money to missions | Money to people | Money to causes |
| In-depth Bible study and prayer | Practical Bible study, prayer/share | Issue-oriented, Bible study, prayer/share |
| Loyalty to denomination | Loyalty to people | Loyalty to causes |
| Minister out of duty | Minister for personal satisfaction | Minister to confront issues |
| **Program** | | |
| Relate to missions | Relate to people | Relate to causes |
| Stress in-depth Bible study & prayer | Stress fellowship & support groups | Stress Bible studies on issues |
| Maintain stability | Use variety | Use variety |
| Focus on marriage & retirement | Focus on marriage & family | Focus on marriage & singles |
| Be formal | Be relational | Be spontaneous |
| Encourage contact with baby busters | Encourage involvement in small groups | Encourage involvement in community issues |
| **Worship** | | |
| Quietness | Talking | Talking |
| Hymns | Praise songs | Praise songs |
| Expository sermons | "How to" sermons | Issue-oriented sermons |
| Pastoral prayer | Various people pray | Various people pray |
| Guests recognized | Guests anonymous | Guests anonymous |

| Organ/piano | Guitars/drums | Jazz ensemble |
|---|---|---|
| Low audience partici- pation | Higher audience partici- pation | Lower audience partici- pation |

### Implications for Future

| Ability to carry on pro- grams and projects will wane | Support of people-ori- ented projects will continue | More involvement with issue-oriented projects |
|---|---|---|
| Giving will continue un- til retirement | Giving will be related to people projects | Giving will be related to issues & causes |
| Revivalistic evangelism will continue to de- cline | Friendship evangelism will continue strong | 12-Step evangelism events will grow |
| Loyalty to institutions will continue to de- cline | Loyalty to people will continue strong | Loyalty to issues or causes will grow |

## Traditional or Contemporary?

"Help! I'm confused. After reading all of this, I'm not sure what is traditional and what is contemporary in my church. Some things seem to fit in one category and others in another."

This is one situation where confusion is good. Confusion is a valuable step toward recognizing that every situation is unique. No two churches or communities are alike, and there are no easy shortcuts to determine what is appropriate. The process of evaluation is not only necessary to determine what is contemporary but also for implementing what is appropriate.

In order to diagnose and prescribe for a particular situation, consider these questions:

*What are the traditions?* Start with your own list of all the traditions of your church and your community. Examples may include Sunday school picnic, Fourth of July community parade, and taking an offering every Sunday. The list should be long. Ask others to add their traditions. Be as inclusive as possible.

*What do these traditions mean?* What are the values behind each of these traditions? Why did they begin? Why have they contin- ued? Who are they important to? What do they mean for different people? For example, the tradition of baptism may have different meanings to different generations in the church or between church members and community citizens from another church. Ask around—but listen more than talk.

*Which traditions are helpful? Harmful?* Evaluate each tradition in terms of its contribution to fulfilling the specific purpose of the church? Which ones help make more disciples for Jesus Christ? Which ones are effective in evangelizing? Which ones reach the community? On the other side, which traditions are harmful for fulfilling the purpose, making disciples, evangelizing, and reaching the community?

*What should be done with traditions?* Some are just wrong—work on getting rid of them. Some may die from neglect—so don't make a big deal out of them; just starve them out of the church program. Some are wonderful—emphasize and elevate them.

Remember that people need traditions. When an old tradition is removed, a new tradition should replace it. Seek to remove ineffective and counterproductive traditions and replace them with effective and productive traditions.

Some traditions are not as concrete as a Sunday school picnic or the Sunday morning offering. They are traditions like inflexibility or openness. They should also be identified and dealt with. In the whole process, aim at establishing (or reinforcing) a strong church tradition of ongoing purpose-driven reevaluation. This is a tradition that helps the church to renew itself.

*What is contemporary for us?* Don't focus on success stories from California, Georgia, Rhode Island, or North Dakota. See them as ideas in a catalog—some fit and some don't. Draw a profile of what is contemporary for the unique mix of your church and community—traditions, culture, concerns, region, and generation. Along the way, continually test your design against the standards of the Bible.

All of this should lead to an effective church that celebrates its best traditions and is creatively contemporary in reaching its community.

## Chapter 9

# *Is Yours a Shopping-Center Church?*

WARNING: The concept of the Shopping-center church can be upsetting.

### The American Mall

The shopping center is a central institution to American life. Its convenience, comfort, frequency, and familiarity have impacted more than the way we shop. It has also influenced the way we think about how an institution ought to be. Not surprisingly, many twenty-first-century churches are now considering this way of doing things.

The first enclosed shopping mall opened on October 8, 1956, in Edina, Minnesota. The Southdale Center began a nationwide revolution in the way Americans shop and meet.

Southdale was a modest beginning compared to the new Mall of America in neighboring Bloomington, Minnesota. The new mall boasts that it is the largest shopping mall in the world, costing $625 million and covering 4.2 million square feet. Since an acre is 43,560 square feet, the mall totals over 96 acres of floor space!

Besides the anchor department stores of Bloomingdale's, Macy's, Nordstrom, and Sears, there are fourteen movie screens, six supper clubs, and a seven-acre Knott's Berry Farm "Camp Snoopy." The indoor amusement park includes a log flume and a roller coaster that is 70 feet high. Expectations include millions of tourists each year in addition to regular shoppers.

"Why Kids Can't Stay Away From THE MALL" reported a study and analysis of why teenagers are so attracted to shopping malls.[1] They spend an average of at least three hours per week at the mall because (1) there's no place else to go; nothing else to do; (2) the food, folks, and fun are addictive; (3) it's a safe place away from parents; (4) it's a place to belong.

There is much more to a mall than a teenage hangout. It is the new town square, the community marketplace, the crossroads of human travels, the source of supplies, the place for entertainment, a major employer, and one of the few remaining common denominators in a fragmenting society. The shopping mall is a living microcosm of culture. Consider five major characteristics of the typical regional shopping center:

1. VARIETY: The food court has a wider variety of menu choices than almost any restaurant—pizza, tacos, hamburgers, chop suey, ice cream, frozen yogurt, popcorn, and cookies. Other restaurants offer table service and a full dinner menu.

Walkers, joggers, and runners are welcome at many malls during early morning hours. They can exercise for free in a climate-controlled atmosphere, where they are safe from robbers, dogs, and cars.

Entertainment can run from the expensive to the free, from a few video game machines to a whole indoor amusement park. Theaters have the latest movies. Free shows in common areas mark the seasons, display products, present music, and even give away complimentary samples. You can have a lot of fun at a shopping mall spending little or no money.

The biggest variety is seen in the number of stores—everything from sporting goods to lingerie, specialty shops for the petite and the plump, and services from dentistry to barbering. It's true that you can't find everything you need at a shopping mall, but there is probably more there than anywhere else.

2. CONVENIENCE: Shopping malls are designed with the

shopper in mind. They are the opposite of warehouses that are designed with the product in mind. Warehouses are inconvenient for people but convenient for trains, trucks, and merchandise. Malls are inconvenient for the same big trucks and exclude trains, but they are easy for people.

Convenience includes ample parking with well-lighted lots and many exits and entrances. There are reserved places for the disabled, clear direction signs ("Camel-Lot" is where you park), and loading docks for customer pickup.

Shopping centers usually have excellent locations—they are easy to find, easy to see, and easy to get into and out of. The locations are so good that other businesses cluster nearby, and many directions are given in relationship to the mall.

Even the mall hours are convenient. Long after the downtown stores are closed, you can stop at the regional mall and shop until 9:30 or 10:00 P.M. At Christmas time or other special occasions, the hours are extended for the shopper's convenience. The determining factor is not what is easiest for the stores and employees, but what is easiest for the customers.

3.   ANONYMITY AND IDENTIFICATION: The average person can be completely anonymous at the shopping center. No one asks you to join, to sign, to give, who you are, or what you are doing there. If you like, just wander around and check out everything before you buy anything. This is very important to many shoppers—they do not like strangers coming in too close, watching every move or pressuring them to buy. Today's customers want to gather information and decide for themselves; pressure scares customers away.

The same shopping center can offer identification for those who want it. Regular customers at a restaurant or a clothing store are recognized and called by name. Boutiques have special mailing lists for their regulars. Dress saleswomen often send thank-you notes to those who buy from them. But the greater value of identification in a shopping mall is that the customer can pick and choose the stores that are a match and ignore the others. No one expects you to even know about all the stores, much less shop in them. Out of a hundred stores, you can frequent the four or five that meet your needs and skip the rest. If you have a bad experience at one men's clothing store, you can switch to another men's clothing store while shopping in the same mall.

Rarely are shopping centers known by "mall brand names." There are companies that own chains of malls, but almost all customers are unaware of the connections. Individual stores may carry the McDonald's or Sears name, but the overall center name is generic. Shoppers like that because they don't feel controlled by some distant headquarters; they feel that their own integrity and freedom of choice is respected and maintained.

4. SIZE: There is a critical size necessary for a mall really to be a mall. Visitors immediately know whether the size is right or not.

Some towns "play mall" and don't fool anyone. They take a traditional downtown area and build a roof over a few shops and call it "The Downtown Mall," but everyone knows it isn't. There isn't the feel. It isn't large enough. There are too few services.

At the other extreme are those overbuilt behemoths with a million square feet and only fifty leased spaces. The size is there, but the services are not. Most of the stores are boarded up, and many have not been rented since the mall opened. The leases are low-grade, seasonal, and filled with "fly-by-night" businesses. Every time you visit, there is a different product being sold in the same little rented space.

No one expects a city of 10,000 to be home to the Mall of America with a Knott's Berry Farm amusement park inside, but they do expect a decent shopping center appropriate to the size of the city that offers all of the basics in variety, convenience, anonymity, and identification.

5. LIMITATION: The mall doesn't sell everything. Most don't have car dealerships, medical clinics, construction companies, cemeteries, gas stations, high schools, or swimming pools. They are very broad and diverse, but they know they can't do everything for everyone.

Shopping centers do not have evenness of excellence among *all* businesses. Some stores in the mall are better than other stores in the mall. If the system works well, the best stores expand, and the worst stores are closed down. In almost all malls, stores come and go over the years. It is a normal and healthy part of mall life.

Modern shopping-center churches share a great deal in common with these regional shopping malls. People are comfortable in them because of their similarity to the mall, which is such a part of their lives. The transfer is nothing new. In small towns in earlier generations the basic institutions were the town meeting, the one-room schoolhouse, the general store, and the local church. While serving different purposes, they were all similarly configured and run. Thus, it was natural and comfortable to move from one to the other. The same comfort continues today with the shared characteristics between the shopping mall and the shopping-center church.

## Variety

Hope Chapel in Hermosa Beach, California, started out as a surfer church, holding services on the beach. It has changed to become a shopping-center church, offering more than sixty identified ministries that include jogging, skiing, special programs for substance abuse, a divorce-recovery ministry, and van service for the disabled.

Beaverton Christian Church in Beaverton, Oregon, provides parent education training in homes. The trained teachers are single parents who have gone through the training themselves and now disciple other single parents right in their own homes.

Central Presbyterian Church in St. Louis, Missouri, has "Lucy Program" (named from the Peanuts cartoon where Lucy plays the psychiatrist), providing counsel and spiritual help for children. The target group is kindergartners through high schoolers whose parents are alcoholic or divorcing.

Johnson Ferry Baptist Church in Marietta, Georgia, has an extensive prayer ministry administered by a full-time staff member. There is a 24-hour prayer program with church members on site in a prayer room for an hour each. Billboards with the 981-PRAY phone number invite anyone in Atlanta to call in their prayer requests and be assured of personal prayer. There are prayer chains throughout the congregation. Specially designed and folded prayer-request brochures are available to the congregation. There is a system for reporting God's answers to prayers.

St. Mark's Evangelical Lutheran Church in University City, Missouri, ministers to "skip generation" parents. These are grandparents who are raising the children of their single-parent children. The church has a monthly meeting for "Grandparents Raising Grandchildren." The gatherings include sharing needs, ideas, and resources.

Wooddale Church in Eden Prairie, Minnesota, and Preston-wood Baptist Church in Richardson, Texas, both have ministries for "blended families," where remarried parents each bring children from previous marriages.

Willowcreek Community Church in South Barrington, Illinois, provides a special parking lot for cars with children and only one parent. The location provides close-in convenience for those who have to both park the car and manage children into the building.

Crossroads Christian Church in Corona, California, gives "respite care" to families with disabled children. Caregivers come into the homes two Saturday mornings and one Saturday evening each month, allowing parents time away without worrying about their disabled kids. There is no charge.

Fairview Avenue Brethren in Christ Church in Waynesboro, Pennsylvania, joins generations through a Sunday school class for entire families. It is a 250-member church.

Mission Ebenezer Church in Carson, California, reaches out to families whose children are in trouble with teenage gangs.

New Hope Community Church in Portland, Oregon, has parents in dysfunctional families attending support groups. At the same time, there are support groups for their children called "Positive Action for Kids." The idea is to help the children through the stress, especially showing them positive Christian adult role models.

Youth activities in First Presbyterian Church in Wichita, Kansas, periodically include the parents of teenagers, especially in fun programs together.

Trinity Baptist Church in Wheaton, Illinois, offers bulletins for children in worship services—not adult bulletins, but bulletins designed for the age and interests of children.

College Avenue Baptist Church in San Diego, California, is a megachurch with a long tradition of ministry to college students, but it also has an accredited theological seminary on campus. College Avenue's "Moms by Choice" is a Sunday school class that is part of an overall ministry of support to pregnant teens and those who give birth.

The list of other special programs and ministries offered by shopping-center churches across the nation is really more of a catalog than a list—visiting nurses for the elderly, translation services for the deaf, counseling centers, AIDS hospice care, schools of music for children to learn to play instruments and sing, athletic teams and leagues, travel programs for mission and vacation trips, financial programs to teach budgeting, support groups for cancer patients and their families, camping programs for all ages, MOPS ("Mothers of Preschoolers") clubs, telephone contact services for shut-ins, audio and video cassettes of services, bookstores, and recreation centers with gyms, bowling alleys, swimming pools, and food service.

There is something for almost everyone. These shopping-center churches have looked around to determine the needs and interests of those they want to reach and provided some type of relevant program or ministry.

Many churches have special ministry and programs. There is no special number that qualifies a church for shopping-center status. More churches are adding new ministries to be effective. Additions may be first stops down the road to becoming shopping-center churches or may be applying shopping-center church lessons to another type of church.

The inevitable question is, "What does this have to do with religion?" On the surface it may seem that these churches have abandoned their central mission of making disciples for Jesus Christ. In most cases they have not. Active shopping-center churches have gone to such variety out of a powerful motivation for ministry and evangelism. They usually top the list of churches that are most effective in winning the non-Christian and unchurched to Christ and the church. There is a risk that they will become focused on the method rather than their mission, but that same thing can happen in traditional churches that eschew these special ministries and keep to the programs of worship services, pastoral visitation, and Sunday school.

The biblical model for such variety comes from the New Testament book of Acts. The apostle Paul came to communities and evaluated the needs and interests of those who lived there. If there was already an established synagogue, he used the synagogue approach (Corinth, Acts 18). If there was no synagogue but religious Jews and Gentiles were meeting outside of the town for prayer, Paul used the riverside approach (Philippi, Acts 16). If the people were pagans, he went to their marketplace and quoted their poets to establish a common ground for evangelism (Athens, Acts 17). It was all part of the Holy Spirit's strategy to "become all things to all men so that by all possible means I might save some" (1 Cor. 9:22).

This model is very different from the single-cell church that targets only one audience and expects everyone in the church to participate fully in every activity of the church. The father of a friend of mine hasn't missed a single event in his church during the past forty-five years—including every wedding and every funeral. The shopping-center church does not expect anyone to go to everything. Not even the pastor is expected to show up for many or most activities.

A survey of baby boomers asked what they would do if they were given some free time. The number one answer was "sleep." We are tired. We work longer hours. Our lives are busy. But our needs are great. Shopping-center churches address both areas by saying, "You don't have to come to a lot of things, but come to those that will help you meet your needs."

Shopping-center churches intentionally provide more services than any one person needs. Some are free and for all. Others cost money and are only for a few. Those who come to these churches take delight in inviting friends with different needs, knowing that there will be a place for them. There is also a personal satisfaction in knowing, "If I ever have cancer, go through a divorce, or face some new challenge in life," my church will be ready to help me.

When a Lutheran church offered worship services on Thursday and Monday nights, the inevitable question must have been, "Why?" After all, isn't Sunday service enough? Why not just have more services on Sunday?

That's an old way of thinking. Participation in church worship services is determined by more than the number of seats available. In Minnesota many suburbanites own lake cabins that become their summer weekend homes. If their home churches have only Sunday services, they will miss worship from May until September. The typical pattern is to drive to the cabin after work on Friday afternoon and return late on Sunday night. Churches offering services on Thursday and Monday evenings provide an opportunity for worship before leaving or after returning.

More churches are offering 24-hour phone answering service, much like physicians, so that a pastor can be contacted at any time. Beepers and fax numbers are no longer tools just for business, but for ministry as well.

The shopping-center churches think less about their own convenience and more about parishioners' convenience. They don't say, "You can change your plan to fit our schedule," but try to say, "We'll change our schedule to fit your plans." Gone are the harsh critical words that condemn Christians as uncommitted for not always doing it the church's way.

The convenience factor is easily understood within the shopping-center church but sometimes misunderstood by those in other churches. It appears to the critics as a compromise. Theologically, it is incarnational. When the Son of God became human, he came to our time and place. He fit into our humanity because he knew we could never otherwise make it to his heaven or his eternity.

Examples of convenience are many. The list usually begins with a look at the church through the eyes of strangers. Old-timers know where to park, when to come, how to act, and where the rest rooms are located. Strangers have no idea and may stay away.

Have you attended classical orchestra concerts? If not, you probably don't know how to go about it. Several symphony orchestras have run cartoon ads in newspapers explaining how first-timers can come to a concert. The ads explain how and where to buy a ticket, what to wear, how long a concert lasts, and what the program will be like. Churches can do the same, because outsiders have little notion of whether they should dress up or be casual, arrive early or on time, or even where to find the building.

One man visited a church for the first time in his life and didn't realize that most of the people in the audience knew one another. He thought churches were like restaurants and theaters where people go alone and seldom meet. He had no idea that he was the only visitor and that everyone else knew he was a visitor.

Therefore, the shopping-center church has lots of signs. There are signs along the driveways, in the parking lot, and outside the building. They point a driver where to park. They indicate which is the main entrance. They explain the location of offices, auditorium, classrooms, gym, and rest rooms.

Signs, however, are not enough. Most shopping-center churches have kiosks or information booths at several locations so the stranger can ask another person for help. Lots of literature is available to explain the programs, schedules, and teachings of the church. Coat rooms, public telephones, lounge areas with seating, beverage service, and clocks on the walls are typical. For nighttime activities the parking lots and entrances are well lighted. So are the signs. Buildings are well heated in the winter and adequately air-conditioned in the summer.

Some shopping-center churches offer valet parking, umbrellas for rainy weather, canopied drop-off areas, and beepers for parents whose children are in the nursery. The infant nursery is often the showpiece of shopping-center churches. Parents come to a well-lighted, fully equipped, and professionally decorated nursery center. Trained attendants give warm welcomes and lots of specialized attention. Parents fill out questionnaires about baby's habits. Claim checks are given to assure that no stranger will be given their child. Diapers are changed shortly before the parents return. Sanitary procedures include attendants wearing latex gloves when changing diapers, changing crib sheets with each new child, and segregating sick children. Nursing rooms are provided for mothers to feed their infants.

Location is a significant convenience factor. If a church campus is hard to find, many won't bother. Hundreds of churches make the important decision to sell old properties and relocate to more convenient locations because they are willing to surrender their traditions and comforts in order to reach new people. The best locations (1) are easy to find, (2) have smooth ingress and egress from major highways, (3) provide ample parking, (4) are large enough for growth. Such sites can be very expensive and very hard to find. Since it is such a long-term and significant investment, would-be shopping-center churches often take the time and spend the money to acquire the best location even if it means starting with less square footage in the first phase of building.

The times of church activities can be the greatest inconvenience of all. Are they set by tradition? By the preferences of pastors and custodians? The best way is to ask those people the church wants to reach.

The inevitable question arises: "Are we going to let the world change the church, or is the church supposed to change the world?" A statement is often added before there is a chance to answer: "All of this sounds a lot like compromise. If we cater to the whims and wants of non-Christians just to make everything convenient for them, we'll risk ruining the church." Such questions are valid, and the concerns are real. The answer requires a deeper understanding of what the church really is and how the world can be changed. The church is not a time, a place, or a nursery committee procedure. The church is the body of Jesus Christ in this world; it is powered by the Holy Spirit, and it communicates a life-changing message of eternal salvation. On those essentials there should never be compromise. To compromise the essentials is to make the church no longer the church.

However, to make access easier and more pleasant for those we want to reach is logical and biblical. Jesus fed the crowds. Jesus preached from the deck of a boat or on a grassy field so his listeners could better see and hear. Jesus changed the water to wine for their convenience. And convenience is merely a means to reach people and become all that God wants the church to be. What is the other choice—to be intentionally inconvenient? Who would recommend that the building be hard to find, that the signs confuse the visitor, that the nursery be dirty, or that the services be held when no one can come?

The shopping-center church thoughtfully and thoroughly caters to the convenience of others.

## Anonymity and Identification

"Will all visitors please stand?" someone says at the beginning of a Sunday morning service. "We have a gift packet the ushers will bring to you. Please take the red ribbon and pin it on so that we can all see who you are and greet you after the service."

The announcement is well intentioned but potentially offensive. It isn't that newcomers don't want attention and recognition. It's just that they want to choose rather than have it imposed upon them. Modern Americans value their privacy and power of personal choice. They don't like other people deciding for them. Most want to check out new situations from a position of anonymity before they are asked to say or do anything.

Our family visited a church on vacation. The pastor asked for visitors to identify themselves. I kept my hand down and stayed seated. Since it was a church of about one hundred in a small community, and since there were six of us filling a whole pew, I figured they already knew who the visitors were. The pastor kept on asking and I kept on sitting. One of our children whispered, "Dad, he's talking to us. DO something!" So I raised my hand. An usher rushed to my side with a gift pen, a red ribbon, and a visitor's card, which the pastor then publicly asked me to fill out and place in the offering plate. But it was already filled out with the name and address of a previous visitor who went through this same process. Someone had recycled the card. Subsequently, I put it back into the offering plate with the other guy's information on it. You may be surprised that we went back. Many people would never return.

Public recognition better fits an older generation in yesterday's churches. The younger generation in the shopping-center churches wants to stay anonymous until they decide to go public. There is far more to this than the words of announcements and the offering of red ribbons to visitors. It is mostly a matter of respecting the other person's right to choose.

The first-time visitor shows up and finds a user-friendly facility. Sensitive greeters and hosts/hostesses are helpful, but the best approach is a visitor-sensitive congregation. A church member casually introduces herself or himself to the visitor and immediately seeks to understand how much attention is desired. If the visitor wants to talk, time is taken to talk. If the visitor signals "leave me alone," that is respected. The shopping-center church lets the visitors decide whether they want to sign cards, receive calls, have home visits, or be publicly recognized. If not, there is no pressure. The newcomer is given time to walk through the "shopping center" and check out what is going on before making any kind of a commitment.

The opposite of anonymity is identification, which goes two ways: The newcomer may want to be identified by the church *and* identify with the church. Shopping-center churches are often high commitment organizations. Their standards for membership and ministry may be among the highest in the nation. Typically they require clear evidence of Christian faith, membership classes, interviews, spiritual gift discovery, special-ministry training, faithfulness to assignments, and rigorous accountability. The appeal and the rewards of belonging to and working with an organization that is serious about its mission, powerful in its ministry, and excellent in its execution draw many otherwise uncommitted Americans into full identification with shopping-center churches. Many are looking for a cause, for a purpose, for high expectations, and for success.

Think of these shopping-center churches as funnels. They are very wide and open at the top, but the farther a person goes in the tighter the circumference becomes. The first experiences are broad and anonymous; the later experiences are focused and identified. The key is that the person, and not the church, decides how deep and how far to go into the life of the church—much like the shopping mall.

## Size

Can only large churches be shopping-center churches? The answer is a qualified yes. Nevertheless, it depends on how you define "large." Since half of the churches in America average seventy-five or less at worship on Sunday mornings, it is technically correct to welcome newcomers to a church of seventy-six, saying, "You have come to one of the largest churches in America!"

There is a "critical mass" necessary to become a shopping-center church. That number varies, depending on the size of the community, the region of the country, and the style of the church. For example, a church of 250 has a better chance of being a shopping-center church in a rural area or in the Northeast than in a metropolitan area or in the Southwest. Ratio of church size to community population is also a significant factor. Large Protestant churches are more numerous in the Southeast, Southwest, and parts of the upper Midwest than in many other parts of the nation.

One interesting example is the 5.24-million-member Evangelical Lutheran Church in America, which didn't grow between

1983 and 1990. In 1990 the 1,959-member increase was comparatively small, but this denomination still grew. Analysis, however,
shows that the growth was not even. The denomination grew the
most where it has the most congregations and the largest congregations, which is the Midwest. In the northeastern United States
the ELCA actually lost 10,000 members in 1990.

Some of the ELCA churches are far larger than the denominational average of 473 members per church: Mt. Olivet Lutheran
Church, Minneapolis, Minnesota, has 13,450 members; Zion Lutheran Church in Anoka, Minnesota, has 7,690 members; Calvary
Lutheran Church in Golden Valley, Minnesota, has 7,069 members; Prince of Peace Lutheran Church in Burnsville, Minnesota,
has 7,010 members; and, Bethel Lutheran Church in Madison,
Wisconsin, has 6,836 members. All of these are shopping-center
churches with multiple staffs and a wide variety of programs. They
tend to have large size for anonymity and small-group ministries
for identification. Most interesting is that analysis by ELCA leadership doesn't set the determining number at 2,000 but at 200 for
a church to be large. According to the Reverend David Lindbolm
of the Minneapolis Area Synod:

> We have more than 90 congregations that have multiple
> staffs. They can provide many tracks in programming that
> are very attractive, particularly to young families. We have
> done a lot of work in evangelism, particularly with congre-
> gations that reach 200 worshippers on a Sunday morning.
> That's a critical time. Either they stay small then or they
> grow beyond that. Some folks want to keep it small. It's a
> difficult time sometimes to teach people to serve and wit-
> ness to Christ beyond that, to accept and get involved.[2]

What is so special about the number 200? It represents a major
change in the way a church works as a social organization. The
primary difference between a church of 200 and 2,000 is not the
number of people, but how they relate to one another and the
complexity of the system.

Start with the pastor. Most churches averaging less than 240
at Sunday worship function as a hub-and-spoke relationship system with the pastor at the hub. While people have relationships

with one another, they all relate to the pastor just as all spokes are connected to the hub of a wheel.

When I was the pastor of a church with 200 in attendance, I felt very important in parishioners' lives. I stopped by the community hospital every day whether anyone from the church was there or not. I checked the admission roster just in case. When babies were born in the middle of the night, fathers often called me before calling the grandparents. I knew everyone by name and I was integrally involved in many lives. I performed all church weddings and officiated at every church funeral. I was present at every church committee meeting and almost every church activity. Now, as the pastor of a church of thousands, I am not nearly so important to most people. Since it is impossible to have a hub with thousands of spokes, the large majority of parishioners are relationally connected to someone else. Other pastors do the majority of baptisms, weddings, and funerals. I cannot call most people by name. I can't remember the last time I received a call in the middle of the night, announcing, "It's a girl, and you're the first one I've called!" Now they call someone else. There are days when I grieve the loss of earlier relationships and importance, but I have chosen to continually modify my style of leadership and set of relationships to fit the needs and growth of the church.

The other alternatives are clear: (1) limit the size of the church to the leadership style and relationship needs of the pastor, (2) push a pastor to keep adding more spokes to the hub until he or she burns out, (3) change pastors so that the church can get a pastor who relates differently, while the outgoing pastor can find another church to fit his or her style. Since most pastors and churches opt for number one, 95% of America's churches have 250 or less at worship on Sunday morning. Even if they grow larger, they often downsize within a year or two to the 250 level. Very, very gifted and hard-working pastors sometimes stretch the hub-and-spoke model up to an attendance of 500, or even 800. Usually this requires 80+ hour workweeks, extraordinary commitment, and eventual exhaustion.

Shopping-center churches may have more visible pastoral leadership on the public and organizational level but far less visible leadership on the relational level. The style switch moves from "farmer," where one person does everything, to "rancher," where a leader works with and through others. Shopping-center churches involve many leaders, much delegation, and greatly shared responsibilities.

What happens when the leader of a very large church dies, retires, or resigns? Isn't the danger so great that churches should avoid the risk by never becoming so large? Careful study shows that few churches collapse with the loss of a senior pastor. Actually, few of the relationships are disturbed because most people are tied to another hub that continues. The greater loss is in the unifying voice, vision, and presence that the visible leader provided. More shopping-center churches are addressing the issue of succession in advance. They are preparing for the present leader to leave and another leader to come long before it happens. Since these churches usually have a multiple staff and capable lay leadership, others are prepared to step into the vacancy on at least a temporary basis.

The old system of pastoral placement does not work well with large shopping-center churches. That system expected recent seminary graduates to begin in small rural churches. After a few years of experience, the pastor would be appointed or called to a larger church in a bigger city. Throughout one's ministerial career the brightest and best kept moving up until they arrived in a large-membership metropolitan congregation. This assumes that large churches are big versions of small churches, which isn't so. In his book, *Looking in the Mirror*, Lyle Schaller describes the church of fewer than 35 as a "cat" and the larger church of about 35–100 as a "collie." One of his primary points is that a collie is not a big cat—it is a completely different kind of animal.[3] Likewise, the shopping-center church is completely different from the small single-cell rural church. Pastoral experience in one size of church may not be helpful in pastoring a different size of church; it may actually be counterproductive. The better route to succession in the senior pastorate of a large shopping-center church is to call or appoint an associate pastor from that church, an associate pastor from a different shopping-center church, or a senior pastor from a different shopping-center church.

In addition, organizational complexity and relational diversity keeps increasing with the size of a church. Like very large shopping malls, hospitals, universities and other institutions, the large shopping-center church requires a leader who feels comfortable and deals effectively with complexity and diversity.

These social dynamics also apply to the lay leadership and overall membership of churches. For example, there are some church members who define the quality of a church in terms of their personal knowledge and relationship to every other member. Since few of us have the mental or social capacity to relate to more than 200, those church members insist that the church be restricted to their personal relationships and capabilities. It's not that they veto a newcomer's membership application. Rather, they subconsciously raise fences and establish exclusive systems to keep the church small and outsiders away. They oppose making the church more comfortable and convenient for outsiders, who don't already know where the rest rooms are and what time meetings begin.

By contrast, the church that sets out to become a shopping-center church and is willing to make the necessary changes has a far greater likelihood of getting there. Bishop Lowell Erdahl of the St. Paul ELCA Synod says, "The two kinds of congregations that grow are the new ones and the larger ones that provide a whole range of services."[4]

New churches grow for a number of reasons: They are strongly missional; they often have a cluster of energetic entrepreneurs; they need to grow in order to survive. At first they are not likely to be shopping-center churches. They grow like a new business until they face a critical choice. Are they willing to give up acquired resources and relationships in order to move on to the next level of complexity, size, and relationships? Many are not willing. They stay the same size. Some are willing, and they become small shopping-center churches around the 200 level. This change starts a new beginning, sometimes calling for new leaders. At the 200 level the church chooses to add services and switch to a decentralized system of relationships. It is then on its way to becoming a larger shopping-center church.

Is it worth it? Many proponents of small stable churches conclude, "Small is better." They argue that large shopping-center churches are not only impersonal but also qualitatively inferior. In other words, it is spiritually superior to grow up in a small church compared to a large church. That is the small church myth.

Consider the results of research by the Barna Research Group
reported in the *Evangelical Press News Service* on March 1, 1991:

> While about half of all churches in America are made
> up of fewer than 100 people, a study recently released by
> the Barna Research Group suggests that these small
> churches may be having an even smaller impact on the
> spiritual lives of the teenagers in their congregations.
>
> The study "Today's Teens: A Generation in Transi-
> tion" details some of the differences between teenagers who
> attend a church with fewer than 100 people and those who
> attend a larger church. The findings reveal some striking
> differences in the spiritual beliefs and involvement between
> the two groups of teens.
>
> For instance, while 69 percent of the teens from larger
> churches called themselves "religious," only 48 percent of
> the respondents from smaller churches would use this term
> to describe themselves. In looking toward what they want
> their adult life to be like, teens from larger churches were
> more likely to regard having a close relationship with God
> as a very important priority (69 percent to 49 percent).
> They were also more likely to place a high priority on being
> part of a local church when they are adults than were teens
> from smaller churches (49 percent to 34 percent).
>
> Teenagers who attended a church with 100 or more
> people in the congregation also tended to have a more active
> involvement in the life of the church than did teens from
> smaller congregations. Among the teens from larger
> churches, 33 percent read the Bible in the week preceding
> their interview, and 62 percent went to church. Among
> teenagers from smaller churches, only 20 percent read the
> Bible in the week before their interview, and only 40 per-
> cent had attended church.
>
> Not only were teens in larger churches more involved
> but they were also more likely to agree strongly with a
> number of statements about basic Christian beliefs. For
> example, 79 percent of the teens in larger churches agreed
> strongly, "Jesus Christ rose from the dead and reappeared
> on earth after his resurrection," compared to 55 percent of

the teens from smaller churches. Among teens from larger churches, 56 percent agreed strongly, "Jesus Christ is alive today," compared to 34 percent of the respondents from smaller churches.

In general, the study notes, "We must wonder what is happening in our small churches. The evidence overwhelmingly points out that teenagers affiliated with small congregations may fail to grow spiritually as much as teens associated with larger congregations." The report also points out that this is not a danger to be associated just with this generation of teens—respondents from smaller churches were half as likely as other churched teens to feel that when they have a family, it will be a priority to include religious training as part of their family life.[5]

There is an axiom for churches that want to grow: "Act the size you want to become." While some moderation is necessary to comply with reality, the principle is sound. A church that seeks to be a large twenty-first-century shopping-center church should begin by acting like one. This starts with the offering of services, conveniences, anonymity, and identification that will pave the path to the larger size of the shopping-center church.

## Limitation

Smart managers know that deciding what not to do is just as important as deciding what to do. No person, business, or church can do everything. Every need cannot be met. Every need does not require a ministry. Those who try to do it all seldom do anything very well.

Shopping-center churches are very good at saying no. Some have refused to start parochial schools, undertake radio or TV ministries, begin counseling centers, buy or build summer camps, and add other programs that are not central to their primary purpose.

One of the toughest tasks for shopping-center churches is turning down designated gifts. What if a generous donor comes along and says, "I'll give up to $250,000 as a matching grant for a new television ministry. If the rest of the people in the church will donate $250,000, we'll have a half-million dollars to kickstart our

TV program." Most churches don't like to refuse money. Many pastors want to appear on television. But there are key questions to be answered first: (1) Is someone else already doing it so that we don't need to do it? (2) Will this fulfill our purpose as a church? (3) Whose needs will be met? (4) What won't be done? The last question forces us to reality. Since we can't do everything, there must be a choice between what will be added and what will be subtracted.

As churches grow larger, they may be able to add programs that smaller churches can't do. However, as churches become larger, there is also a growing weight in maintaining existing programs. Sometimes the ability to make something work is confused with doing the right thing. There are churches whose greatest strength is that "they can make anything work," which is also their greatest weakness. Efficiency is doing things right. Effectiveness is doing the right things. Outsiders often see shopping-center churches as efficient, but churches should be more concerned about being effective.

One time-management principle suggests that an individual write down everything she needs or wants to get done in a day. When the list is finished, number each item in terms of importance. After the numbering, begin to accomplish the first and then the second and then the rest in order. If she never gets past number two, that is okay because the most important need or task has already been done. Shopping-center churches figure out everything they can do and then begin doing what is most important, knowing the entire list will probably never be accomplished.

At the top of a Christian's list should be the essentials of biblical Christianity: honoring God, correct doctrine, right relationships, and evangelism. Also high on a church's list should be knowing the people God has called that church to reach and ministering to them in terms of their needs. Needs come in two categories: (1) The ultimate need for salvation through Jesus Christ, knowledge of God, and obedience to Christ's commands; (2) Felt needs that vary with time, place, and personal circumstances. Felt needs are primarily a means toward meeting ultimate needs. There is an old African saying that "empty stomachs have no ears." Missionaries help feed the hungry so that they will listen to the gospel and have their ultimate needs met. Food is the felt need; God-in-their-lives is the ultimate need. At the same time, we must be careful not to be manipulative. It is always right to do good even when it does not bring the end we desire. Jesus healed those who never bothered to thank him. Jesus fed many who never believed in him or followed him as disciples. Healing and feeding were good in themselves. For us today, doing good in the name of Jesus Christ is valuable and has merit of its own. Nevertheless, Christians should love others enough to desire God's ultimate good for them.

The shopping-center church that sets out to meet every felt need is setting itself up for failure. Some people have so many felt needs that a lifetime is not long enough to meet them all. The resources are not available. Instead, the primary felt needs of the most people and of people otherwise not reached should be targeted. If the needy are few, or if the needs overlap or can be met by another church, make those needs a lower or excluded priority.

Not every church can or should be a shopping-center church. The shopping centers of America have certainly had their critics. These malls have contributed to the decay of inner cities and the loss of economic and social stability in neighborhoods. Some predictions indicate that very few new regional malls will be built as neighborhood strip malls become more popular.

Frankly, similar criticisms may be launched at shopping-center churches that have drawn parishioners away from smaller churches and accelerated the decline of neighborhood relationships. Still other critics argue it is inappropriate for the church to be compared, much less align, with such a commercial concept.

There is validity to these and other critiques, but don't allow the negatives to overshadow the significance of the shopping-center church phenomenon. Recognize that shopping-center churches will be major ministries and primary pacesetters for the twenty-first-century church. Just as downtown cathedrals, Sunday schools, and frontier chapels greatly influenced all churches of earlier generations, so will shopping-center churches influence this generation.

## Chapter 10

# *Who Are We Here For?*

THOMAS AQUINAS CLAIMED, "If the primary aim of a captain were to preserve his ship, he would keep it in port forever."

The same goes for the church. If our goal is to preserve it, we will defensively protect it. If our goal is to reach out, to go somewhere, and to do something—we will willingly risk it.

Recently I sat in an airplane next to a man who was reading an aeronautics magazine. I looked over his shoulder long enough to see a picture of a Boeing 777 and read the article headline: "Boeing Risks the Company—Again." Politeness and inadequate eyesight kept me from reading the rest of the article, but I can guess what it said. Boeing had moved commercial aviation from propeller aircraft to jets by introducing the Boeing 707 in 1958. It was a big risk that could have destroyed the company, but it didn't. Boeing risked itself again in 1970 with its Boeing 747, and the age of wide-bodied jet aircraft was born. It must have been hard for a successful corporation to risk stability and profitability with such a new venture. The risk taking, however, did not end. The company would not be satisfied with yesterday's innovations and successes—so along comes the 777.

There is another way of looking at the same changes. Would it have been a greater risk not to have changed? What happened to the companies that stuck with manufacturing wooden ships, horse-drawn carriages, and traditional typewriters? Most are long gone. Those that remain must be aging shadows of their former selves.

Those who have a future are those who look outside of themselves. They risk new approaches. They service new people. They exist for others and not themselves. In some ways, it is the safest route to survival.

Churches of the twenty-first century will not be those that emphasize self-preservation and isolation without risk. The survivors and thrivers will be those who exist for others.

There is a sense in which the church has taken itself too seriously. We have thought that keeping ourselves going is a good enough reason to continue. How different from Jesus, who came to seek and to save those who were lost (Luke 19:10). The church is really a means to an end rather than an end itself. God is the one who is most important. Obeying Jesus Christ is what really matters. Keeping an organization going that meets in a building on the corner of Third Avenue and Main Street isn't really that important. Think about it: How many local churches have lasted anyway? Start with the church in Jerusalem, and make a list that includes the churches of Antioch, Ephesus, Corinth, and a million others—most of them are long gone. What matters is that THE church of Jesus Christ is larger and stronger than ever, that the gospel has more adherents right now than in all of previous history combined, and that the cause and kingdom of the Savior have advanced for 2,000 years.

The parable of the lifesaving station begins with drowning swimmers and sailors along a dangerous stretch of the coast. A few heroes accepted the mission of saving those in distress. They were so successful that their ranks quickly grew. Many of the new lifeguards were those who were themselves saved from the sea. Together they organized into a lifesaving society and built a lifesaving station. It was simple at first, but as their numbers and affluence grew, so did the station. Within less than a generation the membership was large, and a lifesaving club with state-of-the-art facilities for recreation, dining, and entertainment had replaced the lifesaving station. Membership was highly valued. Member meetings discussed finance and membership requirements. Old-timers and their children held the power. Newcomers seldom joined. Every year there was less and less interest in actual life-saving. The membership hired professional lifeguards to do the lifesaving for them. Then came budget cuts, and the lifeguards had to go. It was a fine club but no longer in the lifesaving business.

This parable is a commentary on the church that once existed for others but changed to exist for itself.

Every church needs to answer the question: "Who are we here for?"

## For Whom Churches Exist

There are many possible answers to the question—even within a single local congregation.

DENOMINATION is an older answer but still a common answer. Many churches founded between 1900 and 1970 began to represent their denomination in the community. Northern denominations have sent church planters south, and southern denominations have sent church planters north—both to guarantee that they will have a church for their kind of people. It is somewhat like those cultures where couples have lots of babies to perpetuate the family name and guarantee they will be cared for in their old age.

Unfortunately, denominational representation is a motivation not easily passed down to the next generation. They don't care as much. This attitude frustrates the founders who bemoan the decline of their church and the coming day when "there will no longer be a church of our denomination in this community."

Some denominations are viewed as more inclusive, and others are perceived as more exclusive. Reality and the perceptions can be miles apart, but the perceptions seem to persist. For example, non-Catholics perceive the Roman Catholic Church as just for Catholics. They think that only Catholics go to Catholic churches. It is a perception of exclusivity. The same perceptions are held toward Baptists and Lutherans—you have to be one to go to a Baptist or Lutheran church. Presbyterians are different—non-

Presbyterians think that anyone can go to a Presbyterian church. Presbyterians are perceived as more inclusive. It can be a crazy thing: A very inclusive church can be regarded as exclusive, and a very exclusive church can be seen as inclusive. Overall, denominational churches are considered to be exclusive: You are welcome if you are already one of them. Otherwise, you might not know what to do or might not be welcome. This strange system of church choice can work well for a church that is strong in an area because there are enough people around who think of themselves as fitting in—Roman Catholics in the northeast, Methodists and Baptists in the South, and Lutherans in the Plains states.

Churches that began for their denomination and exist for their denomination number in the tens of thousands. They value loyalty. They think their way is the best way, if not the only way. Almost every denominationalist jokes about his members being the only ones in heaven. For some it is not a joke; they believe it.

There is a paradox to this type of denominationalism. When denomination is primary, it often proves to be too weak a reason for growth and survival. However, denominational churches that have broader and bolder motivation often attract many from outside of their traditions. When those newcomers move to another community, they remember their positive church experience and seek out another congregation of the same denomination. It is ironic that some of the most denominational churches least perpetuate the denomination, while some of the least denominational churches most perpetuate the denomination.

BUILDING can be as strong or stronger than denomination. Churches can become very attached to their facility. Pioneers sacrificed their savings and their skills to turn a dream into an edifice. The walls and halls have become sacred, filled with precious memories of weddings and funerals, baptisms and confirmations, plus ten thousand other emotional attachments.

Endowments are established through major gifts and bequests to assure the care and continuation of the building. Sometimes this means that the facility survives when the congregation dies. It is like leaving all of your money to your house.

At least 10% of the churches in America should sell their buildings and relocate. It is obvious to outside observers. It's also very difficult to pull off. Typically, the best-planned and led church-

relocation attempts require at least two or three failed congregational votes before actual relocation. Even then, there are building
loyalists who are hurt and angry. Some stick with the building
even after their friends and family have moved to a new site.

Some early New England churches were very careful to refer
to their "meeting house" and never call the building a "church."
They had the Bible on their side. Never in the New Testament
does the word "church" refer to any physical structure. The New
Testament church was people. A long-established abuse of words
in the Christian vocabulary confuses the place where the church
gathers with the church itself. Places and things aren't holy; Christians are holy. To make a building the reason for a church's existence is equal to making a house the reason for a family's existence.

In Acts 1:8, the risen Christ commissioned the church to leave
its place and "be my witnesses in Jerusalem, and in all Judea and
Samaria, and to the ends of the earth," but they liked their place
in Jerusalem so well that they didn't budge. Consequently, God
forced them to leave: "On that day a great persecution broke out
against the church at Jerusalem, and all except the apostles were
scattered throughout Judea and Samaria" (Acts 8:1). If they had
stayed in one place, the church would have died there. Loyalty to
a place is no virtue to the church of Jesus Christ.

PASTOR is a very different reason for a church to exist. First
of all, few would ever be bold enough to state a pastor as the
reason. However, we subtly promote the idea by referring to a
church by the pastor's name, by posting the pastor's name on the
outside sign, by publishing the pastor's picture in the newspaper
ad, and by saying, "This church would probably fall apart if Pastor Jones ever left."

Pastor Jones will leave—if not by resignation, then by retirement, disability, termination, or by death.

It can be a fine line between positive and pathological pastoring. No doubt the senior minister is a very important person in
most modern American churches. The style, tenure, appearance,
personality, vision, and preaching of the pastor is the most visible
reason for success in many churches. It may be the number one
reason why newcomers visit and stay in a church.

Many pastors like the attention and enjoy thinking of themselves as very important. It can reach the point where the pastor

can't tell where he or she ends and the church begins—it is some-thing of a blur. Identity is tied to the church. As a key leader, he or she consciously or unconsciously accelerates the myth that he of indispensability. The church begins to exist for the pastor.

The clearest way to cut the myth and refocus the church is for every pastor to ask and answer honestly: "Would I leave right now if that were in the best interests of this church, even if it is not in my best interests?"

There was a controversial elementary school on the West Coast. Parents petitioned the school board for freedom to enroll their children elsewhere. Teachers fought the proposal out of fear that a significant drop in enrollment would cost them their jobs. The school board came up with a compromise: Parents could choose any school in the district during the coming school year; teachers would be guaranteed a job no matter how few students enrolled. School opened in September, and there were no stu-dents. Teachers came every day anyway. It continued that way for the entire school year. For that year the school existed for the teachers and not for the students.

Churches must beware of the danger of existing for the pastor and staff rather than for the people and purpose.

MEMBERS may be the number one reason most churches exist. They exist for those who are already part of the church. Their church has become a dearly loved fellowship, a home away from home, a comfortable place to go, a source of hope, a gath-ering for worship, and a safe fortress in a world that is increasingly hostile.

It is not uncommon for churches more than twelve years old not to want newcomers. If newcomers are incorporated, they come through marriage, birth, or other family relationships. Those who are not related come to the church only when they are very similar to those who are already there. Strangers who look, sound, act, or think differently may be superficially welcomed but ultimately excluded.

Many churches that would never admit to such exclusivity nevertheless perpetuate it by the decisions they make. Outsiders are excluded by secrets, rules, doctrines, traditions, and politics. When a hard decision is made, the exclusive church generally votes for its own comforts and others' discomforts. Others must "bend to fit with us" rather than our "bending to fit with them."

Rarely is this done with malice. It is more a function of avoiding change. Churches, like people, narrow their comfort zones as they grow older. We become very comfortable with present people and ways. We become very uncomfortable with new people and new ways. We like the room temperature at 70 degrees, the familiarity of our same third pew, the tunes of the same hymnal, and the security of a paid-up mortgage. Very few of us choose discomfort unless we have very good reasons.

COMMUNITY is a very different reason to exist. It is external rather than internal. It is for others rather than for self.

There are, however, different ways to exist for community: One is for servicing of others' needs, and the other is for evangelism and incorporation into the church. Both may exist side by side, although one is usually a priority over the other.

Dean Kelley, a United Methodist who serves as counselor and researcher with the National Council of Churches, divides the priorities between Group A churches and Group B churches in this way:

> Into Group A, I'd put such priorities as winning souls for Christ, providing worship and religious instruction for congregants and ministering to members' needs for services, counseling, weddings and sacraments.
>
> Into Group B, I'd put priorities such as helping the needy, social conscience, supporting minorities and influencing legislation.
>
> I conclude that members are not dropping out of churches because they object to clergy doing Group B ministry, but because they object to clergy doing Group B ministry to the neglect of Group A.[1]

I wouldn't give all the credit or blame to the clergy. The social fabric and traditions of churches that exist for the community can either be Group A or Group B—independent of clergy.

## The Blessing Principle

Ralph Winter has popularized the analysis of biblical Israel as a nation that wanted to be blessed but didn't want to be a blessing. The result was their destruction.

Compare the Sea of Galilee to the Dead Sea. The Sea of Galilee has water flowing in and out; it is full of life. The Dead Sea has water flowing in but not out; it is full of minerals.

Churches that give away blessings are much more likely to be blessed. They are focused on others rather than themselves, open to outsiders with their new ideas and ways, inclusive rather than exclusive, outreaching rather than self-fortifying, an army of life-savers rather than a club of those once saved. These churches are for the twenty-first century.

It is never an easy decision to be a blessing to outsiders. Nor is outreach painlessly implemented. When an inward church decides to give birth to an outward orientation, there will be pain. Some people will misunderstand. Anger may flare. A few might leave the church. Certainly the problems should not be sought, but they shouldn't be avoided either.

There is a basic principle of church growth: "For a church to grow, it must want to grow and be willing to pay the price." The price is least counted in dollars. It comes in the more costly currency of change. It is doing church in new ways, incorporating new people, moving out of comfort zones, and existing for others rather than for self.

Becoming a blessing to others and existing for those to be reached requires a definition and description of the target audience. Churches should welcome any who come but target those they are specifically called to reach. The target audience will be unique to each church. Churches of the same denomination and neighborhood may target very different people in their community.

## Who's There?

Fishing for mackerel in Lake Michigan or for northern pike in the Southern Pacific Ocean is a waste of time. They are both good fish, but they live only in certain places.

Fishing strategy begins with knowing the kinds of fish that live in your lake or ocean, knowing their habits and preferences, and using the appropriate bait to hook them.

The first step in becoming a church for others is to know who's there. People, like fish, tend to live in some places more than others.

Ethnically, African-Americans are concentrated in the southeastern United States—the highest percentages of population being in Washington, D.C. (65.8%), Mississippi (35.6%), and Louisiana (30.8%). Asian-Americans are concentrated in Hawaii (61.83%) and California (9.56%), plus major cities of the northeast. Native-Americans are primarily in the West: Alaska (15.58%), New Mexico (8.87%), and South Dakota (7.27%). Hispanics are most numerous in the Southwest: New Mexico (38.23%), California (25.83%), and Texas (25.55%). Whites are 80.3% of the US population and live in large concentrations in all states but in higher density in Vermont (98.6%), Maine (98.4%), and New Hampshire (98%).[2]

New Mexico is the nation's most diverse state. *USA Today* developed a Diversity Index, "based on the chance that two randomly selected people in a particular area are different from each other racially or ethnically."[3] In New Mexico there is "a 60% chance that any two randomly selected New Mexicans are different either racially or ethnically."[4] The most diverse metropolitan areas in the United States are the following: Los Angeles-Long Beach, Miami-Hialeah, New York, Jersey City, Houston, San Antonio, Albuquerque, Honolulu, Chicago, Fayetteville, Fresno, and many other California cities.

Ethnicity is only one measurement of who's there. It is like measuring a person's height. There are many other measurements to make—weight, age, blood pressure, blood type, and gender.

Generations have become a distinctive set of groups in the North American culture. William Strauss and Neil Howe have written the popular and influential book *Generations: The History of America's Future 1584–2069*, in which they argue for a cycle of four generational patterns: Civic, Reactive, Idealist, and Adaptive. The idea is that when you were born greatly influences your approach to life. It also influences your approach to church. Take their Civic Generations as an example. In 1992 these are young people aged 10 and under and older people aged 68 and up. They like each other. They are similar in perspective. They are confident, upbeat, and decisive. They are quite different from the Reactive Generation now in their teens and twenties—a generation described as coming to a world that is like a beach trashed by a summer party, and they are being fined for littering.

How much money a family has and earns, the rate of mobility into and out of the community, religious preferences and patterns, level of education, political and cultural conservatism or liberalism may define who is there. Are the residents nearby mostly married or single? Are families small or large? Is school enrollment increasing or decreasing? Is unemployment high, or are jobs easy to find? Are more people moving into the area or moving out of the area? The list may be long, but answering these questions goes a long way to knowing who they are and then determining how they can be reached. For they all need to be reached for Jesus Christ and his church.

Realistically, few churches or church leaders will undertake a serious in-depth study of the demographics and psychographics of the people in their area. There are some simple practical steps, however, that can be taken. A few hours in the local library or gathering literature from the Chamber of Commerce will profile the people within the geographic area of any church. Huge amounts of fascinating information are easily available.

An easier approach is to buy the research ready made. Church Information Data Service (CIDS) will do all of the research for any church in the United States.[5] They will provide color maps pinpointing the church's location and profiling everyone within one, three, and five mile radii. From their printouts a church can learn the lifestyles and preferences of the groups in their neighborhood.

## Who's Not Here?

Peter Drucker, writing in his syndicated column about "Marketing 101 for a Fast-Changing Decade," used department stores as an illustration of how not to do it:

> Another lesson born of failure: the precipitate decline of the big-city American department store. The cock of the walk in 1980, it is in severe trouble, if not in bankruptcy, 10 years later. The decline is not—as is widely believed—the result of financial manipulation and miscalculation burdening the stores with crushing debt. If department stores today had the same share of the market they had 10 years ago, they could carry the debt. What brought them low is

the most common of all marketing sins: ignoring the people who should be customers but aren't.

No one better understands customer data than the big department store or studies them more assiduously. But these data are all about people who already shop at the store. During the 1980s the department stores, by and large, held on to their old customers. But their share of new customers was shrinking steadily—especially their share of the most significant group, the educated and afflu-ent two-earner families. They never learned that these peo-ple shop together, shop in the evenings, and are far more value-conscious than the traditional department store cus-tomer. Sooner or later the total number of customers always goes down, and with it the customer base, if an industry's or business's share of new customers declines. By then it is in serious trouble.

Marketing starts with *all* customers in the market rather than with *our* customers. Even a powerful business rarely has a market share much larger than 30%. This means that 70% of the customers buy from someone else. Yet most businesses or industries pay no more attention to this 70% than the department stores do.[6]

A frequent practice among churches that are talking about change is to survey the members of the church. Typical questions ask about their preferences in pastoral characteristics, programs they would like to have instituted, and complaints they want ad-dressed. Like the department stores, these churches are gathering more information about people they already know well and "ig-noring the people who should be customers but aren't."

Think about what such surveys tend to do. They focus the attention and energy of the congregation inward on themselves rather than outward on others. They perpetuate the way things already are because the most loyal parishioners are the ones who respond to surveys. They give statistical reasons which keep in-ward churches inward. They put problems rather than opportu-nities at the top of the church's agenda.

Does this mean that churches should not conduct surveys of their constituents? No. But a once-per-decade survey is no sub-

stitute for ongoing opportunities for communication and feed-
back. It is far better to have open channels of communication all
the time. Critique every sermon, service, class, and program on
a regular basis. Teach that openness is a virtue and that criticism
should always be constructive and purpose-driven.

The church that seeks, surveys, and reaches out will quickly
learn how others see everything in the church. It may be threatening at first, but it can become a powerful positive catalyst for
change.

I have sat behind the glass of focus group meeting rooms and
listened to unchurched people talk about the issues they think are
important. It changes my sermons. I have observed as they talked
about the way Wooddale Church nursery workers care for their
babies, ushers guide them into services, parking lot attendants
help them find parking places, and friends talk to them about their
church relationships. What a learning experience! Otherwise, I
would think that the people inside the church represent all of
reality when they are actually only a small part.

Of course, churches that exist for themselves do not need to
listen to outsiders. They can cater to those already in the church.
But watch out for the downside risk. Inside our churches are
millions of Christians who want to be part of a vital growing fellowship that is impacting this generation. In order to please many
on the inside, we must incorporate many on the outside.

## How to Connect

Michael Silva, National Director of Evangelism for the Conservative Baptist Association of America, gives suggestions for
connecting to outsiders:

> In many neighborhoods today, you'd think the neigh-
> bors were in hiding. People seem to be so busy with their
> own lives that they don't have much time to get acquainted
> with others. Here are some ideas to put you "in touch"
> with your neighbors.
> *Moving day*—The best time of all to become acquainted
> is when someone first moves to your neighborhood. Your
> appearance at their door is sure to be welcome—especially

if you bring along snacks, a meal, a city map, or a strong back for the piano!

*Evening walks*—If you or your family take the same route for a regular walk, folks will begin to notice, and even expect you. Eventually you're bound to find someone who will notice and chat for a while.

*Garage and yard sales*—What better place to meet folks than over a table of "better-than-blue-light specials"? Don't forget neighborhood parties for selling housewares, cosmetics, jewelry or whatever.

*Community groups*—Does your area have a neighborhood association? A baby-sitting co-op? A garden club? How about the area school PTA?

*Backyard volleyball*—One neighborhood has an informal volleyball game played every Thursday night in warm weather. Newcomers to the area are always invited.

*Block party*—Keep it simple. Make it fun. Churn ice cream, eat watermelon, pull taffy, or barbecue. Take advantage of every opportunity to pull neighbors out of hiding and into your life.[7]

Other ways to read the culture and connect with people include Christmas Coffees, service clubs, attending city council meetings, watching court proceedings, volunteering for community services, and reading the community newspaper (not the large city or national newspaper).

There are two purposes for such undertakings: (1) information and (2) pre-evangelism.

Information is learning about the people outside the church. The eventual goal is to describe the unchurched and non-Christian persons in the area. What is an overall general description of the average person's thinking, activities, fears, hopes, and needs? Profile a typical person from your town. These are not negative descriptions or names. Most of the unchurched persons in the area would listen and say, "Sure, that's me you're talking about!" Pastors and leaders of churches existing for others should be able to describe their Miami Millie, Joplin Joe, or Local Larry.

Pre-evangelism refers to the preliminary steps toward building a relationship with someone who will later be reached for Jesus Christ. It is much like Jesus' conversation with the Samaritan woman in John 4. He first talked to her about water. They became acquainted. Then he talked to her about her personal relationship with God. It was a long conversation that began with where she was and ended with where Jesus wanted her to be. Outreaching churches invest heavily in pre-evangelism, knowing that these are bridges to later evangelism. Pre-evangelism is never enough. Christians must either know how to introduce non-Christians to Jesus Christ as Savior and Lord or connect them with people and programs where they can become Christians.

In an interview in *The Win Arn Growth Report*, Dr. George Hunter, Dean of the School of World Mission at Asbury Seminary, described the kind of church that reaches persons outside the church:

Churches that are effectively reaching secular people . . .

1. . . . know that people who aren't disciples are lost.
2. . . . know that lost people matter to God.
3. . . . see their church as primarily a mission to lost people; rather than a gathered colony of the faithful.
4. . . . have high expectations of their members.
5. . . . know what to change and what to preserve.
6. . . . understand secular people.
7. . . . accept unchurched people.
8. . . . use music secular people understand.
9. . . . start new congregations.
10. . . . are involved in world mission.[8]

## Changing Outward

How does an inward church become an outward church? It is not easy. For some the price tag will prove to be more expensive than their willingness to pay.

Begin with multiple means of change over a period of time. Communicate the value of becoming a church-for-others through sermons, church newspapers, Sunday school curricula, and regular conversations. Plan pre-evangelistic events that have a high predictability of success. For example, rent a local amusement park for a special day when church members can invite friends, neighbors, and co-workers. Don't incorporate an evangelistic meeting (or any meeting for that matter); just become acquainted and have a good time. Design a step-by-step process of increasingly incorporating outreach experiences.

Don't neglect those already in the church. Minimize the potential backlash from those who will say that their needs are not being met and that they are neglected. But also remember that some will always feel neglected and will never sense their needs met—regardless of anything their church does. Walk the fine line of balance at the beginning, but more and more make choices that favor those outside over those inside.

A crisis will come. Seldom is there a smooth process that transforms an internal church into an external church. The crisis point cannot always be predicted, but there are some common occurrences:

*Breaking the rules.* A church that forbids smoking at church activities may permit smoking at some events targeting outsiders.

*Dividing the budget.* Does the money go to hiring an evangelism pastor for outreach or a counselor for church members? Should the new budget have literature money to invite the community to church or bus money for our kids to go to camp? Is it better to put extra funds into advertising or debt retirement?

*Accommodating strangers.* Should Bible reading be announced with page numbers or just book/chapter/verse? Should newcomers get the best room for a "Welcome Wagon" reception or should the established adult Sunday school class be allowed to stay in that room? Should the music fit the tastes of those who are here or those who will come?

*Pastor's time.* Does the division of the pastor's time tilt toward serving insiders or reaching outsiders? Is it okay for a layperson to do the hospital visitation so that the pastor can have time for contacting new residents?

*Name of the church.* Few decisions focus the issue more sharply. Does the name of the church best serve insiders or outsiders? Is it for the denomination? For the traditions? For outreach? In many cases the apparent issue is not the real issue. The congregation seems to be voting on a few words for the sign but is really voting on whom the church wants to serve.

As the church changes toward outreach, there are some measurements that can be charted. Compare the past and present percentage of church expenditures going to outreach. In most inward churches it is less than 1%. In some outward churches it is 10% or higher. While money to foreign missions is a secondary sign of outreach, it should not be included in the percentage comparison. In other words, how much money is going to reach people for Jesus Christ in the local community in connection with the local church? Where Americans spend their money is a primary indicator of their priorities. If most money goes to servicing the existing church, or the percentage to outreach is not growing, those signs probably reflect an inward church.

Compare the present and past content of church communications. Does the church newsletter have a growing number of articles on ministries for outreach, or do most promote church programs for present members? Do sermon topics and illustrations give attention to outreach or to internal issues and interests? Are people talking about outreach more in their hallway conversations and social gatherings? Do church board and committee minutes indicate that the decision makers are dealing with evangelism issues or maintenance issues? Are prayers exclusively for those within the church or increasingly for those outside the church?

Determine when most of the people inside the church first came. If the majority arrived more than twenty years ago, rate the church inward; if the majority arrived less than ten years ago, rate the church outward. If 10–20% of the church has come in the past twelve to twenty-four months, celebrate the high outward orientation of the congregation. Another check is on leadership positions: When did leaders join the church? The older the date, the more difficult it is for new people to assimilate and gain ownership; the more recent the date, the more open the church is to new people. Even first-time visitors will sense whether the church is open or closed—and for whom the church exists!

# Chapter 11

# *Should the Sermon Beat Up or Lift Up?*

PREACHING HAS CHANGED from the days when the parishioner at the door said, "Thanks, pastor. You really stepped on our toes today, and I loved it." The church of the twenty-first century is dealing with a generation that is discouraged, depressed, tired, lonely, and feeling guilty. They are more interested in learning what to do about their sins and struggles than being told they are sinners and strugglers.

This has already changed the approach to preaching that is emerging for the twenty-first-century church.

## Hope

Gospel means "good news," and that news is what people are listening for. They want someone to tell them that God loves them and will rescue them from their circumstances and destiny.

This approach does not mean that today's churchgoers won't listen to sermons against sin, prophetic words from the Bible, or confrontation of what is wrong with their lives. They will listen and agree, but they insist on hope from God at the end. In fact, lack of reality in sermons that are all positive and upbeat turn many of them off. They know from experience that life is not like that.

Some preachers strongly condemn the shortage of sin-naming and condemnation in twenty-first-century churches. They try to balance the distribution by maximizing the negative from their own pulpits. My guess is that they have misunderstood the needs of today's generation, and they risk alienating the very people God has called them to shepherd.

Mike Bellah, author of *Baby Boom Believers* and pastor of Evangelical Fellowship in Amarillo, Texas, encourages us to "be generous with hope":

> Baby boomers desperately need hope. The church that reaches this generation will be one where hope is frequently dispensed. However, it is important that the church offer real, not contrived, hope. The kind of hope promised by the success gospel is looked on with a deserved cynicism by most baby boomers. Similarly, the hope offered by sincere but unrealistic Christians, which ignores real pain and suffering, will not help disillusioned baby boomers. This generation will not respond to religious platitudes and cliches that minimize the hurt found in a fallen world. The church that offers hope to baby boomers will proclaim the God of Joseph, Daniel, Elijah, and others like them. It will reveal a God who does not always remove us from our crises, but who supports us in them and brings us through them."[1]

Pastors who want to check their preaching should ask parishioners whether they are receiving the hope of God. They should listen to tapes of their own sermons to determine whether they have an overall message of condemnation or encouragement, and whether the hope they offer is genuine and comes from Jesus Christ.

Some of the best preaching for the twenty-first-century church comes from pastors who have faced their own sins and struggles and discovered the grace and hope of God through the Bible and a personal relationship with Jesus Christ. Sermons born out of this reality communicate to hearers: "This preacher has been there and knows what I'm going through, and has personally encountered God the way I want to encounter God."

G. Campbell Morgan was a famous preacher of an earlier generation who seemed to understand the needs of this generation. He once listened to an articulate young preacher as he delivered his sermon. A bystander later asked him for his evaluation of the preacher and the sermon. Morgan answered, "He is a very good preacher and when he has suffered he will be a great preacher."

The preachers who will communicate well to the twenty-first-century church will be those who not only speak well, but also who have suffered and found hope in Jesus Christ, whom they delight to share with others who are hurting.

## Content

Both Christians and non-Christians listening to twenty-first-century sermons are smart. They often have a lot of education, but even if they haven't been to all the schools, they are often sophisticated and well informed. Information has bombarded them all of their lives. Through television (if not through actual travels) they have seen the world, witnessed wars, heard the latest ideas, and been exposed to the best communicators. They will not tolerate sermons that lack meaningful content.

In a world with experts there is an expectation that the preacher be an expert as well. Physicians are supposed to know about medicine; pilots are expected to know about flying; lawyers should know the law; and preachers should know the Bible. Rarely do people listen to a sermon expecting expertise on current events, politics, stress management, or psychology—not that sermons shouldn't relate to other issues. Sermons that are based on biblical revelation and modern relevance will inevitably connect to most disciplines and most life experiences, but the connection needs to be appropriate. Bible first, everything else second.

Consider second things first. Every Sunday when I preach at Wooddale Church, I recognize there are people in the audience who know more about whatever I'm talking about than what I know about it. If I mention cancer, there are people listening who have had cancer, who have cancer, who treat cancer, and whose family members have died of cancer. There is nothing I can say about cancer that they don't already know. The same goes for truck driving, Shakespearean literature, rock music, the Baltic republics, farming, computer technology, brick laying, home remodeling, finance, management, Spanish, and meteorology. Nor am I the top expert on the Bible and theology. Every Sunday there are parishioners who carry their Greek New Testaments, teach in Bible colleges or seminary, are pastors, theological writers, or otherwise better informed than I am. Needless to say, this can be intimidating!

My responsibility is to relate God's truth to all of them in an effective and interesting way. But I must also be credible. If I say that the Bolshevik Revolution happened in 1817 instead of 1917, I will lose credibility with those who know world history. If I confuse the difference between a psychiatrist and a psychologist, I will risk the disdain of both. If credibility is lost in some secular area outside of my expertise, they will doubt my accuracy and credibility when I teach the Bible. Therefore, I must undertake the necessary research, or I must talk to some of these experts in advance so that I have accurate information and adequate documentation. When I am accurate, my credibility is enhanced. For example, I recently preached on Jesus' conversation with the leprous man in Matthew 8:1–4. I researched both biblical leprosy and modern Hansen's Disease. I related the ancient fears and struggles with leprosy to modern fears and struggles with cancer. Afterward several physicians stopped to talk with me, speaking positively about the medical accuracy of my sermon. A young family also stopped to talk—the mother wearing a scarf on her head. The woman explained that she had cancer, was undergoing chemotherapy, had lost her hair, and identified with what was said in the sermon.

The integrity of the content of sermons is vital. If any part doesn't make sense, is inaccurate, or otherwise doesn't ring true, listeners may reject the whole sermon as incredible.

Even more important, the primary content of sermons for the twenty-first-century church should be the Word of God. This is theologically necessary because the Bible represents God's communication to humans and the source of our information on salvation and life. To omit the Bible or merely use the Bible as a "jumping-off spot" for the preacher's opinion is presumptuous.

It assumes that what we have to say is more important than what God has to say. Indeed, on a practical level people are weary of the bombardment of human opinions. Modern Americans feel so attacked by multiple messages that they are not likely to come to church for one more. They want an authoritative message from God that is distinctively different from all the others. They come to hear what God has to say.

Different churches will take different approaches to teaching the Bible. The lectionary is a systematic overview of the Bible's major themes and messages designed into an annual calendar. There are Old Testament and New Testament lessons for each Sunday. The major Christian holidays are celebrated so that the Scripture matches with the calendar. It is common practice in liturgical churches to annually follow the lectionary. In other traditions sermons are often preached in series organized by text or topic. They may systematically teach through a book of the Bible, select the Lord's Prayer for a line-by-line series, or study the Sermon on the Mount. Topical series may focus on prayer, salvation, family life, or prophecy. In topical series the sermons tend to draw from multiple biblical texts, while textual series stick to single texts.

Recognizing that the audience may include growing numbers of biblically illiterate persons, pastors often build their sermon titles and organization on words more familiar to an unchurched audience. Titling a sermon on Luke 18:18–27 "The Guy Who Had Everything and Still Wasn't Satisfied," rather than "The Rich Young Ruler," doesn't make the sermon any less biblical. It makes it more relevant.

There are two traps to avoid in preparing the content for a twenty-first-century sermon: (1) inadequate understanding of the biblical text and (2) overload of information on the biblical text. The preacher's preparation needs to include research, questions, answers, and fundamental understanding of the teaching of the text and issues related to the text. However, most of the information learned usually doesn't appear in the public presentation. Compare it to a surgeon explaining a procedure to a patient. There was a time when surgeons explained very little—they said, "Show up for the operation on Tuesday," and that was about it. Most patients demand much more today. Patients ask questions and expect adequate answers. If the answers aren't adequate, they may look for another doctor. Nevertheless, a surgeon should not explain everything he knows—that would take too long and almost require a medical school course. There is an underlying assumption that the surgeon fully understands the procedure and patient and that an appropriate amount of information is selected to teach the patient all he or she needs to know. The test comes when the patient asks a technical question beyond the explanation. If the answer is easily offered, confidence soars and learning increases. Likewise for a sermon—lots of preparation with adequate but not complete explanation.

In Tex Sample's book *U.S. Lifestyles and Mainline Churches*, he argues that too much education can become a barrier to communication. He gives examples of preachers who understood their people and were understood by them until they went off to seminary. Their identification was broken as they became scholars with too much theory and too little practicality. This problem strengthens the argument of those who insist that higher theological education is best when directly tied to ongoing parish ministry or is undertaken over a longer time from parish ministry rather than separately in the cocoon of the seminary. The training of physicians closely connects the clinical experiences with patients to the laboratory and lecture hall. When I was a seminary student, my wife and I ran children's churches for 2 to 3-year-olds and for 4 to 5-year-olds. Each week I attempted to give a five-minute explanation to the children of what I had learned the previous week in systematic theology classes. It was a humbling experience that may not have bridged the chasm but regularly reminded me that the "real world" was more like children than professors.

The best tests concerning content are in the results: (1) Did the listeners experience God? (2) Was God's Word learned and better understood? (3) Is the content clearly connected to the listener's life?

Because this approach to content is so demanding, it is hard work for the preacher. The inexperienced preparer will devote as many as twenty or more hours of preparation per sermon. The skilled and experienced preparer may need as few as six to ten hours per sermon. Nevertheless, the longer the same preacher talks to the same audience, the greater the need for adequate preparation and credible content. It is easier to sound fresh to strangers than to long-time friends. Both the church and pastor must be committed to the priority of preparation and preaching in the twenty-first-century church. While it is true that great churches can no longer be built solely on preaching (if in fact they ever could), the great twenty-first-century churches cannot be built without good preaching.

## Goal

What is the goal of good preaching? Knowing the target is essential to knowing how to shoot.

The primary goal is to change lives to be like Jesus Christ. According to Matthew 28:20, it is to make disciples who obey all that Jesus commanded. In other words, preaching is pointed at transformation.

Transformation is usually a process rather than a point in time. We must take individuals from where they are to where God wants them to be. The starting point may be hostility, apathy, seeking, or commitment. Where the audience is must determine how we communicate.

Because of the spiritual diversity in the population, churches have chosen to specialize. Some target "seekers" and begin at an elementary level that is essentially pre-evangelistic. Others aim to be "seeker sensitive," but recognize that the majority of the audience is already nominally Christian and needs to be discipled. Some go for "advanced disciple making" and assume that everyone in the audience is a committed and informed believer.

When the sermon and service target a specific level, the rest of the programming of the church tries to service the other levels. Thus, seeker churches have other gatherings targeted for believers, while disciple churches program for the non-Christian through investigative Bible studies or special pre-evangelistic and evangelistic programs.

In every case there should be a mix of theory and practice. Again there is a gamut in American churches. Some have been heavy on theory and offer almost no application—"figure it out for yourself." Others go to the opposite extreme, telling everyone how to behave and what to do (or what *not* to do), but they never mention why. Rick Warren, who understands the baby boomer culture very well (especially in Southern California), gives wise advice for preachers when he says, "Tell them why; show them how." Most modern churchgoers require both explanation and application. On a very practical level, that means teaching the Bible's truths and principles and then showing how they can be translated into transformed lives. The ratio could be 50/50, maybe 60/40, but it rarely ought go beyond a 70/30 distribution. In other words, half of the sermon content and time goes to theory and half to practice, but not more than 70% to either theory or practice.

When walking out of a church service and reflecting on the sermon, most want to have a clear idea of what they are supposed to do. They want to decide for themselves whether they will do it or not, but they still want a clear picture of what is expected of them.

## Style

Henry Ford said that Model-T customers could buy "any color they want as long as it is black." Those days are long gone. Today's customers don't buy many black cars and resent a lack of choice.

A friend bought a beautiful green Cadillac as a gift for his wife. He drove it home, parked it in the driveway, and called her out to see it. She wouldn't even get in it. She said she wouldn't be seen in a pink Mary Kay car. Her husband is color blind; he had to sell the car.

Sermon styles are like car colors. Different people have different preferences. When someone told me, "He is the best preacher in the English language today," I thought to myself, "Sure, and pink is the best car color in the world today!" It all depends on what you like. There is no such thing as "the best preacher" or "the best style." It is a matter of preference. But just as some colors are much more popular than others, so are some preaching styles. Just as the color needs to be matched to the preference of the customer, the sermon style needs to be matched to the church and community. What is wonderful in one context can be a constant irritant in another context.

Yesterday's style was oratorical, formal, loud, polished, intense, used significant historical illustrations, and told people what to do. Some churches and listeners still like this style very much. Most, however, associate it with wind-up alarm clocks, black-and-white TV's, and rotary-dial telephones.

Today's style is much more conversational, much like the monologue of Johnny Carson or Jay Leno on the Tonight Show. Management author and popular speaker Tom Peters says, "The whole issue with public speaking at any level is loosening up and getting comfortable." Today's speaker is more of a "communicator" than a "preacher." Today's style is more of a "conversation" than a "lecture."

Words like "ought," "should," and "must" punctuated the older style in which the preacher told the audience what to do. The new style explains the issues, presents the alternatives, and then seeks to persuade—but clearly leaves the decision up to the listener. Modern Americans don't want their politicians, doctors, or pastors telling them what to do. They want to be well informed and decide for themselves. Persuasion takes place when the speaker describes the way things "could be" if right decisions and responses follow. It is the difference between saying, "Quit smoking today, or you will be dead tomorrow!" and saying, "You're going to feel great and live a long healthy life if you'll stop smoking right away."

One of the reasons the old style doesn't relate as well to the twenty-first-century church is because of the heightened issues of authenticity and hypocrisy. Leader credibility has nose-dived in the second half of the twentieth century. Public officials, businesspeople, professionals, and pastors have fallen from heights of prominence to the depths of discredit. They appeared to be something up front that they were not in real life. Today's people listen to and believe public persons who model honesty and integrity both in their public and private life. I suppose that someone who shouts in the pulpit and also shouts in restaurants and rest rooms might be considered consistent. Most people don't shout, tell complicated historical stories, have alliterated outlines, or perfectly polished gestures and phrases in everyday conversation. The preacher who talks with a style few use in everyday conversation is suspected of hypocrisy—and hypocrites aren't very popular or respected.

Ronald Reagan has been called "The Great Communicator"

of late twentieth-century politics. The reason is because he talked
to the nation in the same way he talked to individuals. Watching
him on television was like listening to someone sitting beside you
in the family room. He told a lot of stories, and much of his humor
was aimed at himself. He seldom laughed at others or asked you
to laugh at others.

Yesterday's style was deductive; today's style is inductive. Deductive reasoning starts with a premise and then explains it. Inductive reasoning starts with explanations and then states the conclusion. Deductive approaches work best with those who are
already convinced. Inductive approaches are better for the un-
decided and the hostile. A deductive sermon states its thesis in the
first few minutes ("God loves you!") and then defends it
("#1 = God is love; #2 = The Bible says God loves you; #3 = God
demonstrated his love by sending his Son; #4 = God still demonstrates his love with grace today.") An inductive sermon may
start talking about our need for love, give stories and examples of
God's love in people's lives, explain the greatest demonstration of
love when God sent Jesus, and reach the conclusion—"God is
love!" One style is not right and the other wrong—they are different. However, one style may be right for a specific audience
and wrong for another.

Stories are especially important to the twenty-first-century
preaching style. We increasingly deal with a generation that thinks
more in images than in points. Stories stick. They are memorable.
They are easy to identify with. Ask any generation of churchgoer
to repeat the points of a six-weeks-ago sermon and few can do it.
But ask for a rerun of the stories and illustrations, and a high
percentage remember in detail. There is a strong theological prec-
edent in the preaching of Jesus. His communications were full of
stories—related to everyday happenings and practices. The par-
ables were not only strong for the first century and the Bible, but
they also have become a part of modern conversation and culture.
Even people who don't know from where the phrase originated
speak Jesus' metaphor of a "prodigal son."

Simplicity is another element of style. In an increasingly complex world listeners are drawn to simplicity. In an increasingly
complex world, however, simplicity is harder for a preacher to
produce. In an introductory journalism class at Northwestern

University in Illinois, my professor started his first lecture quoting Genesis 1:1, "In the beginning God created the heavens and the earth." Although most of his vocabulary and illustrations indicated he was not a religious man, he said he chose this example of excellent writing because "you can't say anything more profound, and you can't say it more simply." Today's communicators need to be both profound and simple, which requires a lot of work.

How can all of this be done for an audience that ranges from the young to the old, the high school dropout to the Ph.D., the rich to the poor, and many of the other diversities in today's urban congregations? One way is through M*A*S*H preaching. M*A*S*H refers to "Mobile Army Surgical Hospital" and is the name of one of the most popular television series ever to run. Reruns continue in most broadcast markets today. In a typical half-hour episode there are multiple story lines that are parallel and simultaneous. "Hawkeye" the surgeon and "Radar O'Riley" the private have a string of one-line jokes woven through every show. Head Nurse "Hotlips" and her doctor lover Frank carry on a banter of passion and sexual innuendoes. There is usually a medical theme that deals with surgical procedures, patient problems, and other medical matters. Finally there is some type of social commentary—like the triage officer who has to decide which of the incoming casualties will be treated first: a white American Second Lieutenant who was commissioned out of an Ivy League college ROTC program, a veteran black American sergeant from the Deep South, a teenage draftee in the North Korean army, or a Communist Chinese regular army officer sent to train and lead the North Korean troops. At least four different stories in the same script: comedy, passion, medicine, and social dilemma.

Different viewers relate to different themes. Some laugh from one-line joke to one-line joke and miss the serious messages. Others are caught up in the medical matters and don't pay attention to the rest of the story. Some are attracted to the passion, and others are deeply involved in the struggles of race, class, and rank. The same show speaks on various levels to different audiences.

Sermons in the twenty-first-century church will have to seek to do the same. In thirty minutes or less the fabric of the presentation must simultaneously draw contrasting audiences into the same experience. It is not easy to do and cannot always be done, but the challenge must not be ignored.

As an example, suppose that the sermon text is 1 John 1:9: "If we confess our sins, he is faithful and just and will forgive us our sins and purify us from all unrighteousness." Since the topic is confession, the preacher might say:

> The Bible was written in Greek in which the word for "confess" is *homologeo*.
>
> *Homo* means "the same as"—like in homogenized milk or homosexual. Homogenized milk is all the same. Homosexuals are attracted to persons of the same gender.
>
> *Lego* means "to say" something.
>
> Put it together, and "confess" is "to say the same thing."
>
> When we confess our sins to God, we are saying the same thing about what we did as God says.
>
> Now, pick something you've done. Anything—good or bad: from praying to robbing a bank. What does God say about what you did? If you tell God you agree with him, you've confessed. And if it's a sin, God promises to forgive.

In this example, although it is not a story, it is multiple level. The person who has studied Greek hears and understands the Greek word. Learning and credibility take place. The person who doesn't know Greek probably tuned *homologeo* out and won't remember that the word was spoken. Older listeners who remember when milk bottles came with the cream at the top quickly identify with the sameness of homogenized milk. Adult listeners, especially younger ones, are drawn into the explanation with reference to homosexuals since homosexuality is a frequent current topic, and they immediately understand the idea of two persons together who are the same gender. They will also follow a thought pattern that asks what God thinks about homosexual behavior and whether or not they agree and say the same as God. The open-ended opportunity to select any activity from praying to bank robbing allows participation by every level and variety of person in the audience. Each chooses one's own (rather than the preacher doing the choosing for you). It communicates that not everything is a sin, but that it is important to decide what God thinks of our actions. If it is a sin, do we agree with God or not? If we agree,

God promises to forgive. It is an example of M*A*S*H preaching, an effective style for the twenty-first-century church.

## Audience

Every audience is unique. That is one of the reasons a sermon may be good one time and poor another time. Thomas Long, Frances Landey Patlon Professor of Preaching and Worship at Princeton Theological Seminary, gets it right when he says:

> . . . the best preachers may never become known beyond their own congregations.
>
> If you were on a baccalaureate or church conference committee responsible for selecting a speaker a generation ago, you could come up with lots of names of nationally known preachers.
>
> You can't do that anymore. You'd be hard pressed to come up with more than a handful of nationally known preachers today.
>
> Some people think that's evidence of preaching's decline. I think it's evidence that good preaching is now much more local.
>
> It's being done by this preacher, standing in front of these people, whom he or she loves, speaking this text to their mission in this place on this day. That doesn't travel; it doesn't print. That's local and specific. And that's good preaching.[2]

The communicator must know the audience, and the sermon must be customized to fit that audience. Harry Emerson Fosdick was one of America's most famous preachers during the first half of the twentieth century, and perhaps the most controversial. His sermons were preached at Riverside Church in New York City and broadcast over the National Radio Pulpit. His office was literally in a tower, and there was the risk that he could become far removed from the everyday lives of his congregation. He chose to spend a limited number of hours each week in pastoral counseling—not because it was a requirement of his job or because he thought he would make a major difference to his counselees, but because he needed to know people's needs for sermon preparation

and delivery. He saw "preaching as counseling" and thought of
his large congregation as a group of individuals whom he was
counseling on a one-to-one basis. Fosdick intentionally understood his audience.

Pollster George Gallup, Jr., says that every pastor should know
at least seven needs of the average American:

1. The need for shelter and food.
2. The need to believe life is meaningful and has a
purpose (a need cited by 70% of the respondents, with two
thirds believing most churches and synagogues are not effective in meeting it).
3. The need for a sense of community and deeper relationships (nearly one third of Americans say they have
been lonely for a long period of time in their lives).
4. The need to be appreciated and respected ("the
closer people feel to God, the better they feel about themselves").
5. The need to be listened to and be heard ("Americans
overwhelmingly think the future of the church will be
shaped by the laity more than by the clergy. . . . they believe it will happen, [and] they believe it should happen").
6. The need to feel one is growing in faith.
7. The need for practical help in developing a mature
faith.[3]

We all start with where we are and what our needs are. The
sermon that informs and persuades links up with listeners' present
circumstances and current needs. There is a sense in which those
needs are basic and permanent. That's one of the reasons why
Jesus' words are so timeless; he masterfully touched the central
core of human experience. In another sense, the circumstances
and needs are highly specific—changing with the economy, politics, weather, age, health, and expectations. Effective sermons
connect with both—much like a battery in a car. The battery has
two posts, positive and negative. Connecting to only one will never
start the car or get it moving. The positive post of preaching should
connect with the truths of the Bible, and the negative post of
preaching should connect with the present needs of the audience.

When both are connected the sparks fly, the electricity flows, and the car starts.

Today's audiences are more connected to speakers through the heart than the head. That is to say, preaching to connect emotionally is usually more important than preaching to connect intellectually. Nevertheless, absence of either is a disaster. Both are necessary.

Connecting to hearts begins with the preacher's heart. In the prayer and preparation for the sermon, is there a stirring of emotions? Is there a personal laugh, a private fear, an individual tear? Once experienced, it is important that those emotions naturally flow through the communication.

Just before Christmas I was preaching an Advent sermon from Hebrews 10:5–10. The text was used as a picture of the dialogue between God the Father and God the Son prior to the Incarnation. The Father who loves the world commissioned his Son to leave heaven, become human, suffer, and die on the cross for human salvation. The Son, who had always existed as God in heaven, replied, "I have come to do your will, O God" (Heb. 10:7).

I tried to imagine the emotions in heaven at the moment of departure—those last minutes before the eternal Son of God was gone from heaven and in the womb of Mary. I thought about how hard it must have been for even God to say goodbye. It made me think of the last time I saw my father face-to-face before he died. He had been ill for about six months, and I had traveled to Florida several times to be with him. That last stay was near his end. The last minutes were precious. We both knew time was running out. I helped him to his feet, and he walked me to the door, where he said, "I wish you didn't have to go. Please don't go." I explained to him that I had people to serve and a job to do. After his own sixty years in ministry, he understood what I had said, but he said it again, "I don't want you to go. Please stay longer. Please don't go." But then I left. Those were his last words to me the last time I saw him alive.

As I read Hebrews 10 and thought about the Father and the Son in heaven, all my own emotions of that last time with my dad flooded back to me. It was not an intellectual experience. It was pure emotion. The tears flowed.

I wondered whether I dared tell that story in the next Sunday's sermon—not because it might be inappropriate but because I didn't know whether I could tell it without breaking down. I decided to do it. I practiced it many times, to control my emotions as best I could.

In a church with baby boomers, there are many whose own parents are aging and dying. They have spoken their final words between parents and children. They felt my emotions. They got the point—the incarnation was a costly experience for the Father and Son, and for us.

Or I think of the sermon about following Jesus, not out of duty, but out of devotion. The speaker told a story about Abraham Lincoln, who went to visit a slave auction one day and was appalled at the sights and sounds of buying and selling human beings. His heart was especially drawn to a young woman on the block whose story seemed to be told in her eyes. She looked with hatred and contempt on everyone around her. She had been used and abused all her life, and this time was but one more cruel humiliation. The bidding began, and Lincoln offered a bid. As other amounts were bid, he counter-bid with larger amounts until he won. When he paid the auctioneer the money and took title to the young woman, she stared at him with vicious contempt. She asked him what he was going to do next with her, and he said, "I'm going to set you free."

"Free?" she asked. "Free for what?"

"Just free," Lincoln answered. "Completely free."

"Free to do whatever I want to do?"

"Yes," he said. "Free to do whatever you want to do."

"Free to say whatever I want to say?"

"Yes, free to say whatever you want to say."

"Free to go wherever I want to go?" she added with skepticism. Lincoln answered, "You are free to go anywhere you want to go."

"Then I'm going with you!" she said with a smile.

I've forgotten the text. I don't even remember who the preacher was. But I can still feel the emotions of the story. It touched my heart and made me want to go wherever Jesus Christ went because he is the one who set me free.

Sermons in the twenty-first-century church will know their audiences well and connect to their hearts as well as their minds.

## Atmosphere

Preaching does not take place in a sterile vacuum. It is and always has been a total experience. The record of Jesus' sermons often mentions the surroundings in which he preached them. Modern Americans are especially attuned to total experiences: Classrooms are designed for learning; restaurants succeed because of ambiance as much as food; airplane seats and food are important parts of the passenger's choice.

A certain atmosphere is more comfortable and conducive to effective communication. Johnny Carson insisted his audience have 66-degree temperatures because that's the balance between keeping people comfortable and alert. Church services in very cold or uncomfortably warm rooms make preaching difficult and distractions many.

Buildings are easily dated. Any facility that hasn't been updated, refurbished, or redecorated in more than twenty years probably feels old to most people today. Real estate experts have a name for commercial properties in this condition: They look "tired." The styles have changed from pastels to earth tones to current colors. Microphones more than twenty years old appear to come out of a black-and-white TV comedy show. Platforms used to have a living room appearance with everything carpeted (shag?), but they currently are more like a stage with hard surfaces. Lighting once was dim but now is bright. Buildings without windows were built in the 1960s and 1970s, but outside light is more highly valued today. A smaller room that is fuller enhances communication compared to a larger room that is emptier. Volume that is louder works better than volume that is softer (older listeners may have diminished hearing and younger listeners are used to loud music).

The length of services and sermons is a significant part of atmosphere. Unless there is a strong tradition for lengthy services, most Americans expect the program to be over in an hour. Some African-American churches have traditions of services lasting several hours, although there are indications that some of the fastest-growing African-American churches are now holding services of 60 to 75 minutes in length. It has to do with television and school.

The majority of TV shows have a maximum length of 60 minutes. The number one rated television program in much of 1991 and 1992 is even named "60 Minutes." School classes last 50 to 55 minutes and are called "hours" ("What class do you have during third-hour?").

Some pastors object. They say that the Holy Spirit should not be bound to our clocks, which is true. Actually, TV shows aren't bound to the clock either. When a President is shot or the country goes to war or some other exceptional event occurs, length of coverage has no limit. But that is the exception, not the norm. It seems strange to parishioners when the Holy Spirit regularly takes a set amount of time that seems long to them.

Another objection is that it is hard to get everything done within an hour. That doesn't ring true to those who see so much packed into an hour on TV. It doesn't take long to figure out that greater preparation usually reduces time and lesser preparation often increases time.

How much of the hour goes to preaching? Churches with great emphasis on liturgy and sacraments often have sermons of 15 minutes or less. Churches heavy on teaching may have sermons lasting 45 minutes or more. Ask the average listener and the answer is "twenty to twenty-five minutes maximum." Thus, the answer is within a range, but few preachers or churches can handle much more than 25 to 30 minutes. If the speaker is an extraordinary communicator with outstanding gifts, longer may work. Less than 1% of pastors fit into that classification, however, while the rest of us need to stay under half an hour. When the sermon becomes too long, it begins to defeat its own purposes by alienating listeners. They may still be physically present, but they have mentally departed.

An old church joke had the preacher saying, "This sermon will be over when I'm finished or you leave—whichever comes first." Everyone laughed, but today some will leave. It's still not socially acceptable to get up and go when you are bored, but it increasingly happens.

There is no end to the list of items that create the atmosphere. It is the ushers and architecture, the weather outside, and the kind of people inside. Few of them are all-important, but all of them make a difference in the effectiveness of communication. All need to be viewed and evaluated. The ideal is when all aspects of atmosphere converge to make the sermon succeed.

## Personality

How does any preacher pull off all these elements? The obvious prerequisites are godliness, Bible knowledge, cultural sensitivity, and a lot of hard work.

Less obvious is how to be interesting. Some boring people try to be interesting by looking for interesting things to say. It seldom works.

The twenty-first century is an exciting and interesting time. No one wants to be bored because there seem to be no good reasons to be bored. Therefore, boring sermons are definitely out.

The way to preach interesting sermons is to be an interesting person. That requires getting out and doing something—having fun, meeting people, reading books, watching television, playing sports, visiting homes, hosting parties, traveling, pursuing hobbies, asking questions, and listening. Phillips Brooks defined preaching as "truth through personality." The truth is God's responsibility, and he has given us the Bible. The personality is our responsibility, and we need to be interesting.

Abraham Lincoln stands as a good example of the kind of communicator twenty-first-century preachers can be. In *Lincoln on Leadership: Executive Strategies for Tough Times*, Donald T. Phillips points out that Abraham Lincoln was the first president of the United States elected by a minority popular vote. Not even the majority wanted him, but he did a very good job:

> He excelled in communications on several fronts: He had a wealth of stories at the ready for any occasion, he could speak extemporaneously quite well, although he prepared most of his major speeches, and his ability to persuade was so effective that he rarely had to give orders outright.
>
> His ambition triumphed over continual adversity, from being ridiculed as a gawky youth to achieving the preservation of the Union at great expense.[4]

Some would add that his greatest speech, "The Gettysburg Address," was very short—two minutes!

## Chapter 12

# *Do We Really Need More Leaders? Or More Followers?*

THE STORY can't be true, but it is funny:

The commencement speaker at Yale University was challenging the graduates to be leaders. He outlined his commencement address with an acrostic based on the name of the university. He spoke 20 minutes on the "Y" for "Youth," 30 minutes on the "A" for "Ambition," 15 minutes on the "L" for "Loyalty," and another 20 minutes on the "E" for "Enthusiasm." At the end of the 85 minute speech, one of the graduates was overheard saying, "It's a good thing this isn't the Massachusetts Institute of Technology."

Long graduation speeches on leadership are common. But how can every alumnus be a leader? Doesn't someone have to follow? Few commencement addresses challenge the graduating seniors to "followership."

The twentieth century has had many leadership books, leadership courses, and would-be leaders. Yet, complaints about a shortage of qualified leaders are common.

Perhaps, along with all the leadership courses, a followership course should be offered. Organizations searching for qualified

leaders to fill executive positions should ask whether they have
enough qualified followers in their ranks.

It should surprise us that so much is said about leaders and so
little about followers, especially among Christians committed to
the Bible. The Bible says comparatively little about leadership and
a great deal about followership.

Jesus did not invite Peter, Andrew, James, and John to become
leaders. He said, "Follow me!"

The New Testament books often were named, not for leaders,
but for followers like Timothy, Titus, Philemon, the Corinthians,
the Thessalonians, the Galatians, and the Ephesians.

Our generation has long argued about who should be the boss
in a Christian marriage, but less has been said about the call of
Ephesians 5:21 for all Christians (including husbands and wives)
to "submit to one another out of reverence for Christ."

The great Old Testament saint, David, demonstrated his followership long before his leadership. He obediently cared for the
family's sheep, played his music at the king's command, and was
known as a loyal soldier in King Saul's army. When David became
a famous general, he acknowledged that the reason he won battles
was because of soldiers whom he called the "Mighty Men" who
had developed followership to an art.

Jesus was the greatest follower of all. He clearly stated that he
came not "to be served, but to serve" (Matt. 20:28). He is described as

> being in very nature God,
> did not consider equality with God
> something to be grasped, but made himself nothing,
> taking the very nature of a servant,
> being made in human likeness.
> And being found in appearance as a man,
> he humbled himself
> and became obedient unto death—
> even death on a cross. (Phil. 2:6–8)

The whole meaning of being a Christian is wrapped up in being
a disciple, and being a disciple means being a follower.

## Leadership Without Followership?

Ask a class to write down what makes a leader. The answers often include: integrity, vision, prayer, fairness, intelligence, courage, and good speaking abilities. Certainly these are wonderful traits, but not all leaders possess all these traits. Hitler certainly lacked integrity and fairness, and Moses wasn't a good speaker, but they were both leaders.

For the first half of the twentieth century, leadership studies focused on "trait theory." While the professionals in leadership study moved beyond trait theory around 1950, there are many who still adhere to it.

Careful analysis shows there is no definite list of consistent leadership traits. Some leaders are geniuses; some have average intelligence. Some leaders are extremely outgoing; some are painfully shy. Some leaders are articulate; some leaders struggle to get their words and ideas across. Some leaders are physically attractive; most leaders are quite average looking. Some are educated; some are uneducated. Some are good; some are bad.

Therefore, what makes a leader? The answer is, "Many things make a leader." It is a complicated mix of the leader, the context, and the followers. One leader's skills and traits may be great for one time but wrong for another. The context varies from boom to bust, war to peace, modern to ancient. The followers may be the most important ingredient of all. They are the ones who determine which would-be leader will be followed and whose vision will be implemented. The 1960 presidential election was one of the closest in history. John Kennedy narrowly defeated Richard Nixon. Americans chose who would be their leader and when he would lead. Kennedy was elected, the Cuban missile crisis was resolved, the Bay of Pigs invasion was a disaster, the United States' build-up in Vietnam began, and the President was assassinated. In 1968 Nixon was elected, the Vietnam War ended, astronauts landed on the moon, vice-president Spiro Agnew resigned, the Watergate break-in rocked the nation, and the President resigned. How different history might have been if Americans had chosen Nixon in 1960 and Kennedy in 1968.

The twenty-first-century church needs some first-rate followers. Perhaps we need good followers more than we need good

leaders. It could be effectively argued that church leadership classes should be replaced with followership classes in order to strike
the right balance.

We often have a mistaken notion of followership in North
America. We think of followership as a stepping stone to leadership. We sometimes say one must first be a follower before one
can be a leader. The truth is that followership is a high and noble
calling all by itself. Besides, roles of leadership and followership
can switch back and forth. At church I am a leader, and the doctor
and pilot are the followers. At the hospital, the doctor is the leader,
and the pilot and I are followers. On the plane, the pilot is the
leader, and the doctor and I are the followers. Only a fool claims
to be *the* leader in every situation and all the time.

Not everyone can be a leader. It takes only a few leaders to
fulfill God's goals. But it takes many followers.

This puts followership on a very high level. Therefore, followership must be done right, or it is not worth doing.


## Wisdom

The best of followers are wise. It may be the most important
characteristic of all.

The Borg-Warner Building along Lake Michigan in Chicago
was the site for a one-day seminar for presidents and board chair-
persons of American colleges and seminaries. The guest speaker
was a consultant from the American Management Association. He
claimed there is one primary consideration in the selection for
school boards of trustees: "good judgment"—not wealth, not
alumni status, not age, not gender. He said it is always great if
you can recruit board members who have everything, but you
should never forego good judgment in order to get something else.
If board members have good judgment, they will deal appropriately with money matters and all other matters. If they have wealth
and everything else but lack good judgment, the school will soon
run into trouble. Good judgment is wisdom.

There are always would-be leaders clamoring for a following.
Foolish followers have chosen the rhetoric of Adolf Hitler and
created the Third Reich, the expansionism of Saddam Hussein
and marched to sure defeat, and the poison of Jim Jones and

committed mass suicide in the name of religion. Wise followers have chosen to follow reformers like Martin Luther, John Knox, and John Calvin. Wise followers with forgotten names went after David Livingstone to Africa, Hudson Taylor to inland China, and Jim Elliot to South America.

Followers seldom have famous names; yet, they are the ones who determine the course of history.

Josheb, Eleazar, Shammah, Abishai, Benaiah, and three dozen others with equally unknown names were called the "Mighty Men of Israel." Any one of them could have been a general or a king in his own right. When civil war threatened ancient Israel, these soldiers faced the toughest decisions of their careers. Should they follow King Saul on the throne or the shepherd-turned-soldier from Bethlehem named David? Wisely they chose David. They followed him until he became king.

The twenty-first-century church needs more men and women who will choose to follow right leaders. Because the world is at a critical time of transition, the wise choosing of leaders cannot be more important. We need godly men and women in our churches, schools, and communities who will pray for and practice the wisdom of God. If we have no wise followers, we are doomed to share the destinies of worthless leaders.

Where does this needed wisdom come from? God has gifted some Christians with wisdom (1 Cor. 12:8), and they should be listened to. Those with the gift of wisdom are confirmed in a local church by the demonstration of wisdom over many experiences and many years. They are the ones who apply God's truth to current situations in ways that bring God's results. But wisdom is not limited to a gifted few. It is too important to be limited. James 1:5 promises, "If any of you lacks wisdom, he should ask God, who gives generously to all without finding fault, and it will be given to him."

James 1:5 was the chosen verse for the calling committee that invited me to Wooddale Church in 1976. The committee began every meeting praying on their knees for wisdom. They recruited over 400 other Christians to pray daily for God to give them wisdom. When they chose me to give pastoral leadership, they had already demonstrated wise followership. Wise followers produce good leaders.

## Priorities

The twenty-first-century church will need followers who know how to prioritize. Because we are an increasingly diverse, heterogeneous, and pluralistic culture, our generation is constantly being pulled in hundreds of different directions. Some in our churches say our resources should go to feed the starving millions in Sub-Sahara Africa. Others tell us to pour our energies into fighting abortion-on-demand. Another says the first priority is to stop illicit drugs and immoral pornography. A louder voice calls Christians to evangelism rather than social action. A softer voice calls the church to prayer.

Too often the result is fragmentation and polarization. The number of choices and the magnitude of the needs paralyze too many followers. Some choose their one issue and ignore the rest.

I'm not saying all of these issues aren't important. It's just that some things take precedence over others. There is a story out of Moscow during the 1917 Bolshevik Revolution. Leaders of the Russian Orthodox Church were gathered for a conference to debate the colors used for their clergy vestments. The colors were important, but not as important as their relationship to the revolution occurring around them.

The twenty-first-century church has a revolution occurring around it and can't afford the luxury of petty differences and individual preferences. Blessed is the church with followers who are willing to set aside their personal priorities and align with the greater priorities of the body.

Clark Morphew, religion editor of the *Saint Paul Pioneer Press*, describes well the importance of prioritization:

> Let me tell you the story of First Church on Main Street, Anywhere, U.S.A., a 40-year old congregation with a bad attitude and no way to cast out the demons that have stalled its mission.
>
> In the past six years, three pastors have left the parish in a huff. The lay leadership of the congregation is divided over several issues, but conflict over its mission surpasses all others.
>
> As pastors were hired and fired, the leadership listened patiently to plans for drawing the unchurched into the con-

gregation. But at every step, those plans were sabotaged by a lack of enthusiasm among top leaders or by insufficient funds.

Oddly, older members of the congregation, who have been the core of leadership for four decades, have never complained about proposals for new programs. But underneath their calm demeanor lies a smoking cauldron of resentment. Those in the older power group feel their leadership is not appreciated, and the time and money they have given the congregation is now seen as inadequate.

The younger members, eager for programs that will benefit their children, have said the mission of the church is stalled and stagnant.

The fascinating thing about the First Church conflict is that nobody talks publicly about the true reason for the schism. In private groups, the church's problems are often discussed. But in open meetings of the church council or the congregation, the rift is kept hidden.

The first victims of this kind of silent schism are the pastors who serve the congregation. They are caught in the cross fire. They become the scapegoats, enduring blame from both sides of the conflict.

Hundreds of congregations are experiencing similar rifts, and many have never figured out a solution. And no key to unlocking the conflict will be found until some people begin to talk things through to a resolution.

The keys that will unlock a church split are compromise and communication. Someone has to bring the conflict into the open where the real issues that divide a congregation can be discussed.

But too often, religious organizations mask the conflict and pretend that smaller issues, such as the cost of the new roof or the color of the new carpet, are the straws breaking the congregation's back.[1]

He describes a typical church in which followers are unwilling or unable to prioritize. They can't agree on what is really important. They won't rally around a primary mission for the church. Pastors come and go because no one can lead when no one will follow.

What a contrast to a formative experience during my early pastoral ministry in Colorado. We had a dirt parking lot next to our small church building. When it rained, the parking lot became a mud pond. The church considered a proposal to spend money for the purchase of gravel. Farmers would haul the gravel from the gravel pit, and volunteers would spread it on the parking lot. For reasons I have long ago forgotten, this turned into a serious debate. Different members had different ideas on ways to spend that amount of money. The proposal passed the congregation, but by a split vote. I vividly remember a member who had spoken and voted against the recommendation coming to speak to me immediately after we adjourned the meeting. She said, "Pastor, I voted against it, but I'll be here on Saturday to help carry the rocks." She was a follower who knew how to prioritize. She wisely considered support better than dissent. She was the kind of follower who makes leaders succeed.

The twenty-first-century church needs followers who evidence knowledge of Scripture, practice of prayer, and courage of soul to make hard decisions and choose right priorities. We need men and women who can figure out what is first, second, and third—and then be the kind of followers who make the most important things happen first. Blessed is the church whose followers can prioritize. Otherwise, believers in a Christian community become so divided and weakened that they become ineffective.

## Loyalty

Loyalty is not a common characteristic of the post-World-War-II-generation. We are a generation of consumers, who like to have our needs and wants satisfied. As a result we are quick to change leaders, especially when things don't go well.

Jesus had twelve followers constantly with him at the peak of his popularity. There were thousands more around the periphery of his ministry. When popularity switched to adversity, the ranks of loyal followers considerably thinned. Judas decided he was more loyal to money than to the Master. Peter denied he even knew Jesus. But John stood at the foot of the cross—he was the kind of follower who was not fickle when times got tough.

David's mighty men were also loyal followers. They stuck with him through defeats as well as victories. They were loyal to him even when he failed them.

It takes extraordinary unselfishness to remain loyal. When a church is growing and successful, pastors can count the followers by the hundreds, if not the thousands. But it takes a different kind of follower to remain loyal when the criticisms outnumber the congratulations.

Such calls for loyalty trigger a negative response in some who want to shout back, "Blind loyalty never did anyone any good." Blind loyalty is not good, but neither is critical disloyalty. The twenty-first-century church needs followers who are bent toward loyalty.

Let me put it in another way. Most computer programs have what are called "defaults," which means automatic choices. The program will automatically write in English, double-space, and print the next page of a multi-page letter. Sometimes those defaults are not appropriate and then may be overridden. The operator then chooses Greek or single-space or a page at a time. You accept the default unless you have a very good reason to override it. So should it be with wise and loyal followers who are self-programmed to choose loyalty in every situation, unless there is clear reason to override.

Some churches have members who are self-programmed to criticism, reaction, and disloyalty. They insist on clear and compelling reasons to override their negative defaults. Such churches can be impossible to lead. They are like computers with an internal destructive virus.

I had just turned thirty-two when I was called to the senior pastorate of Wooddale Church. My predecessor had a successful nineteen-year pastorate. While I had read about the difficulties of such a transition in Lyle Schaller's excellent book *Survival Tactics in the Parish*, I thought I was different, and the transition would be easy. Instead, I discovered that I became an unintentional "interim pastor" for the next thirty-two months. Probably there was no one who thought of it in this way at that time, but it seemed to me that the church was willing to let me do what my predecessor did well, yet wouldn't let me do what I could do well. In other words, I had a two-and-a-half year opportunity to perform poorly. It was not a totally pleasant experience.

One of the down days was when a man in his twenties made an appointment and came to see me. He started out by handing to me several pages from Bill Gothard on "How to Handle Criticism." I knew I was in for it. The room was silent as he waited for me to read what those pages suggested. Then he brought out his own pages of criticisms of me and my ministry. It pretty well covered everything—from an inappropriate prize awarded in a youth program to incorrect grammar I used in a sermon. When he had completed his lengthy list, I honestly asked whether he considered my primary problem to be incompetence or ungodliness. He thought for a while and said, "Both!" He wanted me to quit. I thought maybe he was right.

Those were hard days, and I don't think I was much of a leader.

Nevertheless, let me tell you about the members of the church board. They were committed to my success. They dealt with my critics. They prayed for me. They encouraged me. They loved me. They were loyal when others in the church thought they were stupid. They put their own credibility on the line for my sake.

As I now reflect back on those experiences fifteen years later, as I count the amazing changes for good that have continually transformed Wooddale Church, I realize none of it might have happened were it not for those board members and their loyalty. Some have moved; some have died; some are still active in the church. I have personally thanked each one.

The twenty-first-century church will require strong leaders. One of the ways to make them strong is through loyal followers.

## Support

Moses was one of God's most magnificent leaders, but he never would have made it without the support of faithful followers. When he dared to defy Pharaoh, others stood with him. When he could not handle the load of leadership, the responsibilities of judging were shared. When his hands grew weary in upholding military victory, his followers supported his arms for him.

Leaders know the importance of support. It comes in many different forms—regular prayer, encouragement through calls, conversations, and notes, interacting on ideas, and communicating what is going on in the organization. Often it is as simple and straightforward as asking the leader, "What can I do to help you?"

Support, however, is more than doing nice things. It also includes holding leaders accountable. Over the past decade we have witnessed too many tragic stories of followers who did not hold their religious leaders accountable. The consequences went far beyond misspent money and former leaders going to prison. The real consequences were the dishonor to God and the damage to innocent people.

The best of followers ask the hardest questions. They ask their leaders whether they are spending adequate time in prayer, whether they are filled with the Holy Spirit, whether they are resisting sexual temptation, whether they are faithful to the Bible, whether they are correctly handling their money, whether they are getting enough rest and exercise, and whether they are growing intellectually. Such questions are direct and personal. Thus, how they are asked makes a great deal of difference. Followers must first earn the right to ask accountability questions.

When my wife asks me a very personal question that could be interpreted as a criticism and could be taken as a threat, I appreciate her asking. The reason is because I know she loves me and has my best interests at heart. She has earned the right to ask me anything.

The same principle applies to churches and other organizations. Followers who have proven their wisdom, priorities, loyalty, and support have earned the right to ask their leaders accountability questions.

God's standards for leaders are high, and it is the responsibility of the followers to insist that God's standards are kept.

Unfortunately, leaders and followers in churches often hold different views of support. For example, one pastor in Alaska was confronted by a church member who owned a fishing boat. He told the pastor that he should get up and go to work early like the rest of the people in his church. The fisherman warned against perceptions of laziness because the lights were out in the parsonage when all the fishermen walked by on their way to the docks. He probably thought he was being supportive. The pastor probably thought he was being abused. That fishing fleet always went out with the tide, which sometimes meant 1:30 A.M.

A far better approach is to ask church leaders what kind of

support they need. Ask elders how and what to pray for. Ask the pastor what kind of support you can give. Adapt the support to the leader's needs rather than subjecting the leader to inappropriate attempts at support.

There are some special-case churches in retirement areas that draw elderly new residents from across the country (especially parts of California, Arizona, Arkansas, and Florida). Churches may be composed of veteran church members from various traditions who have very strong opinions that their old way is the right way. Often they have been longtime leaders in their former churches. The first mistake is thinking that leadership points are transferable from one church to another. They aren't; you must start over. The second mistake is assuming that what worked back home will work here. It probably won't. And the greatest mistake is assuming that the relationship with a former pastor can be duplicated with a different pastor. That seldom happens. To truly provide support requires humility, a servant's heart, and a willingness to see it from the other person's perspective *and* do it the other person's way. That's hard but helpful.

For the church of the twenty-first century to be the church God wants it to be will require large numbers of wise, prioritizing, loyal, supportive followers. Great leaders aren't born, they are made—by great followers.

How does followership happen? It may sound self-serving for a leader to tell others to improve their followership. That is why the place to begin is with demonstration on the parts of leaders, who teach followership by following in areas outside of their leadership. Leaders don't need to pretend they always know everything nor that they must always be in charge.

Nevertheless, modeling is not enough. Church leaders also should *teach* the biblical principles of both followership and leadership. Encourage open discussion—first on what the Bible says and then about how it is applied to specific situations. Leaders and followers can give each other permission to lead and follow, and then hold each other accountable to do what each is supposed to do.

Accountability is best done in groups. If one person on a church board needs help leading or following better, the others can confront and enable. This approach is better than one on one.

Consider a covenant where a dozen fellow Christians will learn, grow, and help one another be good followers and demonstrate Christian followership in the rest of the church. It could cause a healthy contagion!

# Chapter 13

# *God and Change*

WHAT IS THE ROLE of the spiritual and supernatural?

It may be the question people most frequently want to ask: "What does God have to do with all of this?"

When we talk about major changes and human responses, do we risk sinful manipulation of Christ's church? Is it possible that we will adapt to the ways of the world and forsake the ways of the Lord? Is there enormous danger in reshaping the church for the twenty-first century?

Yes. There is risk, and there is danger. That is why we must take great care to be sure that we have the mind of Jesus Christ (Phil. 2:5) and are obedient to the direction of the Holy Spirit.

It is a healthy thing to fear God. It is still true, "The fear of the Lord is the beginning of wisdom, and knowledge of the Holy One is understanding" (Prov. 9:10). I believe such great changes are taking place in our world that anyone who is sane and informed should be scared of what is happening. Nevertheless, our fear of God should be greater than our fear of circumstances. If ever we needed the wisdom promised in James 1:5, it is as we enter the twenty-first century:

If any of you lacks wisdom, he should ask God, who gives generously to all without finding fault, and it will be given to him.

Fear is a healthy emotion as long as it does not immobilize us. Fear of God can cause us to do nothing; fear of God can cause us to do the wrong thing. Righteous fear of God should motivate us to do the right things.

## Syndromes

Syndromes are usually medical maladies that have no single test to document them. The dictionary says a syndrome is "a group of signs and symptoms that occur together and characterize a particular abnormality."

Throughout Christian history faith without works or works without faith have been considered abnormalities. Anyone who has faith that is not evidenced in works is probably not a Christian—because faith always shows itself in works. Anyone who has works without faith is surely not a Christian—it is actually impossible to have truly Christian works without faith.

Even New Testament authors have been accused of one syndrome or the other. Paul is accused of the Faith Only syndrome because of his words in Ephesians 2:8–9: "For it is by grace you have been saved, through faith—and this not from yourselves, it is the gift of God—not by works, so that no one can boast."

It sounds as if Paul sees no place for works in the Christian life. Individuals may declare they have faith and never evidence it through a transformed life, the fruit of the Spirit, or deeds of righteousness. Faith only.

Obviously that is not what Paul was teaching as evidenced by the next verse (Eph. 2:10): "For we are God's workmanship, created in Christ Jesus to do good works, which God prepared in advance for us to do."

Paul was not guilty of theological abnormality, and careful diagnosis shows no Faith Only syndrome.

The accusation of a Works Only syndrome is usually leveled at James. Some have even tried to drum his little epistle out of the New Testament because they smelled a salvation-by-works theology. After all, James wrote (2:18): "But someone will say, 'You have faith; I have deeds.' Show me your faith without deeds, and I will show you my faith by what I do. You believe that there is one God. Good! Even the demons believe that—and shudder."

Faith folks point out that any so-called Christian who brags about "What I do" and writes about the faith of demons has to be suspect. But that risks another misdiagnosis. It is James who tells us to pray for wisdom from God (1:5). James, the brother of Jesus, writes to Christians who are "my brothers, as believers in our glorious Lord Jesus Christ" (2:1). He insists that those in trouble "should pray" (5:13). Accusing him of Works Only syndrome is a clear misdiagnosis.

## Checking Ourselves for Syndromes

It is certainly possible that we may be abnormal on the extremes of faith or works. Therefore, consider a self-check:

Symptoms of the Faith Only Syndrome:

- No answers to prayers of faith.
- Disobedience to the commands of Jesus Christ in the Bible.
- Lack of responsible behavior in exercising one's spiritual gifts.
- Basing belief primarily in outcomes that are self-serving rather than in outcomes that will honor God and build Christ's church.
- Opposition to other Christians in the church who act out their faith through bold obedience to the Scriptures and the Spirit.

Symptoms of the Works Only Syndrome:

- Failure to pray consistently in faith.
- Praying for God's blessing after the decisions have been made.
- Speaking and behaving as if one is responsible for the ultimate outcome—either in self-pride or self-blame.
- Claiming spiritual security on the basis of behavioral success.
- Pushing other Christians to conform to one's own plans rather than encouraging them to be followers of Jesus Christ.

## Striking the Balance

New Testament Christianity is firmly rooted primarily in faith and secondarily in works. We begin as sinners with a gracious God, who forgives our sins and transforms us through Jesus Christ. As transformed persons we are indwelt by the Holy Spirit and thereby empowered to do God's good works in our world. The works we do are really the works of God through us. In fact, we are privileged to participate in God's activity on earth.

Therefore, good works are good because they are God's. They are the evidence of God's grace, not the cause of God's grace.

Some churches pray and wait for God to do something. Other churches do something and pray that God will bless what they do. One appears to be more spiritual, and the other more sociological. The balance is struck when the church prays and acts, seeks God's direction and does something about it, trusts God fully and behaves responsibly.

Consider some principles for living out the divine plan in an era of change:

### 1. *God is sovereign.*

God knows the end from the beginning. He is never surprised. He works in us "to will and to act according to his good purpose" (Phil. 2:13). The good that he purposes "does not, therefore, depend on man's desire or effort, but on God's mercy" (Rom. 9:16).

Belief in the sovereignty of God is not fatalism because God is good and just, and he orchestrates every detail of history to fulfill his ultimate purposes. We participate in God's sovereign processes and results, but we do not determine them.

Besides being a cardinal doctrine of orthodox Christian faith, belief in the sovereignty of God is a source of great comfort and confidence. We know that God is involved in history and that he will be the ultimate victor no matter how circumstances may otherwise appear.

I am convinced that we are at a great transition point for both the history of the world and for the church of Jesus Christ. But I am equally convinced that God is in charge and will bring all the changes together for good. This fact means that I am not respon-

sible for the outcome; I am only responsible to God for obedience
and faithfulness. He has already determined the outcome.

## 2. *Christ heads the church.*

Jesus Christ is the Head of the Church (Eph. 4:15–16; 5:23–
24). The church of Jesus Christ was founded by Jesus, is owned
by Jesus, and is run by Jesus. It is a theocracy, and we are citizens
under orders. We are stewards who have been entrusted with the
care of that which belongs to Jesus.

The practical implications are significant. The church does not
belong to any denomination, synod, presbytery, association, session, diaconate, pastor, or membership. It is his to do with as he
sees fit.

However, do not risk the misimpression that Jesus started the
church and abandoned it to us. He is as active as ever. He controls,
empowers, disciplines, and rewards.

One part of us needs to become more serious about the church
than we already are, recognizing that our accountability is to the
Son of God himself. Another part of us needs to lighten up, recognizing that the church is his responsibility and not ours.

When the Son of God came to earth in the Incarnation, he had
a body that began at conception in Mary's womb. For approxi-
mately thirty-three years, that body was the primary location for
the work of God on earth. Call it Body #1.

When Jesus ascended to heaven (Acts 1:1–11), Body #1 tem-
porarily left earth (although there is a promise of return). With
the birth of the church in Acts 2, Body #2 was born. The church
is Body #2 of Jesus Christ (Eph. 4). Body #2 is now the primary
location for the work of God on earth. Just as Body #1 had all the
necessary gifts to do God's work, so does Body #2. Just as Body
#1 stayed the same (human, divine, sinless) and changed ("grew
and became strong . . . grew in wisdom and stature, and in favor
with God and men"—Luke 2:40, 52), so Body #2 stays the same
(headed by Jesus Christ and eternally destined to Christ's con-
formity in heaven—Eph. 1) and changes (from a Jewish congregation of 3,000 in Acts 2 to every part of the world in A.D. 2000).
We are the body of Christ—doing the work of God on earth today.
The only success we have is because Jesus is at the head.

## 3. *The Great Commission continues.*

The Great Commission in Matthew 28:19–20 continues today. It contains only one imperative in its original statement: "Make disciples!" The organized church is a significant means for fulfilling Christ's commission, but the commission was not to build the church. The commission is to make disciples who are characterized by obedience to all of Jesus' commands. "Therefore go and make disciples of all nations, baptizing them in the name of the Father and of the Son and of the Holy Spirit, and teaching them to obey everything I have commanded you."

The power for fulfilling the command to make disciples was made clear in the restatement of the Great Commission in Acts 1:8: "But you will receive power when the Holy Spirit comes on you; and you will be my witnesses in Jerusalem, and in all Judea and Samaria, and to the ends of the earth."

Only with the power of the Spirit can the work of Christ be done in all the places he has listed. But, again, there is no mention of the local church. Certainly the strategy that followed throughout the Book of Acts was church planting and building from Jerusalem to Judea to Samaria to the ends of the earth, but it was God's means by which to witness and make disciples.

Much has changed since A.D. 33, but the commission continues. Since the job to be done is disciple-making, the primary means is the church, which can be compared to a health clinic where the goal is healthy patients. The means is medicine and surgery, but the clinic must never think that it exists for either medicine or surgery. It exists for health. Although medicine and surgical procedures and forms change, the goal of health stays the same. So it is that the church changes in order to fulfill the Great Commission of making disciples (see 1 Cor. 9:19–23).

## 4. *Church change is normal.*

The book of Acts quickly established that church changes are normal. It changed from the very beginning: (1) Many of the established early leaders faded, so that we know nothing of Andrew, Thomas, Bartholomew, or Matthew after Acts 1:13; (2) expected leaders failed (Judas); (3) carefully chosen leaders didn't rise to leadership (Matthias, Acts 1:15–26); (4) former enemies assumed leadership roles (Saul became Paul).

Changes are what the book of Acts is all about. At Pentecost Jews became Christians by the thousands (Acts 2). When conflict came, the church adopted a new form of organization to monitor money (Acts 6). The church that failed to spread its witness outside of Jerusalem according to the commands of Acts 1:8 was persecuted and scattered throughout Judea and Samaria in Acts 8:1. The once unintegrated church added blacks—the Ethiopian in Acts 8:26–40 and Simeon called Niger (black) in Acts 13:1. Peter was *very* reluctant to change the rules and traditions for appropriate behavior until God forced him to in Acts 10. The whole church took on controversy and accepted an uncomfortable change in rules at the Jerusalem Council in Acts 15. The rest of the Book of Acts relates the adaptations of the church to different lands, traditions, languages, schedules, and people.

Yes, there are transcultural truths woven into these changes. But we must recognize that God planned and reported change as normal in the church. If anything, the unchanging church is the anomaly and not the other way around.

Interestingly, none of those New Testament churches have continued until today. Like people, churches have life-spans. Churches die and are replaced. Peter M. Senge in *The Fifth Discipline* claims that most American corporations live only half as long as the expected human life-span—most die by the time they are forty. Could it be that the normal life-span of churches is fifty years? Some live longer, and some live less. The purpose of a local church is fulfilled in its generation and its geography. Churches should give birth to new churches that will carry on just like the children of parents. Maybe their buildings should also be sold, or their children's churches should move in as the church dies. It is not failure to die—death is a normal part of the life cycle.

## 5. *Different circumstances require different responses.*

There are two different highways from Denver to Estes Park, Colorado. They are both about the same distance, one through Boulder and the other through Longmont. The choice is yours—depending on weather, scenery, and whom you want to see enroute. However, the rules are the same for both highways—drive on the right side, keep to the speed limit, and pass only with a broken center line.

The goal of making disciples for Jesus Christ may be reached by different roads. One is not right and the other wrong. The choice depends on the circumstances. But God's rules for Christian behavior, faith in Jesus Christ, and dependence on the Holy Spirit are the same for every route.

Paul insisted that Timothy be circumcised (Acts 16:3), risking the criticism of those who said he was a legalist. Paul did not insist on Titus being circumcised (Gal. 2:3), risking the censure of those who accused him of lawlessness (Acts 21). The circumstances were different—Timothy was half-Jewish, Titus was all Greek. Paul was no less Spirit-filled nor less obedient to God in the one relationship than in the other.

Godly Christians who are sensitive to God's will often have different responses to different circumstances. For example, we can understand this by observing Americans who go to start churches in foreign cultures. They design different architecture, speak a new language, adapt to a very different style of music, and wear completely different clothes. Likewise, we must be equally responsive to the changes within our own culture.

## 6. *Emphasize core values during transition.*

There is a basic principle in Conflict Management Theory, which says, "During times of organizational upheaval, the leader should call the organization back to its norms." That's a complicated way of saying we all need to practice the basics during changing times.

When football teams start losing too many games, the coaches call the teams in for extra practices and review the fundamentals. Hours will be spent on running, blocking, lining up, hiking, and passing. It sometimes seems silly that such basics should be required of players who have been in the sport for years. Yet a return to the basics can keep a team alive and get it through its most difficult season.

In the New Testament church this principle was also practiced. Acts 2 is loaded with disconcerting changes. Conversions by the thousands. Miracles. Conflict with the authorities. Indeed, more severe changes were coming as the church faced such discipline as the deaths of Ananias and Sapphira (Acts 5), the martyrdom of Stephen (Acts 7), and the dispersion of the church (Acts 8). How did God prepare them for these changes in their period of transition? By calling them to the norms of Acts 2:42: "They devoted themselves to the apostles' teaching and to the fellowship, to the breaking of bread and to prayer."

Our American church needs the same devotion at the start of the twenty-first century. If we are to stay strong, healthy, and responsive to God in this period of transition, we need to practice daily the fundamentals of teaching, fellowship, breaking of bread, and prayer.

The same principle is applied in Hebrews 13. Look at the list of Christian norms:

1. Keep on loving each other as brothers.
2. Do not forget to entertain strangers.
3. Remember those in prison and those who are mistreated.
4. Marriage should be honored by all.
5. Keep your lives free from the love of money and be content with what you have.
6. Remember your leaders, who spoke the word of God to you.
7. Do not be carried away by all kinds of strange teaching.
8. Through Jesus, offer praise and confession.
9. Obey your leaders and submit to their authority.
10. Pray.

One of the most challenging changes in the history of Wooddale Church was in the early 1980s when the leadership called on the congregation to sell its long-established site and relocate three towns and nine miles away. It was upsetting to the church and its people. Some said it would bring disaster. There were predictions that most of the people wouldn't even move; they would stay with the church that bought the old building.

The first Sunday at the new site was July 22, 1984. I wondered who would show up. The new facility was smaller than what we had left behind. We had ventured out on a journey of faith that I believed was right, but I was scared anyway. One of the first decisions was what to preach on that first Sunday morning. I had been preaching through Hebrews 13 and would be expected to interrupt the series for this transition Sunday. Instead, I chose to preach on the text of the next verse to come. It was Hebrews 13:4: "Marriage should be honored by all, and the marriage bed kept pure, for God will judge the adulterer and all the sexually immoral."

I am sure some thought I was crazy. I think it was a wise choice because of what it communicated:

1. The ongoing teaching of God's Word is much more important and significant than the relocation of one local church.

2. Our church's values are at the core of what we do. Morality and marriage are central to the church, and it is to the central values that we must constantly return as everything else around us changes. The central values of the church are honoring God, biblical doctrine, godly living, effective evangelism, and making disciples. They are the fundamentals. They are always important, but even more important when the church and culture are in transition.

### 7. *Trust God for the outcome.*

All of these principles add up to trust, for God is in charge, and we are ultimately responsible to him. Since the results are his, we need not worry, knowing God always does his job well.

Gamaliel was a wise rabbi who faced great change with great trust. He considered the apostles and all they were doing and advised his colleagues, "Let them go! For if their purpose or activity is of human origin, it will fail. But if it is from God, you will not be able to stop these men; you will only find yourselves fighting against God" (Acts 5:38–39).

The thirteenth chapter of Hebrews with so many core values for changing times gives a wonderful benediction for the twenty-first-century church: "May the God of peace, who through the blood of the eternal covenant brought back from the dead our Lord Jesus, that great Shepherd of the sheep, equip you with everything good for doing his will, and may he work in us what is pleasing to him through Jesus Christ, to whom be glory for ever and ever. Amen" (Heb. 13:20–21).

# Chapter 14

# *Where Do We Begin?*

Dear Leith,

Thanks for all you've written. You've encouraged me and given me hope for our church's future. I appreciate your love for the church, insights into society, and practical perspective as a pastor.

I'm in a church that really needs to change. If we don't change soon, I just don't know how much longer I can last.

I know you can't tell me exactly what to do, but could you just outline the basic steps I should follow to get started?

Thanks. I greatly appreciate your help.

Your friend,
Jerry

Dear Jerry,

Your words are kind. Your letter encouraged and challenged me. I'll try to help.

#1. *Pray*. This is more than the spiritually correct thing for

me to say and for you to do. If we really believe the church and
the world belong to God, we must begin with God. Share your
heart. Ask for wisdom. Commit to a specific length of time to pray
about the future of your church—perhaps six weeks or more.

After those first six weeks, keep praying but invite a few godly
trusted Christians to share your prayers. They can be in your
church or somewhere else.

*#2. Write a contract.* Write out what you would like to see God
do in your church. Be as specific as you want. Put down a set
amount of time that you will stick with the church—I'd suggest a
minimum of twenty-four months. If evidence of change doesn't
begin by then, prayerfully consider leaving the church or extending the time. Keep the contract private between you and God.

*#3. Talk to church leaders.* Ask them to join with you in looking
to the future for your church.

Invite them to share common positive experiences—praying
together often, reading several books on church renewal and
growth, visiting several churches that have already changed and
serve as positive models for your church.

*#4. Diagnose.* You may need some outside help on this one.
If so, ask a lay leader or pastor from another church or someone
from your denomination. Pick a person you respect and trust.

Aim to write out a description of your church the way it now
is and the way it should become. Ask your church leaders to share
in this process so that they own this process.

*#5. Prescribe.* List what needs to be done. Keep the list short.
Begin with simple things that are likely to work. You can always
expand this list later.

*#6. Broaden.* Ask your leaders to spread the word on what the
church is going to do. Make this a team effort. Don't do it all
yourself. Get as many as possible involved.

*#7. Review and recycle.* Keep repeating and extending this
process. Trust God for wisdom, power, and results. In many ways
it is more important to be moving in the right direction than worrying about how fast you are progressing. Be sure to celebrate
successes and give God his glory.

Jerry, I hope this is helpful. May God give you grace to see
great good come to his church through you.

In Christ,
Leith

# Notes

## Chapter 1

1. Robert B. Tucker, *Managing the Future* (New York: C.P. Putnam's Sons, 1991), p. 9.
2. Jeff Davis, "Breathing Space: Living & Working at a Comfortable Pace in a Sped-Up Society," *USA Today* (January 8, 1992), p. 4D.
3. Steven R. Covey, *The Seven Habits of Highly Effective People* (New York: Fireside, 1990), pp. 30–31.
4. Ellen Foley, "Atheists Plan to Regroup," *Minneapolis Star-Tribune* (October 17, 1991), p. 1E.
5. Oscar J. Serrat, "A Pentecostal Wave on a Catholic Continent," *The Clarion Ledger* (Jackson, Mississippi, January 4, 1992), p. 1D.
6. C. Eric Lincoln and Lawrence H. Mamiya, *The Black Church in the African American Experience* (North Carolina: Duke University Press, 1990) pp. 157–163, 342–343.

## Chapter 2

1. Kenneth L. Woodward, "A Time to Seek," *Newsweek* (December 17, 1990), p. 56.

2. Peter M. Senge, *The Fifth Discipline* (New York: Doubleday, 1990), pp. 13–14.
3. Faith Popcorn, *The Popcorn Report* (New York: Doubleday, 1991), p. 5.
4. Phil Goodman, "Extra! Boomers *Don't* Read All About It!" *The Boomer Report*, Volume 3, Number 2 (May 15, 1991), p. 8.

## Chapter 4

1. Carole Lynn Shew, "Burnout Is Often the Reason Clergy Leave the Ministry," *Twin Cities Christian* (August 6, 1991), p. 7A.
2. Ibid., p. 7A.
3. Hank Whittemore, "Ministers Under Stress," *Parade* Magazine (April 14, 1991), p. 4.
4. Shew, op. cit., p. 7A.
5. Hank Whittemore, op. cit., p. 4A.
6. Ibid., p. 4A.
7. Ibid., p. 4A.
8. Ibid., p. 4A.
9. Ibid., p. 4A.
10. Ibid., p. 4A.
11. David Gelman, "Overstressed by Success," *Newsweek* (June 3, 1991), p. 56.

## Chapter 5

1. Jerry B. Harvey, *The Abilene Paradox and Other Meditations on Management* (New York: Lexington Books, 1988), p. 13.
2. Thomas J. Peters and Robert H. Waterman, Jr., *In Search of Excellence: Lessons from America's Best Run Companies* (New York: Harper and Row, 1982), pp. 202–203.
3. Kevin Perrotta, "An Old Church Finds New Life," *Faith and Renewal* (May/June 1991, Volume 15, Number 6), pp. 5–9.
4. Ibid., p. 7.
5. Ibid., p. 6.

## Chapter 6

1. Quote from manuscript page 56 of John Webb's forthcoming book *The Enabled Congregation* (Abingdon, projected publication date: 1993) on symbols, systems, and sagas. I am indebted to John Webb for his insights and instruction through his writing, personal interaction, and telephone conversations. He has triggered many of the ideas presented in this chapter.

2. John A. Bray, "What Else Can We Do?" *Mandate: A Home Missions Magazine for the Wesleyan Church* (Summer 1991), p. 7.
3. Peter F. Drucker, "Don't Change Corporate Culture—Use It!" *Wall Street Journal* (March 28, 1991), p. A14.
4. Ibid., p. A14.
5. Ibid., p. A14.

## Chapter 7

1. CT Institute preface, "Evangelism in the '90s," *Christianity Today* (December 16, 1991), p. 34.
2. William Ramsden, "Where to Put Your Energies for Church Growth," *Clergy Journal* (September 1991), pp. 40–41.
3. George Barna, *User Friendly Churches* (Ventura, Calif.: Regal, 1991), p. 137.
4. Ibid., pp. 137–138.

## Chapter 8

1. "Paradigms—Are They Working for or Against You?", *The Win Arn Growth Report* (Number 32), pp. 2-3.
2. Clark Morphew, "Church Growth Soars in the Suburbs," *Saint Paul Pioneer Press* (April 7, 1991), p. 6A.
3. Ibid., p. 6A.
4. Ibid., p. 6A.
5. Ibid., p. 6A.
6. Desda Moss, "Practicing or Not, Many Identify With Religion," *USA Today* (April 11, 1991), p. 7A.
7. Ibid., p. 7A.
8. Dr. Gary L. McIntosh, "What's in a Name?," *The McIntosh Church Growth Network*, Volume Three, Number Five (May 1991), p. 2. The McIntosh Church Growth Network, 3630 Camellia Drive, San Bernadino, CA 92404.

## Chapter 9

1. "Why Kids Can't Stay Away From THE MALL," *Group* (June–August 1991), p. 21.
2. Martha Sawyer Allen, "Lutheran Membership Rises," *Minneapolis Star Tribune* (June 26, 1991), pp. 1B–2B.
3. Lyle L. Schaller, *Looking in the Mirror* (Nashville: Abingdon Press, 1984) p. 16.
4. Martha Sawyer Allen, "Lutheran Membership Rises," *Minneapolis*

*Star Tribune* (June 26, 1991), p. 2B.
5. Evangelical Press News Service (March 1, 1991), pp. 9–11.

## Chapter 10

1. Michael Hirsley, "Reinventing the Church," *Wisconsin State Journal* (May 28, 1991), p. 1C.
2. "Analysis Puts a Number On Population Mix," *USA Today* (April 11, 1991), p. 10A.
3. Ibid., p. 10A.
4. Ibid., p. 10A.
5. Church Information Data Service, 3001 Redhill Avenue, Suite 2–2220, Costa Mesa, CA 92626–9664 (714) 957–1282.
6. Peter F. Drucker, "Marketing 101 for a Fast-Changing Decade," *The Wall Street Journal* (December 20, 1990), p. 20A.
7. Michael Silva, "Where Have All the Neighbors Gone?" *CB Update*, Volume 1, Number 2 (June 1991), p. 1.
8. George Hunter, "What Kind of Churches Reach Secular People?" *The Win Arn Growth Report* (Volume 33), pp. 1–2.

## Chapter 11

1. Mike Bellah, "Make Room for Baby Boomers," *The Evangelical Beacon* (April 1991), p. 7.
2. Thomas Long, "Preaching With Ordered Passion," interview, *Leadership Journal*, Volume xii, Number 2 (Spring 1991), pp. 137–138.
3. George Gallup, Jr., *National & International Religion Report*, Volume 5, Number 11 (May 20, 1991), p. 1.
4. Michael Pellecchia, "Abe Lincoln Is a Worthy Role Model for Would-Be Leaders," *Minneapolis Star Tribune* (February 28, 1992), p. 2D.

## Chapter 12

1. Clark Morphew, "Future Doubtful for Congregation That Won't Confront Its Basic Conflicts," *Saint Paul Pioneer Press* (February 1, 1992), p. 5B.